CITIZEN POET

ALSO BY EAVAN BOLAND

POETRY

The Historians
A Poet's Dublin
A Woman Without a Country
New Collected Poems
Domestic Violence
Against Love Poetry
Outside History: Selected Poems 1980–1990
The Lost Land
An Origin Like Water: Collected Poems 1967–1987
In a Time of Violence

PROSE

A Journey with Two Maps: Becoming a Woman Poet
Object Lessons: The Life of the Woman and the Poet in Our Time

EDITED BY EAVAN BOLAND

The Making of a Sonnet (with Edward Hirsch)
The Making of a Poem (with Mark Strand)

EAVAN BOLAND

CITIZEN POET

New and Selected Essays

EDITED BY
JODY ALLEN RANDOLPH

Foreword by HEATHER CLARK

W. W. NORTON & COMPANY
Independent Publishers Since 1923

For information about special discounts for bulk purchases, please contact
W. W. Norton Special Sales at specialsales@wwnorton.com or 800-233-4830

Manufacturing by Lakeside Book Company
Book design by Brooke Koven
Production manager: Gwen Cullen

ISBN 978-1-324-07428-1

W. W. Norton & Company, Inc., 500 Fifth Avenue, New York, N.Y. 10110
www.wwnorton.com

W. W. Norton & Company Ltd., 15 Carlisle Street, London W1D 3BS

10 9 8 7 6 5 4 3 2 1

CONTENTS

FOREWORD

rish poetry, Eavan Boland famously said, was one in which you could "have a political murder, but not a baby." The first time I read this statement, in 1997, it hit me like a revelation. I was a graduate student at Trinity College Dublin, and Boland's first book of prose, *Object Lessons*, had recently come out. As I read Boland's essays about a young woman writing poems in her Dublin garret, I felt less alone in my own damp, cold flat in the Liberties. I was thrilled by the attention Boland paid to women, and I appreciated her clean prose. Unlike the poststructuralist theory then sweeping American campuses, *Object Lessons* was obviously the work of a poet—its language clear and crystalline, a slow-running stream glinting in sunlight. And poetry was all I wanted that year in Dublin. I spent my days discussing poems in class and my nights at boozy poetry readings. But the voices I read and heard belonged mostly to men. *Object Lessons* called my attention to this gap. I knew about Sylvia Plath, Anne Sexton, and Adrienne Rich—all poets who influenced Boland—but I had managed to get an undergraduate degree in English literature without reading any of them. The only woman poet I had studied with any seriousness was Emily Dickinson, whose work I cherished but found gnomic. I had practically memorized James Joyce's *Portrait of the Artist as a Young Man*, but there was no *künstlerroman* for women who wanted to light out for the territory, like Stephen Dedalus, and make art. Now I see that Boland's essays are that guide.

Living in Dublin in the late 1990s, I began to understand what Boland was up against as a woman poet trying to make herself the subject, rather than the object, of the Irish poem. I could see that the Irish poetic tradition made little room for what Boland called "ordinary" women. Irish women did not have recourse to the freedoms that I, as an American, took for granted then. Divorce was illegal in Ireland until 1996, and abortion illegal until 2018. I found these sexist laws infuriating, but not surprising. I had grown up in an Irish American family in which the answer to life's burdens was to "offer it up." I thought I knew about the secrets and silence that abraded women's suffering, but I was not prepared for the revelations that began to surface in the 1990s about the Magdalene Laundries. These Catholic institutions were places of violence and cruelty where unmarried pregnant women were abandoned, shamed, and imprisoned until a male relative came to free them, or until their babies were adopted—often by wealthy American Catholics. I was later shocked to learn that one of the laundries was still operating when I lived in Dublin, a half-hour walk from my flat. I'd had no idea. These were the stories I did not know, because they were women's stories, and no one had told them.

I had heard other stories. One summer during college, I lived on an island off the Connemara coast. I worked long nights in a pub where the crowd quieted as old men stood up and sang ballads of loss, their voices a living register of pain. Islanders still talked about Oliver Cromwell's murderous seventeenth-century campaign through Connaught, and how he had imprisoned priests on the island. His men had tied a bishop to a rock in the island's harbor and watched him drown as the tide rose. All the islanders knew this rock, whose location had been passed down for more than 300 years. On the island, I began to understand that the Irish had a pressing and intimate relationship to history—the "nightmare," Stephen Dedalus famously said, "from which I am trying to awake." That summer, there was a steady drumbeat of stories on the radio about sectarian murders in Northern Ireland. I heard stories, too, about domestic violence and alcoholism on the island. A young woman drowned in mysterious circumstances. But those stories were whispered, not sung. And not passed down.

Boland knew the powerful songs, poetry, and plays that had inspired generations of Irish men and women to fight for independence from Britain. She knew, too, about the dangers of mixing art and politics in Ireland. "Did that play of mine send out / Certain men the English shot?" William Butler Yeats wondered in his poem "Man and the Echo," about his and Lady Gregory's incendiary 1902 drama *Cathleen ni Houlihan*. Boland understood better than Yeats the mythic and seductive role that women had played in Irish nationalist iconography. "Until we resolve our relation to both past and tradition," she wrote in "Letter to a Young Woman Poet," "we are still hostages to that danger." For Boland, resolving that relationship to the past meant telling women's stories, both real and imagined. In her poems and essays, she reinscribes the voices of women who were silenced, and left no trace. We meet Boland's grandmother, dying alone in a Dublin maternity hospital; an elderly woman on Achill Island with a living memory of the famine; a desperate mother and her children fighting for survival in the Clonmel workhouse; poor young women bound for Boston to work as domestics, or forced by hunger into prostitution. Like the water diviners in the Irish countryside, Boland searched for the undercurrents of suffering that coursed below the official histories. Reading *Object Lessons*, I began to see how Irish women had been written out of their own poetic tradition, made into "dehumanized ornaments," as Boland put it, by men. They were queens and muses, reduced to political propaganda, emblems of a colonized nation—Cathleen Ni Houlihan, Dark Rosaleen, the Poor Old Woman. If this truth was hiding in plain sight, it was also, for Boland, a fraught discovery. As she told Jody Allen Randolph in 1999, "There was only one poetry world in Ireland and I seemed to be putting myself at odds with it. . . . [T]he idea of the poet it offered was not mine. I couldn't use this inherited authority and pretend it was mine. I had to make it for myself."

Boland was eighteen when she first wrote what she called a "real poem." It happened during the Big Freeze of 1963, the coldest winter in a century. In *Object Lessons*, she writes about how that experience overlapped with news of Sylvia Plath's death:

> She had died alone in that season. The more I heard, the more pity I felt for it, that single act of desolation. From now on I would write, at least partly, in the shadow of that act: unsettled and loyal. Other poets—men—moved easily among the models of the poet's life, picking and choosing. I chose this one—not to emulate but to honor. Not simply for the beautiful, striving language of the poems when I came to read them. But because I could see increasingly the stresses and fractures between a poet's life and a woman's. And how—alone, at a heartbroken moment—they might become fatal.

The essays in *Citizen Poet* record Boland's struggle to harmonize the parts of herself that she once thought were unreconcilable, and to renew and reshape the Irish poetic tradition through the inclusion of women's voices and stories. Sylvia Plath, Adrienne Rich, and Denise Levertov were inspirations, but, as Boland later wrote in her introduction to Rich's *Selected Poems* (1996), her own feminism was different. Rich's poems "describe a struggle and record a moment that was not my struggle and would never be my moment. Nor my country, nor my companionship. Nor even my aesthetic." Boland had a harder battle to fight in a conservative, Catholic nation where sexism and sexual repression were pervasive, and where the violence in Northern Ireland consumed political and emotional capital that might otherwise have supported a women's movement. Boland would look to Rich's poetry and prose for inspiration, but she would become a different kind of citizen poet. "We need to go to that past: not to learn from it, but to change it," she wrote in "Letter to a Young Woman Poet." "If we do not change that past, it will change us. And I, for one, do not want to become a grateful daughter in a darkened house."

When Boland was an undergraduate at Trinity College Dublin in the early sixties, she spent time with her fellow student Derek Mahon, who would become, like Boland, one of the finest Irish poets of his generation. Though she had been writing poems for years, she saw herself as Mahon's apprentice—a grateful daughter. She remembered, "When I was starting out, over coffee in Roberts', he told me approvingly that one of the real strengths of my poetry was that you could hardly tell it had been written by a woman." She took Mahon's words as a compliment and continued to write what she called "genderless" poems. Dublin then, she recalled, was "not only male. It was bardic." In pubs and coffeehouses, she heard slights from her male friends "that women were bringing into poetry currents of experience which would somehow make it small. One word above any other: autobiography. . . . Women—so it goes—have not lived the lives which fit them to be the central, defining poets that men can be."

After Boland married, moved to the suburbs, and had children, she began to feel disconnected from the Dublin poetry scene. In *A Journey with Two Maps* as well as in *Object Lessons*, she writes about her struggle to reconcile the words "woman" and "poet" as she cleaned the kitchen, sang her children to sleep, and tidied the nursery. These were the quotidian realities of her life as a wife and mother. "The dial of a washing machine, the expression in a child's face . . . I wanted them to enter my poems," she wrote. But: "I had learned to write poetry . . . by subscribing to a hierarchy of poetic subjects." She began to question those hierarchies. In her seminal essay "Domestic Violence," Boland wondered, "What did it mean for generation after generation of poets that the world outside was deemed to be a horizon of moral transcendence and pastoral significance? But not a half-empty cup, a child's shoe, a crooked patch of sunlight on carpet?" Vermeer had captured the inner lives of women in his still, soulful paintings of domestic interiors, but few poets had done the same. Apart from Plath, there was little precedent for the kind of poetry Boland imagined—a poetry in which the child's cry held as much significance as the skylark and the moor. She began to reimagine and redefine the sublime, making room for new moments of grace: "Standing in a room in the winter half-light before the wonder of a new child is aesthetics," she writes in "Reading as Intimidation."

When Boland's one-year-old daughter nearly died of meningitis, she decided she had to become a different kind of poet—one whose words commemorated and validated women's lives, and women's suffering. She realized, with shock, that she knew no poem about a mother watching her child struggle through a serious illness. So many women had endured this grim condition, and yet she could not find the words that would console her. "Sitting there alone . . . my child's life in the balance, I expected to feel abandoned by circumstance, luck and even life. But not by art. . . . [N]ot a line of poetry, not a single poem, came to my mind or memory in that terrible solitude." It seemed absurd to her that she could summon up poems about birds and flowers, but none about a dying child. It was then that she realized with full force how few poems had been written by women, and especially by mothers. In her essay "Daughter," published here for the first time, she wrote, "The power, privilege and consolation of art—why did it leave me and my child so unattended in that room? The more I thought about it, the more the question seemed urgent, huge and ominous. . . . I felt the beginnings of a true intellectual anger." In her darkest hour, she hit against the limits not just of the Irish poem, but of poetic convention itself. She knew she had to expand those conventions, in Ireland and farther afield. This great invisibility needed to be redressed. She had no choice. *I had to make it for myself.*

Boland's late-twentieth-century struggle to write as a woman poet seems almost quaint in the socially progressive, cosmopolitan society that is Ireland today. We now take for granted that women are the practitioners and subjects of poetry. But Ireland has expanded its figurative borders because of writers like Boland, whose works confronted and challenged the nation's endemic sexism. Though there has been an explosion of writing by Irish women since the early seventies, Boland's essays remind us that these reconciliations are a recent phenomenon. They remind us, too, of the change she helped bring about, which is nothing less than the redefinition and expansion of what Irish poetry—what any poetry—can be. The journey was not easy. Her stance was controversial, and she often drew criticism. But Boland understood what she had achieved. In "Letter to a Young Woman Poet" she writes, "On the best days I lived as a poet, the language at the end of my day—when the children were asleep and the curtains drawn—was the language all through my day: it had waited for me. What this meant was crucial. For the first time as a poet, I could believe in my life as the source of the language I used, and not the other way around." When she wrote her best-known poem, "Night Feed," about a suburban mother feeding her infant as the sun rises, she felt no joy afterward. But she thought she had written something "aggressive and solid. As if I was trying to teach lyric poetry a new word," she asserted in "Daughter." She knew the effort was worth the cost, and that more work lay ahead. In her 2001 poem "Is It Still the Same," she asserts that the "young woman who climbs the stairs" to write alone in her flat will now inhabit a "different" tradition: "This time, when she looks up, I will be there."

HEATHER CLARK

EDITOR'S PREFACE

Eavan Boland was a trailblazing poet, critic, and essayist. Her essays influenced how Irish poetry was understood in Ireland and abroad. They also became an essential part of the conversation on how women poets shaped poetry across the English-speaking world. This volume contains essays selected from the prose books Boland published during her lifetime: *Object Lessons: The Life of the Woman and the Poet in Our Time* (1995) and *A Journey with Two Maps: Becoming a Woman Poet* (2011). It also includes pieces published in periodicals, and an unpublished draft of "Daughter," an earlier project that Boland returned to shortly before her death but did not live to finish. As such, it forms the most complete single volume of Boland's essays available in any format.

That Boland's essays speak persuasively to many beyond the borders of her home in Ireland and her career at Stanford University where she taught for twenty-four years is not surprising. Born in 1944, the daughter of a well-regarded painter and a gifted diplomat, Boland learned to walk and talk in Dublin, learned to read and write in London, and arrived at adolescence in Manhattan, before returning to Dublin as an awkward, displaced teenager. The cultural and geographical displacements of her childhood, so vividly described in her essays, produced early estrangements vital to Boland's later understandings of how collective imaginaries are negotiated, contested and remade.

From the start of her writing life Boland published critical prose. She published her first essay before she turned twenty-one and her last shortly before her death at seventy-five. Looking back in 2005, she noted: "All poets face one thing, and they face it alone: the mysterious distance, part cultural and all solitary, between writing poems and being a poet . . . I certainly found the writing of prose essential to managing that distance" (*Poetry Magazine*). Her early essays, reviews and articles reflected her diligence as a young poet as well as the hospitality provided to Irish writers across a broad range of media in the Dublin of that time. As time went on Boland's prose grew clearer in focus and purpose; she argued that a poet's work is not just to write their poems, but also to contribute to the critical conversation in which they will eventually be judged.

She wrote her first prose pieces for the *Dublin Review* in 1965, while still an undergraduate at Trinity. Many more were written for the *Irish Times*, not all of which can be labeled as simply journalism. In the Dublin of that era the line between journalism and literary criticism was blurred. That fine line is represented here by "The Weasel's Tooth" (1974), written in the immediate aftermath of the Dublin and Monaghan bombings. As the earliest essay included, it provides a first glimpse of the thinker, theorist, and writer of position statements we would come to recognize over the next two decades. Her unease at the effects of nationalist politics on the Irish poem is already evident, as is her powerful sense of communal responsibility. Most notable, however, is her effort to use her womanhood as a lens on nationhood.

Forty years and many essays later she would ask: "Why have so few women, in the history of poetry, been citizen-poets? Why have so few set up their poems with country, nation, nationhood, placing themselves at the center of those themes?" ("A Woman Without a Country: A Detail").

By the mid-eighties Boland's prose began to acquire focus and direction using what would become a signature new development—the mixing of autobiography with analysis and argument. Early attempts in this vein, "Religion and Poetry" (1982) and "The Woman Poet: Her Dilemma" (1986), were quickly followed in 1987 by "The Woman Poet in a National Tradition," an autobiographical essay on the difficulties for women poets writing within a national tradition resistant to them and a history that excluded them. What a national tradition offered her as a young woman poet, she would later surmise in *A Journey with Two Maps*, was not the comfort of finding a nation but just "a new way of not belonging."

"The Woman Poet in a National Tradition" led Boland forward into a long, passionate effort to join together those parts of her identity that had seemed impossibly separate: woman, poet, citizen. This happened not in a single leap but in fits and starts as Boland developed and published her arguments, revised them and published again. The scholar and poet Catríona Clutterbuck describes this germinal phase as "bracketed by Eavan Boland's first and final versions of what would become one of the most important essays in Irish literary culture, titled 'The Woman Poet in a National Tradition' in 1987, 'A Kind of a Scar' in 1989, and by 1995, when collected in Boland's [first] volume of prose, retitled again as 'Outside History.'" Here Boland argued Irish poetry had idealized women, enmeshing the national and the feminine in a trope which simplified both. "Women in such poems were frequently referred to approvingly as mythic, emblematic," she wrote in "Outside History," "but to me these passive and simplified women seemed a corruption."

In her turn toward autobiographical essays, Boland had two decisive influences: W. B. Yeats and Adrienne Rich. Boland first encountered Yeats's essays as that estranged teenager just returned from a childhood abroad in London and New York: "unable to name the country I came from," she wrote in *Cross-roads* (1998), "unable to come from it until I could name it." In her first years as a poet, Boland learned from Yeats how to use language to belong to a place. As her autobiographical analysis gathered force and focus, she learned from Yeats that through language a poet could not only claim a place but change it as well.

By the time I came to know Boland in the late 1980s, the fiercely questioning and subversive essays of Adrienne Rich were already spurring her development as thinker and theorist. After marrying the novelist Kevin Casey in 1969, Boland moved to the suburbs where they would raise two daughters, and where she first read Rich in the mid-1970s. She turned increasingly to Rich in the 1980s, as a strong example of a woman poet forging her own critique against a resistant literary culture. In essays describing her growth as a poet, Rich made connections between the life she led as a woman, the works she wrote, and her role as a dissenting citizen and an activist for change. Rich's named intent, "to write directly and overtly as a woman, out of a woman's body and experience, to take women's existence seriously as a theme and a source for art," steeled Boland's resolve to construct a critique for Irish poetry to address the painful distance between being a woman and becoming a poet that she recognized in Rich's account of her experiences as a young writer (*Blood, Bread, and Poetry: The Location of the Poet* [1985]).

By the early nineties Boland's prose was gathering into a coherent narrative. Her radical questioning of the ethics of a poetry which had flourished in the shadow of a powerful national tradition had become an influential critique. Irish, American and British journals now circulated her essays. *PN Review* and *American Poetry Review* regularly featured her longer pieces. In 1995 these culminated in *Object Lessons: The Life of the Woman and the Poet in Our Time*, compiled from essays written over the course of a decade which found their final form there. *Object Lessons* traced Boland's long uncertain route to a poetic self from confusions over nation and belonging, through estrangement to embodiment, as she became a wife and mother in a Dublin suburb, turning away to write poems from a new grounding. Her arguments in *Object Lessons*, about womanhood, nationhood and the relation between the two, came to be viewed as central texts in the theorization of women's writing well beyond Ireland.

If *Object Lessons* followed a young poet as she wrote herself out of a national tradition of heroes and into the silences of women's lives beneath it, *A Journey with Two Maps: Becoming a Woman Poet* (2011) starts out with a map of the poetic past, then offers a second map that charts Boland's reading and writing across several decades, before ending with an address to women poets of the future. Both maps are contoured by self-portraits of Boland as daughter, wife, mother, and citizen. The essays move freely between Ireland and the United States, to post-war Germany and back again. "In the sense that my life as a poet has been marked by boundaries," Boland writes, "this book allows me to unwrite them—moving freely between countries and poems and histories."

The central essays in *A Journey with Two Maps* trace Boland's route to becoming a woman poet through tradition, the canon and change. They are included here, minus Boland's essays on individual women poets—Adrienne Rich, Charlotte Mew, Sylvia Plath, Gwendolyn Brooks, Paula Meehan, and most recently the poetry written by women in Germany at mid-century—which will be published by Carcanet as part of a subsequent volume. Her landmark essay in *A Journey with Two Maps*, "Letter to a Young Woman Poet," forms the rationale for the book as a whole, as well as indicating the anticipatory and wayfinding role these memoirs and essays play for more recent creative nonfiction by younger Irish writers including Anne Enright, Doireann Ní Ghríofa, Sinéad Gleeson, Vona Groarke and Emilie Pine. In Boland's essay, an encounter between an older and younger poet echoes Rainer Maria Rilke's title "Letters to a Young Poet." It also deliberately echoes Boland's poem "The Journey" in which Sappho guides her charge through an underworld so she would "know forever/ the silences in which are our beginnings." The younger woman is the future. The older woman is the past. She enters a room she has made herself of language to explain to a young poet the necessity of engaging with the past, "the place where authorship of the poem eluded us. Where poetry was defined by and in our absence." "Why visit the site of our exclusion?" Boland anticipates the younger poet asking. "We need to go to that past not to learn from it," the older poet replies, "but to change it."

The final section of *Citizen Poet: New and Selected Essays* gathers key essays that appeared outside of Boland's two volumes of prose. It is framed by new readings, new arguments and new narratives of becoming both a woman-poet and citizen-poet, including an unpublished draft of "Daughter" which began as an extended essay before turning into a book project: "a book about a way of life—motherhood—and an art—poetry—which hardly made any room for it." A major stylistic departure for Boland, "Daughter" is composed of fragments in conversation with each other: definitions, quotations from letters, parts of poems, journal entries from her years as a young poet and mother, knit together with sections of running commentary. Conventions of the lyric and the dream vision are raised then confronted and complicated by fragments of poems, argument and personal narrative. The fragments, Boland explains, "echo, retrospectively, the anger, irony and estrangement I felt as a working poet and a mother, and the incoherence I felt would make it impossible to draw these two sides of my life together."

In "A Woman Without a Country: A Detail," published in *PN Review* in 2014, Boland returns to the major theme of *Object Lessons*: how a woman belongs to a country. "Why should women want to be citizen-poets?" she asks. The obvious reason, Boland answers, "is a confirming tradition of national reference in male poetry. More importantly, within that tradition it's clear that male poets in England, Ireland and America are not just drawing on words and names when they refer to their countries. They are also pulling up a deeply sunk reference-hoard of power, nation and poetry." But Boland also insists that reading well outside those national traditions is vital to the future of poetry: "New poetry requires fresh resources. From poet and reader, both. Those resources will be necessary if we are to read an emergent generation of women poets whose poems are rising out of the deepest contentions of history. And who need us to listen."

In her last years, Boland worked assiduously to encourage a new, diverse generation of Irish poets. The final pieces included here are short editorials written in the final three years of her life when she served as guest editor for *Poetry Ireland Review*. At Poetry Ireland, Boland was a guiding presence in a conversation about diversity, inclusion and community, on which she knew the future of poetry depends. These editorials, along with the remarkable body of essays gathered here, became part of Boland's legacy, and, in a sense, part of her poetic canon, where they enrich our understanding of her remarkable commitment to the craft of poetry, to the future of poetry, and to her country, the one she found and the one she helped to shape.

I

FROM

Object Lessons:

The Life of the Woman and the Poet in Our Time (1995)

AUTHOR'S PREFACE

I began to write in an enclosed, self-confident literary culture. The poet's life stood in a burnished light in the Ireland of that time. Poets were still poor, had little sponsored work and could not depend on a sympathetic reaction to their poetry. But the idea of the poet was honored. It was an emblem to the whole culture that self-expression and survival could combine. A contested emblem, certainly—the relation was never easy and may even, in certain ways, have been corrupt—but it existed, it was there. A poet was remarked upon and pointed out, was sometimes quoted, and the habits and sayings of poets frequently found their way into a sort of image file of idiosyncrasy which further reinforced the sense of poetry as something in high relief and set apart.

A woman's life was not honored. At least no one I knew suggested that it was exemplary in the way a poet's was. As dusk fell in the city, a conversational life intensified. Libraries filled up; the green-cowled lamps went on, and light pooled onto open pages. The pubs were crowded. The cafés were full of students and apprentice writers like myself, some of them talking about literature, a very few talking intensely about poetry.

Only a few miles away was the almost invisible world that everyone knew of and no one referred to. Of suburbs and housing estates. Of children and women. Of fires lighted for the first winter chill; of food put on the table. The so-called ordinary world, which most of us had come from and some would return to on the last bus, was not even mentioned. Young poets are like children. They assume the dangers to themselves are those their elders identified; they internalize the menace without analyzing it. It was not said, it was not even consciously thought and yet I absorbed the sense that poetry was safe here in this city at twilight, with its violet sky and constant drizzle, within this circle of libraries and pubs and talks about stanzas and cadences. Beyond it was the ordinariness which could only dissipate it; beyond it was a life for which no visionary claim could be made.

The opposite is now true. A woman's life—its sexuality, its ritual, its history—has become a brilliantly lit motif, influencing the agenda of culture and commerce alike. At the same time the old construct of the poet's life, for which I have such an exasperated tenderness, has lost some of the faith and trust of a society. Increasingly, it is perceived as arcane and worse: as a code of outdated power systems whose true purpose was to exalt not the poet's capacity to suffer but his suitability for election to a category which made him or her exempt from the shared experience of others.

I KNOW NOW THAT I BEGAN WRITING in a country where the word *woman* and the word *poet* were almost magnetically opposed. One word was used to invoke collective nurture, the other to sketch out self-reflective individualism. Both states were necessary—that much the culture conceded—but they were oil and water and could not be mixed. It became part of my working life, part of my discourse, to see these lives evade and simplify each other. I became used to the flawed space between them. In a certain sense, I found my poetic voice by shouting across that distance.

But I was also hostage to it. As a young woman and an uncertain poet, I wanted there to be no contradiction between the way I made an assonance to fit a line and the way I lifted up a child at night. But there were many; they were deep-seated, they inflected arguments of power and presumption which were obvious to me and yet unexamined in any critique I knew.

The relative status of these lives has changed. The power of each to limit and smooth out the complexity of the other has not. In the old situation which existed in the Dublin I first knew, it was possible to be a poet, permissible to be a woman and difficult to be both without flouting the damaged and incomplete permissions on which Irish poetry had been constructed.

The new situation has made a role reversal. Now poetry itself, and the concept of the poet, have been put under severe pressure by any number of factors, among which the emergence of women and the new importance ascribed to a woman's life are a real and powerful presence.

Here and throughout this book these lives remain the themes. These, after all, are the two lives—a woman's and a poet's—that I have lived and understood. They are the lives whose aspirations I honor, and they remain divided. I have written freely about both, and sometimes my pen has skidded on the modest particulars. I am not a scholar, and my historical sense is selective. My working life has been spent not in any aspiration towards knowledge or accuracy but in an intuitive struggle with form. And yet at certain points in writing this book,

I have caught a glimpse of the wider implications of the theme. At these moments it has seemed to me that these lives, with their relation and division, make a sign which is ominous and revealing: about silence and expression, about democratization and oligarchy, about the life a society tolerates and the one it nominates to take it into the future, to both glory and survival.

II

I have put this book together not as a prose narrative is usually constructed but as a poem might be: in turnings and returnings. In parts which find and repeat themselves and re-state the argument until it loses its reasonable edge and hopefully becomes a sort of cadence. Therefore, the reader will come on the same room more than once: the same tablecloth with red-checked squares; the identical table by an open window. An ordinary suburb, drenched in winter rain, will show itself once, twice, then disappear and come back. The Dublin hills will change color in the distance, and change once more. The same October day will happen, as it never can in real life, over and over again.

In various pieces I have returned to the same themes and their interpretation, often to the exact room and the identical moment in the suburb when the light goes out of the sky and dusk comes. I will need the reader's patience as, once again, I go back to the visionary place, the obstructed moment. Not so much because of an aspiration to give a definite shape to the book but because each revisiting has offered me another chance to clarify the mystery of being a poet in the puzzle of time and sexuality and nationhood.

Argument and recollection may not solve the puzzle, but

they have allowed me to note it. They have also allowed me to make a record of the interior of the poem as I found it; its angles of relation to my life and circumstance. There is nothing definitive about this; such angles are subjectively observed and understood. But it is also true that they are not found in textbooks, at least not for a working poet. They are best seen where they have most effect: at the actual moment of writing a poem.

And in a sense it is the very smallness of this moment and the ordinary furnishings which surround it—a suburban dusk, a table by an open window with a book and a pen on it—which have led me to a larger contention. To make it at all clearly here, as against the diffused form in which it appears throughout this book, I will have to return to the argument.

In an odd and poignant way these two lives, of a poet and a woman, have proved to be formidable historical editors of each other. In previous centuries, when the poet's life was an emblem for the grace and power of a society, a woman's life was often the object of his expression: in pastoral, sonnet, elegy. As the mute object of his eloquence her life could be at once addressed and silenced. By an ironic reversal, now that a woman's life is that emblem of grace and power, the democratization of our communities, of which her emergence is one aspect, makes a poet's life look suspect, can make it appear, to a wider society, elite and irrelevant all at once. Therefore, for anyone who is drawn into either of these lives, the pressure is there to betray the other: to disown or simplify, to resolve an inherent tension by making a false design from the ethical capabilities of one life or the visionary possibilities of the other.

It is these very tensions, and not their absence, and not any possibility of resolving them, which makes me believe that the woman poet is now an emblematic figure in poetry, much as the modernist or Romantic poets were in their time. I make this less as a claim than as a historical reading. It does not mean she will write better poetry than men, or more important or more lasting. It does mean that in the projects she chooses, must choose perhaps, are internalized some of the central stresses and truths of poetry at this moment. And that in the questions she needs to ask herself—about voice and self, about revising the stance of the poet, not to mention the relation of the poem to the act of power—are some of the questions which are at the heart of the contemporary form. This does not give her any special liberty to subcontract a poem to an ideology. It does not set her free to demand that a bad poem be reconsidered as a good ethic. Her responsibilities remain the same as they have been for every poet: to formalize the truth. At the same time the advantage she gains for language, the clarities she brings to the form, can no longer be construed as sectional gains. They must be seen as pertaining to all poetry. That means they must also be allowed access to that inner sanctum of a tradition: its past.

At the age of seventeen I left school. I went to university, and I wrote my first attempts at poetry in a room in a flat at the edge of the city. That room appears often in this book. I can see it now, and I have wanted the reader to see it. It was not large. It looked north rather than south. The window beside the table was small and inclined to stick on rainy afternoons. And yet for me, as for so many other writers in so many other rooms, this particular one remains a place of origin.

But one thing was lacking. There were times when I sat down at that table, or came up the stairs, my key in my hand, to open the door well after midnight, when I missed something. I wanted a story. I wanted to read or hear the narrative of someone else—a woman and a poet—who had gone here, and been there.

Who had lifted a kettle to a gas stove. Who had set her skirt out over a chair, near to the clothes dryer, to have it without creases for the morning. Who had made the life meet the work and had set it down: the difficulties and rewards; the senses of lack. I remember thinking that it need not be perfect or important. Just there; just available. And I have remembered that.

LAVA CAMEO

In the early days of October, in the year 1909, a woman entered a Dublin hospital, near the center of the city. The building is still there. If you approach from the south, with the Dublin hills behind you, and look down a tunnel of grace made by the houses of Fitzwilliam and Merrion squares, your view will end abruptly in this: the National Maternity Hospital, red brick and out of character, blocking the vista. The rooms inside are functional and light-eating. They show no evidence of that zest for air and proportion which was the mask of an Augustan oppressor.

October is a beautiful month in the city. If you turn around and go back towards the hills, away from the hospital, the roads are narrow and gracious above the canal. The woman who entered the hospital may have passed them as she made her way to it. If, for instance, she drove around Stephen's Green, having arrived on the late-morning train from Drogheda, she may also have noticed a trick of light peculiar to that time of year: in the dark corridor of Lower Leeson Street, sunlight cuts the houses in half. Halfway up the brick, the reflection of the houses opposite builds another street: chimneys, roofs, gutters made of unglittering shadow.

She may not have come that way. She might have travelled down the unglamourous back streets that lead more directly to the hospital. Fenian Street. Hogan Place. Past the mills. Past the Dodder River on its way to the Liffey. Up the slight gradient which would still, in that year, be cobbled. The prewinter chill, which can be felt on some October mornings, could have struck extra music out of the horses' hooves.

It is not a long drive. But whatever she saw that morning, it is lost. Whatever that journey yielded—the child with a hoop who never existed, the woman with a red hat I am now inventing—they were her last glimpses of the outside world.

This is the way we make the past. This is the way I will make it here. Listening for hooves. Glimpsing the red hat which was never there in the first place. Giving eyesight and evidence to a woman we never knew and cannot now recover. And for all our violations, the past waits for us. The road from the train to the hospital opens out over and over again, vacant and glittering, offering shadows and hats and hoops. Again and again I visit it and reinvent it. But the woman who actually travelled it had no such license. Hers was a real journey. She did not come back. On October 10 she died in the National Maternity Hospital. She was thirty-one years of age. She was my grandmother.

NINETEEN HUNDRED AND NINE. It was a different city and another time. The difference is worth settling on. In just a few weeks George Roberts of Maunsel and Co., the Dublin publishing house, would write to James Joyce promising him the proofs of "Ivy Day in the Committee Room." The proofs would not arrive. A little later Roberts would write again. He would ask Joyce to remove all references to the king in his story. Towards the end of 1910 Augustine Birrell would inform William Butler Yeats that his civil list pension, at last, could be counted on. "I know you don't care about Doctor Johnson," he wrote, "but I always think his pension was the money best spent in England during the whole of my beloved eighteenth century. It is well that the Twentieth should follow suit."

It was a year on the edge of political upheaval. In the next fourteen months England would have two general elections. The second one yielded a result which was important for Ireland. True enough, only 84 out of 272 successful Liberal candidates so much as mentioned Home Rule in their election addresses. Nevertheless, as the results were gradually declared throughout December 1910, it became clear that the Liberals would depend for their majority in the House of Commons on the Irish members there. It was also clear that the driven, ambitious son of a Yorkshire wool manufacturer had changed his mind. Herbert Asquith, now prime minister of England, who had once vowed the Liberal party would never take office again if they were to depend on the Irish members, now accepted the result. Unlike other politicians, his literacy extended to the writing on the wall. In April 1912, by introducing the Third Home Rule Bill, he would set tar barrels and bonfires blazing throughout Ireland.

The city which waited upon these changes was itself changing. In 1909 it was a place of roughly a quarter of a million souls. We have to imagine a town of bowler hats, bicycles, trams and red uniforms. By all contemporary accounts, it was a mixture of occupation and indigenous obstinacy. There were frequent recruiting marches for the British army. New recruits, after all, got a shilling there and then—an amount hard to resist. The police still chased thieves and arrested drunks wearing the uniform of the Royal Irish Constabulary. Horses were everywhere. James Joyce would repeat the city superstition that you never crossed O'Connell Bridge without seeing a white horse. Bystanders tell of the small, daily theatre of watching runaway horses break out of the shafts and even, on occasion, collide into shop fronts. On the corner of Marlborough Street there was a shop which sold pigs' trotters in brown paper bags.

Poverty was widespread. The death rate for Dublin was the highest of any city in Europe. In Britain Street and Gardiner Street and Rutland Street, all north of the Liffey, evictions were a daily occurrence. Trade unionists blamed the bad housing and worse health conditions on a corrupt city council, mainly of Irish nationalists.

A place on the edge. A place of resentment and beauty and conflict. All abstract qualities perhaps, but nonetheless potent for that. In another ten years it would all change again. There would be gunfire in these streets and outside the windows of the building she died in. There would be carts and lorries full of hostages carried to and fro by the Black and Tans. The glittering dances, the genteel imitations of British manners practiced by those who saw no tomorrow in this year of 1909 would be waning ten years from now. The schemes and conspiracies of those who could not tolerate the present moment—the men and women with the "vivid faces" Yeats referred to in his poem— would soon be vindicated.

HOW MUCH DID SHE CARE? Politics and social change, except as it touched her immediate circumstances, could only have seemed a distant drum. The facts of her life are briefly stated; none of them makes an obvious intersection with political change. She came from a large family. She lived in the midlands of Ireland. She married a seaman in her late teens. He became a master mariner and then a sea captain. She had five daughters. She died in a Dublin hospital.

Even the fact that she was the wife of a seagoing husband put her at a remove from some of the most intense national questions. In 1903, for instance, George Wyndham, the chief secretary for Ireland, managed to pass a new Land Purchase Act in the House of Commons. It was easily the most satisfactory settlement yet of the festering question of British landlordism. She and her husband lived in a cottage on the outskirts of Drogheda. I have no doubt it was rented. If they had been tenant farmers instead, living on the estates whose demesne walls ran from one end of Ireland to the other, she would have noticed the change. By a clause in the act, tenants could now buy their lands and the legal cost of transfer would be met from public funds. This was a new and attractive provision. Landlords benefited also. If a whole estate was sold, they were rewarded with a 12 percent bonus on top of the purchase price. In another six years 270,000 land purchases had been negotiated out of a possible half million tenant occupations. And she was dying.

A HUNDRED YEARS AGO she was a child. But where? Strange to think that once the circumstances of her life were simple and available. They have become, with time, fragments and guesswork.

I have pieces, but they are few enough. But she has a name. Three names, in fact. Mary Ann Sheils. There is a faint surprise about the three flat take-it-or-leave-it syllables of the Christian names. Mary Ann sounds more like the name of a younger sister in Jane Austen than a girl from the end of the nineteenth century in Ireland. Then again, it was a time of turmoil and turmoil is easily negotiated into ambivalence. Which in turn can be seen in the Irish endowing their sons and daughters with echoes of the names given to the children of squires and vicars across the water.

I know nothing about her childhood. There are no photographs. No letters. Nobody ever recalled her to me as living memory. It is another erasure. And yet something does survive: a story so odd and strange that it has the power to upstage all those icons and arrangements that survive the recorded childhoods of official family histories. It is a story I heard twice—so improbable that each time I thought of it as one of those signs the past makes when it has transferred its available resources from memory to allegory.

SHE CAME FROM a family of millers. Sometime after the famine they left the small fishing town of Milford in Donegal. Hard pressed as they were, they must have missed the idiosyncrasy of their own place: the sight of Mulroy Bay in February light. The main street with its steep climb up the side of a hill. They moved east and south to the town of Dundalk. There the business failed. And they moved again to Leitrim where her father was born. It was to him that legend clung. And the way I build that legend now is the way I heard it: out of rumor, fossil fact, half memories.

He was a small man, compact and saturnine in the way of many western people. If he was anything like his son, whom I met for a few hours years ago, he had eloquent and strained features. A fine profile. Close-set, obstinate eyes. There was something strained and pinched about it all which kept it well away from beauty. He grew up in Leitrim and some time in his early manhood—I imagine the early 1870s—he had fallen in love with a local girl. I know so little about her or him that I must become the fictional interventionist here and say that she was, of course, winning and expressive and utterly true to him. And that he loved her stubbornly.

But there was an obstacle. She was a younger sister. In the manner of fairytales, her older sister was plain and deserving and on no account to be slighted by having the younger girl marry first.

And so it went around. The parents insisted he should offer his suit to the older sister. They may have offered him inducements, but I doubt it. The inducement can only have been local custom and iron decorum. There were no dowries. These were poor people, reduced in circumstance by a difficult century, utterly vulnerable to the sickness of a heifer or a farthing's change in the price of wheat. They would have brought to bear on him the influence of local opinion and approval. He must marry the older girl and that was that. He was implacable. It would be the younger one, and that was all. The younger girl retained her love for him, and he for her. Finally—and now the narrative quickens, gets unsteady, fills with unknown passages of time and event—the impasse yielded. Love triumphed. The wedding day was set.

I have no document or certificate. I have Mary Ann's marriage certificate but not this one. In any case, the cold signatures of the witnesses and the sacristan could not do justice to the event. The wedding day came. It seems safe to imagine a small, granite church in the middle of a townland and the weather, more than likely, grey and overcast. Perhaps the turnout was a bit more than usual because of the notoriety of the whole thing; the struggle of wills and all the gossip and curiosity incurred on that account. The bride came, dressed in white and heavily veiled. The vows were taken and repeated, said by the bride and the groom. The priest pronounced them man and wife. For a single moment it must have seemed to him that some wound of ill luck and misadventure in his own life had undergone a miraculous healing.

Then he lifted her veil. But it was not—the story turns gothic now—the face he loved. Convention had prevailed. The family had smuggled in the older, plainer girl, and he was bound to her by iron convention and legality for the rest of his life.

THE NINETEENTH CENTURY, especially the second half of it, was a time of restatement in Ireland. After the famine, after the failed rebellions of the forties and sixties, the cultural and political desire for self-determination began to shape each other in a series of riffs on independence and identity. It was an exciting time but not a pure one. Self-consciousness mixed in with improvisation, and not always happily. A new interest in the language and customs of Ireland went hand in hand with instinctive, colonial attempts to metabolize that interest into something weaker and less threatening. The love of a nation is a particularly dangerous thing when the nation predates the state. The danger was partly handled by a tabloid version of it, which suited British drawing rooms and did not put an obvious sell-by date on empire.

From this confused time come the false and synthetic Irish

dances. The suspect emblems of harps and Celtic crosses. And while the Fenians experimented with real terror, the drawing-room version of Irish nationalism became acceptable and even fashionable. A genteel mix of nostalgia and sentiment.

This was the time when legends began to be dignified as myths. Cúchulain. The Red Branch Knights. Maeve. Conchu-bar. They reemerged from a lost scholarly past, but in the shape of a Victorian Round Table. While hayricks burned and gun-fire could be heard at night after evictions, Germanic scholars worked over the old Irish stories and resurrected them in a new European time frame.

In all this, some of the real myths were ignored: those down-to-earth and hand-to-mouth yarns which start in fear and short-circuit into a pure and elaborate invention. Which bind a community together, not by what they explain, but by the very fact that they were forced to explain it. I can only think this must be one of them, this Rachel and Leah fable about beauty and denial. It is a wonderful image for something: a man lifting a veil on a plain and peremptory face. But for what? For history? For fate?

To me—the great-granddaughter whose existence was guaranteed when his was cheated—it seems to be something else. I think of it as the Gothic yearning to find for random misfortune something approaching the ritual and astonishment of the coffins certain enclosed orders lie down and sleep in at night, something which dignifies horror by anticipating it. He was an unlucky man. He had an unlucky daughter.

His vows finished on that lost day, in that small church, before curious neighbours, he accepted his lot and took his wife to his bed. They had thirteen children. It hardly seems an elegy for lost love. Six of those children survived. Mary Ann was one of them.

He died in the asylum in Mullingar. Of mental illness. Or drink. Or that combination of both which in Ireland, as anywhere else, might just cover a broken heart.

THIS IS NOT A STORY about luck, or even memory, but about what replaces them. And whether we have the right to replace them. She survived, but only in fits and starts of oral recollection and memory. Looking back, I can see those fractions, those chances more clearly.

I left school when I was seventeen. A rainy summer intervened before I began my courses at Trinity College. Sometime during these months, my mother showed me the only piece of paper—a letter from her father to her mother— in her possession. It was an unusual act. Unlike most people, she treated the past as an opportunity for forgetfulness rather than a source of definition. She had no photographs, not one, of herself as a child. No copybooks from school. No pantomime tickets. She talked of her childhood rarely and without sentiment. Almost, it seemed, without interest.

I understand this better now than I used to. There are parts of Europe, commentators like Claudio Magris are witnesses to it, where minorities, even nations, jostle in the same square mile. Change a language, turn a signpost, rename a village and the previous identity becomes a figment, a hostage to persistence and stubborn recall. Magris speaks of a woman describing the country she loves, "which like all motherlands," he states, "exists perhaps only in this love." My mother wanted to forget.

Childhood was a place of unreadable signposts and overgrown roads. The language could not be retrieved.

I took the letter from her in the back room of the flat I shared with my sisters. I bent my head to read it. My grandfather had written it at sea; there were references to the weather and the voyage. The handwriting was clear and sloping, and the page was lined. The garden, with its path to a locked wooden door, stayed at the upper edge of my sight. When that splintered door was unlocked it opened onto a towpath and the urban containment of the river Dodder. When you stood there, in the occasional July sunshine, you had a view of a stone wall, trees. You could hear cars and buses. You could see the roofs shelving into the city where she died. Now that landscape faltered. The North Sea raised its grey wall and swell outside the window.

The address at the start of the letter was declamatory, affectionate. My dearest wife? My darling wife? Then there were two things which I remember even now. The first was just a housekeeping detail. It made reference to a collection on board for one of the ship's mates. For a hardship, perhaps, or a gift or a leave-taking. In any case, the tone of the account is apologetic. He had given a half crown. Two shillings and sixpence in old money. It was a good amount, he knew, but he felt constrained to do it. He felt she would understand.

A fraction indeed. Even so, the door opens a crack. I see her more clearly. She must have had three children by now, maybe four, and one was sickly. Milk. Rent. Doctor's bills. Clothes. Every penny counted. A sea captain made respectable money, relative to the unrest and uncertainty in Ireland at that time. But the distances must have made it seem at risk, and all the more important that as much salary as possible returned home intact.

The second detail is clearer. There is a yearning note in the letter. The small talk of money and clothes—I remember some mention of a singlet—is anxious rather than anecdotal. The intimacy is of someone trying to set up house between Drogheda and the North Sea. Then the words I remember most clearly, although not exactly or in sequence. This is a paraphrase: "I don't know why I always fear that something bad will happen, but I do."

It is not a passionate letter. It is an anxious and domestic one, and yet I am certain theirs was a passionate marriage. One detail supports that view. It was repeated to and remembered by my mother. It is the sort of small vignette which is extravagant, and enough out of character with the penny-wise young mother, to be repeated and remembered. Whenever my grandfather's ship docked, often at Cork Harbour, Mary Ann would go and meet him. She did this because she feared the women at the ports.

II

How do we create such figures? What act of love or corruption makes us turn to a past full of obstruction and misinformation? I am forty-nine years of age. She has been there all my life, a maquette of fables and possibilities. And yet at a certain point she ceased to be merely a suggestion and became a presence. In that sense, her story is mine also. Where exactly did I discover her? Or, more precisely, when?

THIS AT LEAST I can be fairly certain of. In my thirties I found myself, to use a colloquial fiction, in a suburban house at the foothills of the Dublin mountains. Married and with two little daughters. I led a life which would have been recognizable to any woman who had led it and to many others who had not. My days were arrayed with custom and necessity, acts so small their momentousness was visible to no one but myself. Season by season, I separated cotton from wool and the bright digits of gloves from ankle socks. I drove the car. I collected children from school. In spring the petals from across the road blew down, strewing the kerbs with the impression of a summer wedding. In February, after a high wind, the village street was littered with slates.

But at night the outer landscape yielded to an inner one. Familiar items blanked out. and were replaced by others. The streetlamp stood in for the whitebeam tree; the planet of rain around it displaced the rowan berries. And in those darknesses I lay down as conscious of love for my children as I would have been of a sudden and chartless fever. And conscious also of how that love spread out from the bed on which I lay, and out further to the poplar trees, to the orange plastic mug at one side of the hedge, to the glint of a bicycle wheel and the half-moon.

I understood then, as any human being would, the difference between love and a love which is visionary. The first may well be guaranteed by security and attachment; only the second has the power to transform. As I lay there, my mind went seeking well beyond the down-to-earth and practical meaning of a daily love. The apple trees. The rustle and click of shadow leaves. The mysterious cycle of plants. In those darknesses it could seem to me that this was not a world in which my love happened but one whose phenomena occurred because of it.

Poetry is full of such transformations. They are, for example, the weather of most love poems. They constitute much of the perspective of the great conventions, such as the pastoral.

I ought to have felt that my experiences, even my half-formed impressions at this time, connected well with my training as a poet. But I did not. As each morning came around, with its fresh sights and senses, I felt increasingly the distance between my own life, my lived experience, and conventional interpretations both of poetry and the poet's life. It was not exactly or even chiefly that the recurrences of my world—a child's face, the dial of a washing machine—were absent from the tradition, although they were. It was not even so much that I was a woman. It was that being a woman, I had entered into a life for which poetry has no name.

NAMES. Every art is inscribed with them. Every life depends on them. I was to find out, as I searched for information about her, just how wounding their absence can be.

I knew that she was buried in a small graveyard outside Drogheda, in the village of Termonfeckin. I drove there one Saturday, on the very edge of the month in which she died. September is a time of mild weather in Ireland. Great swatches of light are draped across stone and fields; there is a misleading stillness. October is different. The zone between the two months can seem to be a season in itself, an emblematic journey from fruition to menace.

I drove out by North Dublin. Beyond Swords is the small seaside village of Rush, with its fine strands and the potato farms which supply the Dublin markets. Then Balbriggan, with its old cotton factory. Then fields with great cylinders of saved hay. Past here the road follows the Boyne estuary into Drogheda.

It was a wild afternoon with a clay-and-mortar sky. Heavy rains the night before had left the Boyne churning. I drove over the bridge into Drogheda, into a town crowded with Saturday afternoon shoppers. I drove up one hill and down the next, then followed a sign into a quiet street.

She must have lived, I thought, somewhere along this road. The distance between Drogheda and Termonfeckin is a brief five or six miles. In her time it must have seemed much longer. Over the century, the town had extended so that at least half the road between the two was taken up with front gardens and bungalows. A school. A post office. Petrol stations and newsagents.

After a few miles, however, it is all rural again. Sycamores and ivy-choked oaks block the roadside. The ditches are full of dead branches and cow parsley. As I started the approach to Termonfeckin, I was halted by a small herd of black and white cows, a harlequin back view of haunches. Two boys and a girl were herding them, gesturing and laughing. I slowed down between towns, between centuries. The queue of cars behind me lengthened. Then a gate opened into a field. I heard a sound of voices, more laughter. The road was clear again.

TERMONFECKIN LIES in a flat landscape between Clogher Head to the northeast and the estuary of the Boyne to the south. As I drove in, I had a ghost-impression of the Surrey villages of my childhood. A self-possessed quietness. A dignified slope of ivy-colored walls and slated roofs. Trees and gates and high, well-trimmed hedges. It is a small town, with a population of a few thousand at most. And yet its history is entrenched and visible. Until the seventeenth century the archbishops of Armagh had their summer residence here. The name itself is an abbreviation of the Irish. *Tearmann Feichin*. St Feichin's sanctuary land.

She must have lived within striking distance of this village.

This is not a deduction so much as simple fact. In Ireland, as elsewhere, it is customary that people are christened and married and buried in the parish in which they are born or wed or die. Not an invariable custom perhaps but a reliable one all the same. She must have kept together her small family of girls within reach of these trees and slopes, perhaps only a mile or so away. She would have known this village with its steep, leafy roads and its rural peace.

The graveyard is on the edge of the town, up a small gradient so steep and narrow that only one car can fit with any safety. It takes two or three minutes to drive there, but with every one of them the shade deepens, the trees seem to darken. Then finally there is a widening out, a quadrangle of grass bounded at one end by an ornate iron gate. On the other side of it are a church steeple and, beyond, a clear view to the Boyne estuary. The church is not especially old. A date of 1904 is above the lintel.

The gate was closed but not locked. Once inside, I could see that the graveyard shelved out above fields and some houses. Two graveyards, to be accurate. One on either side of the church. It was as if the church were flanked by two separate plots, neither of them much bigger than a small back garden. To the left of the steeple there was the appearance of a normal graveyard: polished slate and marble, important lettering, recent flowers and some plastic ones. To the right was a plot which seemed to come from another century, another ethos. Even the grass seemed more unkempt and the whole appearance was of a small field of old and often broken headstones. No granite, no marble. Only unpolished stone and very little of it that could be coherently read. One of the best of the headstones was still cracked diagonally, as if with an arrow through a heart in a child's drawing. The inscription read: "Erected by Widow Rodgers of Parsonstown in memory of her beloved husband Edward who departed this life June 1818."

In the cold afternoon these words seemed to me to have an extravagant dignity. Just the name, the language, the location of a human life in the remembrance of it. What was pitiful all around it were the small clumps of stone, giants' handfuls, tossed around, apparently at random. Occasionally one of these had a name, cut roughly into its surface and thoroughly worn. Most of them did not.

Less than a hundred years after that inscription her coffin had been brought here. Through these iron gates and onto the raised shelf of this ground. None of the scattered pieces of granite was bigger than a man's head. None was polished or even shaped. I began to search through them for her name, reaching my hand down through high grass and moss as if into water, trying to feel a lettering. More often than not, there was none. The stones were rough. Yet, in the heartbroken vernacular of the place, each one stood in for a life, a death.

The wind was suddenly bitter. I had a sense of anomaly and intrusion. Just below the graveyard there was a bungalow, with its garden at right angles to the church. Two dogs, one brown and one black, regarded me seriously: a woman in a raincoat, stooping and searching. It seemed of enormous, irrational importance that I should find her name. Her name, carved against the odds into one of those wretched stone markers. I tried to imagine her funeral as I searched: desolate October weather, the hurried retrieval of her body from a Dublin hospital. And what, if any of this, could the discovery of her name offset? I found other names. Sometimes just initials, sometimes a full Christian name. But not hers.

I was astonished at how much I felt the small, abstract

wound. A woman I had never met and never seen. A woman my mother could only have seen in a period of days or weeks which left no memory. Yet the indignity of her aftermath at this moment in this graveyard was one of the worst parts of her story. Five children. A life of work. A husband whose language had some grace of love and concern about it, even across distance. I was certain, in some more rational part of my mind, that her headstone was indeed here. She had been too much loved and noted for it not to have been. But the fact was I could not find it. Somehow that temporary confusion had become in this dull light a sign for a wider loss. She had turned her head for it, come running to it as a child, hoped for it on a letter and answered it in moments of love. And now she had no memorial because she had no name.

III

Was there really no name for my life in poetry? The question preoccupied me more as time went on. And if not, why not? War poetry. Nature poetry. Love poetry. Pastoral poetry. The comic epic. The tragic lyric. Surely there were names enough there for any and every life. Even if the name of my experience, of what I felt and saw, was not specifically entered there, then why not represent my life as one which those conventions, those traditions could name and therefore recognize? In theory it could be done and had been done. As I walked between the whitebeams on my way to call the children home on a summer evening, I was all too aware of how a nuance here and a shadow there could turn me into a woman already recognized by and therefore recognizable to poetic convention.

The way to the past is never smooth. For a woman poet it can be especially tortuous. Every step towards an origin is also an advance towards a silence. The past in which our grandmothers lived and where their lives burned through detail and daily incidence to become icons for our future is also a place where women and poetry remain far apart. What troubles me is not how difficult and deceptive my relation to this past—and to this figure within it—may be, but that it might not have existed at all.

I began writing poetry at a time when, and in a tradition where, poetry appeared to be granted authentic communal importance. I learned, although not quickly, that such grants are provisory and conditional. The mystique was sustained by prescriptions. Poetry, it was suggested, was something of power and resonance. It was also a good deal removed from that life which was deemed ordinary. Therefore, I began in a poetic world where the names were so established, so imposing and powerful it never occurred to me they might not be equally inclusive. I read Yeats first when I was sixteen. There was a small room in the boarding school where I was a pupil. The window sloped at right angles to the ceiling and looked out on grass and a eucalyptus tree and the Irish Sea glittering through evergreens. Early in the morning the acoustics of water and altitude made the sound of a church bell pure and astonishing.

I read Yeats's poetry in that room. In the morning before classes began. And again at night, under thick blankets and with a flashlamp. I took in, with some kind of recognition, and through the gestures of language, exciting and powerful statements. I did not know enough about what he was doing to identify the enterprise. Later I would know the barriers he had broken: in the dark corridor between the fin de siècle and modernism he had found a door and opened it. To the question of whether the poetic self is created or invented he had given a poignant and effective answer: both.

But there were aspects of that reading which troubled me. It began as a small doubt and widened, in my twenties and thirties, into a pervasive sense of unease. Yes, his best poems showed him nameless and powerless before old age and approaching death. But he had moved to that position from solid recognitions. Before he even lifted his pen, his life awaited him in poetry. He was Irish. A man. A nationalist. A disappointed lover. Even his aging was recorded. The values were set. I was to learn how hard it would be to set different values.

From then on I read poetry eagerly. In college my experience of it widened. Some images remained long after I had closed the book: Keats's Hyperion. His starry tantrum on the edges of day and night. Gawain riding through frozen countryside. Only gradually did I become aware of some kind of paradox slowly developing within this process. That the effect of good poetry—the acute sense of liberation which a command of language and technique brought to me—was offset by a growing sense of oppression. In all that reading, propping the book up against table or bed, I know now I was not only taking in beauties of phrase but also looking for my name. And it was not there.

By the time I left college I knew—it sounds something I should have known much earlier— that I had a mind and a body. That my body would lead my poetry in one direction. That my mind could take up the subtle permissions around me and write a disembodied verse, the more apparently exciting because it denied the existence of the body and that complexity. I knew, in other words, that I was a half-named poet. My mind, my language, my love for freedom: these were named. My body, my instincts—these were named only as passive parts of the poem. Two parts of the poem awaited me. Two choices. Power or powerlessness.

The truth is I began reading and writing poetry in a world where a woman's body was at a safe distance, was a motif and not a menace. For a while I felt sheltered by that. As I read the accepted masters of the tradition, it was all too easy to internalize a sense of power and control. To mistake a command of expression for a resolution of feeling. Such poets handled the feminine image in a way which made the action expressive while the image was silent and passive. I saw nothing wrong with that. I was young. I was growing out of my teens in a literary city. I was walking through Stephen's Green on my way to Trinity College, through flowers and water and ducklings, and by the very grass Yeats had walked on where, as my father once told me, he had been behind him and observed that one of his feet turned in. In Newman House, on the south side of the Green, where I occasionally met friends from the other university, was the room which Joyce described in the tundish chapter of *A Portrait of the Artist as a Young Man*. Literature, it seemed, could have an intimate and even an inherited feel to it.

Everywhere, at least to my eyes, there were signs of the command and ascendancy of poetry. Almost nowhere, at the beginning, did I see its exclusions. Nor did I want to. The exhilaration of language—this is particularly true for a young poet—is almost inseparable from its power. Later the suspect nature of the power would undermine the exhilaration. But not yet.

IT MAY WELL BE that women poets of another generation may not feel these things. And yet I do not think it was purely a temporal moment which made me feel as I did; it went deeper.

I suspect there will be women again who feel, as I did, that, through the act of writing a poem, they have blundered into an ancient world of customs and permissions. That world was The Poem. In it women—their bodies, their existences—had been for thousands of years observed through the active lens of the poem. They had been metaphors and invocations, similes and muses. It had not been done by malice or misogyny, but by an encounter between the power of poetic language and the erotic objectifications poetry allowed and encouraged. Custom, convention, language, inherited image: they had all led to the intense passivity of the feminine within the poem. And to this moment when I found my poetry and my sexuality on a collision course.

For the fact was, in my early twenties, as I bent to write poems in a copybook on a summer evening, I was entering upon a subtle and inescapable crisis. I could write lines on the page. I could type and revise them. I could read them over again and publish them. I could go through the motions and act out the role of every young poet. But I felt an estrangement. I had no words for it, and yet I felt it more and more. Put in the language of hindsight and rationalization, the crisis was this: however much my powers of expression made my mind as a human being the subject of the poem, my life as a woman remained obdurately the object of it.

This was not only bearable while I was a student; it was hardly noticeable. I was young and ambitious. I wanted to learn the craft, and I thought in the usual simplifications: that what was perceived could be learned, that what was learned could be expressed. The syllogism began to break down the more I realized that my body was leading me towards a life for which there was no title and no authorization in the art I had tried to learn, only an intense and customary passivity. I was a poet. But I was about to take on the life of the poetic object. I had written poems. Now I would have to enter them.

Soon enough, I was getting married, leaving the flat. I was about to live a life unrecorded in the tradition I had inherited—in a suburb, with bus timetables and painted shelves and school runs. I was packing my bookcases, putting my books in boxes, wrapping my mugs in newspaper and walking back into the poem to be an ancient and component part of it. A subject silence. The crisis was upon me. I would write poems. My life would threaten to stay outside them. Half of me would be in sunlight and half in shadow.

The only resolution of the crisis was both drastic and isolating. I would have to reexamine modes of expression and poetic organization that I was, in many ways, accustomed to and, until then at least, reconciled to. I would have to reexamine and disrupt and dispossess. Not because of feminism, not because of ideology. But because of poetry.

IV

Here is her name. Written in a sloping, florid hand across her death certificate—the letters of the name thick and thin by turns, where the calligraphic nib pressed down and eased up. It is a wretched document. What else could it be? It describes the death of a young woman, far from her home, far from the sweet chills of a Louth autumn. The National Maternity Hospital was not a natural place for her. She could only have come there in some out-of-the-ordinary way. With disease or fever. The cause

of death—peritonitis—is consistent with a complication of puer-
peral fever, which that year had swept the lying-in wards of the
city. If she did not have it when she entered the hospital, she
was likely to get it during her stay.

The death certificate I have is simply a copy of page 539 in
the registrar's book for the year 1909. Legally she died in the
district of the South Dublin Union. Officially her death was
registered there. In the margin, it is numbered 453. The page
spreads across in a chilling grid: eight checkerboard squares.
Name and place of death. Certified cause of death. Age last birthday. And, most bitterly, qualification and residence of informant.
In other words, the witness to her death was simply an inmate,
S. Murphy, and the address is given as Holles Street. In plain
language, my grandmother had died alone, in pain, away from
her children and her husband and in a public ward. What she
may have feared most and tried to protect against by a small,
helpless deception had happened anyway.

AN UNLUCKY CHILD. Born to an unlucky man. And in a country and a century singularly devoid of that precious substance.
One final, small anecdote makes me think she knew it. Or at
least had that sort of dread which amounts almost to knowledge.

Her last child was born at midnight. There can hardly have
been any excitement about it. This was a fifth child and a fifth
girl at that. In those days children were born at home. A midwife
would come to the house. In some cases she would stay for two
weeks, on either side of the birth.

I wonder how midnight was determined in that house. By
a watch? By a striking clock? It must have been the clock, and

those imagined chimes ringing through the damp of the house, against the closed windows, around the chintzes and stuffed cushions of the cottage, have everything to do with this story. My mother was born at five minutes to midnight on February 13, 1908. It can be a harsh month in Ireland. Drogheda, with its north-facing aspect, can have frost and even snow at that time. The snowdrops are finished and the daffodils can already be clumped under rowans and oaks on the roadside. The Boyne will be thick with mist in the early morning.

A baby cried. Five minutes later the clock struck midnight. For the first twenty years of her life my mother believed she had been born on February 14 and held her birthday on that date.

I can almost see those rooms. Somewhere in my childhood, the tufts and velvets, the antimacassars and worn textures of Victorianism became as distinct as memory. My mother hated those colors. Those maroons and greens that ate daylight and seemed to be in mourning for themselves.

In those rooms a child was born and a clock chimed. Years later my mother's uncle mentioned to her in passing that one of those five children—he couldn't be sure which— had been born on February 13 at five minutes to midnight. And so superstitious was his sister that she changed the birthday and would only allow it to be on the fourteenth.

A woman full of dread, claiming a sanctuary in superstition which, in the end, circumstance would not allow her. Willing to exchange a child's birthday for a small fiction of safety. Like so much else in this story, it has more than pathos for me. It has that quality of insult which an unchangeable past throws at the present. For my mother, hearing it at twenty, it was old news. She changed her birthday to the right date. By then, it was too late for superstition.

V

I began this piece to make a record of a woman lost in circumstance, a text ironically erased at a time when and in a country where the text was just beginning to be written. I have accepted that the story of Irish history is not her story. The monster rallies, the oil-lit rooms, the flushed faces of orators and the pale ones of assassins have no place in it. Inasmuch as her adult life had a landscape, it was made of the water her husband sailed on and not the fractured, much-claimed piece of earth she was born to.

What was her story? The worst of it is I am not sure. No matter how poignant the details, the narrative is pieced together by something which may itself be a distortion: my own wish to make something orderly out of these fragments. To transpose them from a text where the names were missing or erased to one where they were clear.

An emblem can be a name. Not an obvious or recognizable one, perhaps. Nevertheless images, as every poet knows, are themselves a nomenclature. They give identity to something. The provide a short title for the mystery.

I found an emblem for her even before I realized I would find it difficult to name her life. Or my own. It happened one Sunday afternoon when I was married with young children. I went to an antiques fair—really just a collection of different stalls—in a hotel in South Dublin.

I remember the afternoon clearly. Or perhaps, like all such memories, it is a composite of other afternoons like that. In any case, the air seems to have been cold and delicate. I do remember looking with surprise—it was only the third week in February—at the small debris of blossoms on the paths and in the gutters. The hotel was on the coast and looked out on the strand, where in the distance the water was cold, wrinkled metal. Even the gulls looked cold.

I felt the chill and hurried into the hotel. There was a room with long tables and small glass cases. I walked along slowly, staring at lace and frames and cups with cracked rims.

I wish now that I had looked more closely at one item. I remember the dealer pointing and talking. This, she told me, was a lava cameo. An unusual brooch and once fashionable. Unlike the ordinary Victorian cameos, which were carved on shells, this one was cut into volcanic rock. The brooch was a small oval. The face was carved into stone the color of spoiled cream. I looked at it quickly and moved on.

Her name. Her emblem. There was a complexity for me remembering the cameo, and the more I thought about it, the more complex it became. To inscribe a profile in the cold rock. To cut a human face into what had once flowed, fiery and devouring, past farms and villages and livestock. To make a statement of something which was already a statement of random and unsparing destruction. All these acts were very far from being simple. They were ironic and self-conscious. They employed artifice and irony. They put the stamp of human remembrance on the material of natural destruction.

Such acts of irony and artifice were not congenial to me. I could not remember the brooch in detail. Nevertheless, something about it, in memory, had almost the flavor of an elaborate sarcasm. If I remembered her life, if I were to set her down—a half-turned-away face in its context of ill luck and erased circumstance—would I be guilty of sarcastic craftsmanship? Would I too be making a statement of irony and corruption?

The more I thought of it, the more the lava cameo seemed an emblem of something desperate. If it was a witticism in the face of terror, if it made an ornament of it, what else was memory? Yet in the end, in my need to make a construct of that past, it came down to a simple fact. I had no choice.

A FRAGMENT OF EXILE

had no choice. That may well be the first, the most enduring characteristic of influence. What's more, I knew nothing. One morning I was woken before dawn, dressed in a pink cardigan and skirt, put in a car, taken to an airport. I was five. My mother was with me. The light of the control tower at Collinstown Airport—it would become Dublin Airport—came through the autumn darkness. I was sick on the plane, suddenly and neatly into the paper bag provided for the purpose.

I left behind fractions of place and memory, images which would expose slowly. There was a lilac bush I had pulled at so often its musk stayed under my fingernails for days. I would remember the unkempt greenness of the canal where it divided Leeson Street. The lock was made of splintery wood and boys dived from its narrow platform in summer. Fields, fragrances, an impression of light and informality—that was all. I held my mother's hand, got into another car. I was in another country.

Hardly anything else that happened to me in my childhood was as important as this: that I left one country and came to another. That an ordinary displacement made an extraordinary distance between the word *place* and the word *mine*.

————————

WE HAD COME TO LONDON. It was 1950. I have a memory of houses and moving vans, of adult voices late at night. Then we were in a tall house, of dun-colored stone, with a flagstaff fitted to a low balcony. In the hall, through doors which were more like wooden gates, there was a kind of chair I had never seen before. It was black leather, and the top was rounded into a sort of hood, edged with brass buttoning. It was called the Watchman's Chair. I was told a man sat in it all night.

Almost everything about this house was different from the one we had left behind. That had been family sized, with a flight of stone steps and a garden edging out into fields. There had been glasshouses and a raggy brown-and-white terrier called Jimmy. There had been lilac and roses along a stone wall. Nothing about it had the closed-in feel of this street. But that had been the house of a life in Ireland, of an Irishman and his wife and five children. And now my father had gone, all at once, it seemed, from being an Irish civil servant to being an ambassador in London. The life had changed. The house had changed.

I knew I was somewhere else. I knew there was something momentous—and for me alone—in the meaning of the big staircase, with its gilded iron fretwork and its polished balustrade; in the formal carpets, with the emblems of the four provinces of Ireland on them: the harp for Leinster, the red hand for Ulster, the dog and shield for the other two. I knew that the meaning was not good. But what was bad and what was good? Bad, it seemed, was dropping soft toys and metal cars down the stairwell. Bad was making noise and tricking with the fire hoses on every floor. Good was being invisible: spending hours in the sparse playroom on the top floor, with a blank television and the balcony which overlooked a dark, closed-in courtyard.

We turned the armchairs on their side there, day after day, and called them horses, and rode them away from this strange house with fog outside the window and a fiction of home in the carpets on the floor.

EXILE IS NOT SIMPLE. There are Irish emigrant songs which make it sound so; they speak of green shores and farewells. By and large, they fit into Valéry's description of Tennyson's *In Memoriam*: "the broken heart which runs into many editions." Which is not to deny their melody; but it is a marketable one. In most cases those songs were composed in settled and hard-pressed communities of Irishmen and women—most of them in the New World—to reassure them that they still had noble roots as they branched out in a daylight which was often sordid and dispossessed.

I wanted simplicity. I craved it. At school I learned Thomas Hood's poem: "I remember, I remember / The house where I was born." But as time went on, I didn't. Such memory as I had was constantly being confused and disrupted by gossip and homily, by the brisk and contingent talk of adults. "Stop that. Settle down. Go to sleep now."

The city I came to offered no simplicity either. The rooms to the east of the house looked out on gardens and railings. But the vista was almost always, the first winter anyway, of a yellow fog. If the windows were open, it drifted smokily at the sill. If the doors were open and you went into the street, you entered a muddled and frightening mime. Passersby were gagged in white handkerchiefs. The lights of the buses loomed up suddenly. All I knew of the country was this city; all I knew of this city was its fog.

The first winter passed. In the conventional interpretation of exile I should, child as I was, have missed my home and my country. I should have entered the lift and regret of an emigrant ballad, and remembered the Dublin hills, say, and the way they look before rain: heathery and too near. Instead I stared out the window at the convent school I attended in North London. It was March, my first one in England. A swell of grass, a sort of hummock, ran the length of the window and beyond. It had been planted with crocuses, purple, white, yellow. I may not have seen them before; I had certainly never seen so many. There and then I appropriated the English spring.

THIS WAS NOT ORDINARY nature loving. I was not really a nature lover anyway. I resisted walks in Hyde Park whenever I could, and I was restless when we went out at school—paired off in the dreaded "crocodile"—to pick up polished chestnuts or gather acorns. This was different. Not a season but a place. Not an observant affection but a thwarted possessiveness: a rare and virulent homesickness.

Even good poets, Thoreau says, do not see "the westward side of the mountain." They propose instead "a tame and civil side of nature." My concept of the English spring was as makeshift, as simplified and marketable to my spirit, as the vision of Ireland in any emigrant song. English crocuses were always a brilliant mauve or gold. English cows—I had heard this somewhere—only grazed in meadows full of buttercups, flowers so called because they made the milk richer. The chaffinch was forever on the orchard bough. In the big woodlands south of London—I was sure of this, though I had never seen them—were acres of bluebells, harebells, primroses.

If it was a simplification, if it resembled in this the country of emigrant yearning, they had a common source. An emigrant and an exile are not necessarily the same thing. There is at least an illusion of choice about the first condition although, sooner or later, it will share the desolation of the second. But both need a paradigm: the disoriented intelligence seeks out symmetry. I wanted a shape which was flawless. If I had only known it, I wanted a country where I was the sole citizen; where the season was fixed in the first days of April, where there were no arrivals or departures.

The more I imagined that springtime, the more I became, in my imagination, the Victorian child suited to its impossible poise. It was not difficult. If Aristophanes called Euripides, as he is said to have done, a maker of ragamuffin manikins, maybe the remark can do as well for childhood make-believe. Certainly, I had plenty of pictures to work from. There were old encyclopedias in the house with just the images I was looking for: English girls with well-managed hair, with lawn pinafores over sprigged dresses, with stockinged legs and buckled shoes. Alice without the looking glass.

Alice. The Looking Glass. An old England, unshadowed by the anger of the oppressed. It would have made better sense had the country I left behind not been engaged in a rapid and passionate restatement of its own identity. Ireland, after so many centuries, was now a republic. A text was being rewritten. Street names. Laws. School curricula. The writing went on and on. My childhood was merely a phrase in it.

II

My father enters here: a complicated man and, by all accounts, a Jesuitical negotiator. And a Jesuit boy he had been, going to Clongowes, the boarding school south of Dublin, where James

Joyce, twenty years earlier, had wept and broken his glasses. My father may have learned there how to make a concept pliable. Later on, in our adult conversations, he would distinguish between Metternich and Talleyrand; between a diplomat who merely sold himself and one who sold his country.

He was a member of what may have been the last generation of European diplomats whose apprenticeship in pessimism was served between two wars. I see them standing on railway platforms, discoursing and wagering in first-class carriages, taking unreliable planes to theatres of crisis. They offered to chaos their skills of rhetoric and compromise and their unending gifts for finding the appropriate dress. Bowler hats, silk top hats, heavy ivory crepe evening scarves seemed to fill the house, marking my father's exits and entrances. He had been in Paris in the thirties. As assistant secretary at Foreign Affairs he had been one of the caretakers of Ireland's neutrality in the Second World War. During the forties, he travelled from Dublin to London, arranging trade agreements, searching out the language, the exact form of words which would bridge the damage of centuries with the practicality of a moment.

In a sense, he is an anomalous figure against the backdrop of Irish political passion. While argument raged and the injuries of the Irish Civil War healed slowly, he went about his tasks and his travels. Paris. London. Rome. Photographs from the forties show him in a reticent coat of Irish tweed and a brown fedora. His Parisian training is shown only in the way he holds a pair of calf brown gloves, well folded, on the steps of St Peter's.

In these journeys his accoutrements were talk and a pursuit of realpolitik. The Irish, after the war, were in need of coal and food and employment abroad—especially in England. It was not a time for expensive gestures or republican intransigence.

Observe him in the forties, just after that war, discussing coal with the Ministry of Supply in London. His country needs it and he will get it. But the ironies are plentiful. Here is a man who studied classics at Trinity and political science at Harvard. He can quote Thucydides on the costliness of civil strife and Tacitus on the infirmity of rulers. He has a strong sense of the historical absurdity and a true sense of patriotism. He will put all and any of that behind in the attempt to bring heat and shelter from that country to his own. He will search hard for the right formula of words to achieve it. And yet will anything he says, anything he proposes, have the raw force of the nineteenth-century Fenian cry "Burn everything English but their coal?"

There were shadows. His grandfather had been the master of the workhouse in Clonmel. The historical ambiguity of a forebear who had harnessed his pony and culled his kitchen garden in the environs of fever and hunger would not have been lost on him. After all, he served political masters for whom the fever and hunger of the nineteenth century were the most persistent badges of honor. His mother—another shadow—was illegitimate. Married to his father, a respectable and feared civil servant in the British service, she had suffered much. Once or twice, at a later stage, he hinted obliquely at her sufferings: she had kept to the house a great deal; her closest friend was the housekeeper.

And there had been—there always was in Ireland—an eviction. It had happened to the family his mother lived with; she had been a child at the time. They had been evicted from a smallholding near the river Barrow in Kildare. There were almost no details. Just the elegant un-Irish name of Verschoyle was carefully remembered: the hated middleman. But if there were no details, the image of an eviction was a brutal Irish generic. No cartoon, no sentimental drawing has anything like the force or bitterness of folk memory: the dreaded bailiff, the furniture out of doors, the windows barred. The illegitimate child, dispossessed even of a foster shelter, was enigmatically factored into my father's intelligence. Years later he told me of a childhood memory: of standing on Dame Street in Dublin, holding his mother's hand. The viceregal carriage—this may have been in 1910—clattered out of the gates of Dublin Castle. He went to doff his cap, not an unusual gesture on those streets at that time. His mother pulled away her hand. "Don't do that," she whispered.

Now it was 1948, and Ireland, having been a member of the Commonwealth since 1921, was suddenly, almost improvisationally, declared a republic. There was surprise, even shock. But there were pieces to be picked up, loose ends to be tied. The old profession of diplomacy had everything to do with loose ends and scattered pieces, and so my father was in London. It was the Commonwealth conference, and he was speaking to old colleagues as well as an old oppressor. But his speech had an unusual ending. He wished Canada and Australia well—they had decided to remain in the Commonwealth— and he understood that decision; indeed, he respected it. But the Irish would withdraw. "There is not," he said—and I am going on hearsay and his own account in this— "a cottage in Ireland which has not shuddered at the words 'Open in the name of the king.'"

It was negotiating rhetoric; it was appropriate language. He was a trained man and would not have used it had it not fitted both requirements. But there was also, I am sure of it, an invisible darkness in the language: the parish lands of Kilberry to the east of Athy. In any case, Ireland was now a republic and needed an ambassador. And he was it.

I knew nothing. Nothing of nations or that Napoleon said,

"What is history but a fable agreed upon?" The truth was that by such words, such gestures—by hints and transits, negotiations and compromises I was utterly oblivious of—my fate was decided together with my country's. By a strange, compound irony, the same sequence of events which made me a citizen of a republic, had determined my exile from it.

When night came, I balanced a heavy, maroon volume on the sheet—the books had been carefully covered for me by my mother—and I was out in the air of an English spring. Never mind that I was called Ginger and Carrot-Top at school, that I had freckles and an accent. I was wearing muslin and those shoes, or maybe boots with impossible mother-of-pearl buttons joining the silky leather from toe to shin, which needed the curve of a silver button-hook to undo. I was looking for a thrush's nest. I was in those places for which the English had fragrant, unfamiliar names: a copse; an orchard; a meadow. In the Irish usage they would have been mere fields and gardens. I was picking bluebells and primroses, going home with indigo- and lemon-colored handfuls. I was going home to muffins and clear, swirling tea surrounded by flowered porcelain. Then it was time for the light to be switched off; for the room to fill with shadows and lamplight.

"Language is fossil poetry," says Emerson, and it may well be. But it is also home truth. Whatever the inventions and distortions of my imaginings, my tongue, the sounds it made in my mouth betrayed me. I was no English Alice. I was an Irish child in England. The more time went on, the more my confusion grew. I knew, if only by vague apprehensions, what I did not own; I had no knowledge of what I did. The other children at school had a king and a country. They could be casual about the bluebells and chaffinches. They could say "orchard" instead of "garden" with the offhand grace imparted by nine-tenths of the law. I could not. When the king died and the reverend mother announced the fact to the whole school at lunchtime, the other children knew how to weep. I only knew how to admire their tears.

The inevitable happened. One day my tongue betrayed me out of dream and counterfeit into cold truth. I was in the cloak-room at school in the middle of the afternoon. A winter darkness was already gathering through one of the stubborn fogs of the time. A teacher was marshalling children here and there, dividing those who were taking buses from those who were being collected. "I amn't taking the bus," I said. I was six or seven then, still within earshot of another way of speaking. But the English do not use that particular construction. It is an older usage. If they contract the verb and the negative, they say "I'm not."

Without knowing, I had used that thing for which the English reserve a visceral dislike: their language, loaded and aimed by the old enemy. The teacher whirled around. She corrected my grammar; her face set, her tone cold. "You're not in Ireland now," was what she said.

EXILE, LIKE MEMORY, may be a place of hope and delusion. But there are rules of light there and principles of darkness, something like a tunnel, in fact. The further you go in, the less you see, the more you know your location by a brute absence of destination. Later I would read this definition in a nineteenth-century book for children: "Home— the nursery of the infinite."

The trouble was, I was adrift in a place of finite detail. I could have been a character who had woken from a lyric fever in an old novel, unable to remember a name, a place of origin or the faces of those who had kept vigil. And there the chapter ends and a new one begins. A cup of tea is brought; a miniature oil-painting; a sweet-smelling elbow-length glove. The character begins to remember: in glamourous fractions, in lightning flashes of recall.

One day in the playroom, with the television off as usual, but the chairs upright and returned to their nonequine positions, I found a book. It was thick and well bound. The illustrations were drawings of landscape and figures, with stories as well as legends. I was not a particularly enthusiastic reader. My best adventures in comprehension, and all my efforts of attention, were reserved for the maroon encyclopedia at the end of the day. But I was older now, maybe only a year or two, but enough to make me look at things more skeptically, more curiously.

The pages were not glossy. They were matt and pastel, and the pictures were reprints of watercolors. Here was a blue distance; there was a bog with the flat ditch-brown squares neatly cut. At the side of a ditch were clumps of scutch grass and smudges of ivory and green on stilts: the artist's rendering of cow parsley. On the far side were red fuchsias, the flowers of the west of Ireland, veterans of salt air and limestone soil. I could see that it was summer. A cart was drawn up by the roadside with a donkey in the traces. His big ears—they were the black-brown of cocoa, I thought—were up and forward.

I turned the page. This was the story of someone called Michael. This bog, this donkey, these distances were part of his home. But he was leaving home. He was going away from this place with its weedy cow parsley, its shadows of fuchsia. "I am leaving here," he said in the text, "because Ireland has nothing to offer me but a spade."

I turned the page again. Now there was no donkey, no cold brown distance. Instead there was a woman sitting on a throne, holding a harp. She wore loose clothes, draped in folds, and one shoulder was bare. "Hibernia," it said under the picture. And the line "O harp of my country." I put the book down. I was confused and startled. Was this the place I had heard of? Was this what it offered? This strange mix of music and a wooden-handled implement I had hardly ever seen? I thought about it. No one I knew used one. We had no garden.

MY FATHER was a good pianist. At Harvard in the twenties, he had made spare cash as the pianist in a jazz band. At the University of Chicago he continued his studies in political science and his piano playing: thumping out ragtime and Dixie, turning up on winter afternoons in a vicuña coat. One afternoon in rehearsal—the band was preparing for a college dance—the saxophonist stopped playing. He looked at my father. "You play a mean piano," he said. And resumed.

He no longer played jazz. He had to climb up three flights of stairs to get to the piano. It stood against one wall of the playroom, opposite the window, its polished black covers almost always closed. When he opened them, it was not to play songs like "Toot Toot Tootsie"—*if you don't get a letter then you'll know I'm in jail*—though he still whistled them at times. Almost always he came up in the late afternoon, his Sweet Afton cigarette glowing between his fingers, then between his lips as he lifted the cover. Almost always he played the songs of Tom Moore.

POOR TOM MOORE. I have come to think of him that way. Tom Moore, who, according to Byron, "struck his wild lyre while listening dames were hushed." He was born the son of a Dublin grocer, and he had studied law at Trinity, as did my father. He was the friend of Robert Emmet, who lost his life in the aftermath of the '98 rebellion. And who, when I was a teenager, would seem the exemplary Irish hero.

A year later Moore had crossed the Irish Channel, from Dublin to London. He was twenty-one. It was a good time to go and a better one to leave. Ahead of him were the Middle Temple and literary celebrity. Behind him Ireland was in flames. From Dublin to Galway, from Kildare to Wexford, the repercussions of the 1798 rebellion were still being felt. The gibbets remained against the skyline. The terrible stories of pitch-and-tar cappings were still travelling from village to village in Wexford. The heroes of the rebellion, Emmet, Tone, Fitzgerald, were either dead or about to be. And their ideas—what Yeats called "all that delirium of the brave"—were over for a generation.

Poor Tom Moore. In British drawing rooms, with his sweet tenor voice, singing his own Irish melodies, he brought tears to the eyes of his listeners. Most of them were ladies; many of them were the wives of the landlords and militia who were even then, at that very moment, against the backdrop of his songs, looting and burning and murdering and evicting.

My father climbed the stairs. He opened the piano. He began to play. With flat-spread, nicotine-stained fingers. He played "Oft, in the Stilly Night" and "Believe Me, If All Those Endearing Young Charms" and "The Minstrel-Boy."

And why not? A century and a half before he had come to London as a diplomat representing Ireland, these songs had preceded him in the role. They had sweet-talked and compromised their way into British drawing rooms, guaranteeing that the

Irish question would be a matter of cadence and the English response a modicum of sentiment.

The tune lilted up and down. I closed my eyes, opened them, closed them again. I looked away from the smoke. And stood there on the top floor of a building on a fogbound English afternoon—a building that was itself a fiction of nationhood— listening to other fictions.

The expatriate is in search of a country; the exile in search of a self. He or she learns how to look for it in a territory between rhetoric and reality, with its own customs and habits of mind, its preferred speech and rigorous invention. I may have heard the song so many times I was bored by it. I may have felt the malaise and displacement of that upper room, stranded in a city of nowheres. But I was learning something. Tom Moore was a survivor. In a time of transition and danger, he had understood that safety is not a place but a language. In his search for a nation, he had discovered that above all.

FROM
IN SEARCH OF A NATION

I came back to Ireland when I was fourteen. I saw unfamiliar sights: horses and lamplight and the muddy curve of the Liffey. I grew to know street names and bus timetables. I went to live with my sisters in a flat outside the city. I went to boarding school. I studied for exams. I started to explore the word *Irish*, not this time as a distant fact but as the close-up reality of my surroundings. As a word which painted letter boxes and colored trains. Which framed laws and structured language.

Language. At first, this was what I lacked. Not just the historic speech of the country. I lacked that too, but so did others. This was a deeper loss; I returned to find that my vocabulary of belonging was missing. The street names, the meeting places—it was not just that I did not know them. It was something more. I had never known them. I had lost not only a place, but the past that goes with it and, with it, the clues from which to construct a present self.

I had to learn a new sensory idiom. A fog in the mouth, for

example, which was different from the London one: less gritty, with more of an ocean aftertaste. An unkempt greenness on the streets. A drizzle which was inter-seasonal, constant. Different trees. Different birds.

As I learned these things, the last unwanted gift of exile came to me. I began to watch places with an interest so exact it might have been memory. There was that street corner, with the small newsagent which sold copies of the *Irish Independent* and honeycomb toffee in summer. I could imagine myself there, a child of nine, buying peppermints and walking back down by the canal, the lock brown and splintered as ever, the young boys diving from it.

It became a powerful impulse. This slow and intense reconstruction of a childhood which had never happened. A fragrance or a trick of light was enough. Or a house I entered which I wanted not just to appreciate but to remember, and then I would begin. Here was the hall with its parquet floor, the sideboard with white lilac and a gilded mirror. There were the photographs of the children and the kennel outside for the dog. I had been eleven here, playing with a friend in that garden. I had been six. I could remember the croquet game in summer, the skirts of women, the serious and intent faces of the players.

There was a small seaside town outside Drogheda called Clogher Head. I had missed it by a small action, by a form of words. Now I thought myself back into it: summer days when the rain cleared and the roads were vacant. A bicycle lying sideways on the main street, and a brown and white dog barking. Red lemonade sold in long bottles. And the vista full of bathers and fishing boats, and the grit of sand as it came out of shoes and towels. And I, in a room where light came through the

curtains until an hour before midnight, lying down to sleep.
An Irish child.

.   .   .

Irish. If I could not remember a country, I could at least imagine a nation. I was not searching for a dialogue; I was looking
to disappear into powerful images: the narrow back ways of a
British town where a shot was fired, a man was captured and
the refrain of a ballad was made inevitable. A channel of water
where French sailing ships creaked and heaved. A gibbet, its
outline visible for miles against a Wexford horizon.

Imagination. The word itself has the poignance of opposites.
By imagining a nation, I was beginning the very process, awak-
ening the very faculty which would bring me into conflict with
it. I was building a strength which would discover a weakness
in these images. But at the same time those oppositions seemed
unlikely. I had returned home. The country was changing. Nevertheless, the external reality still supported something very like
patriotism. There were festivals and remembrances. Newspapers
referred easily and often to the past. The city was marked with
buildings, corners, alleyways where a hero had died; a point
had been proved.

I listened out for the references. I looked intently at the buildings. I read book after book and remembered names and actions.
But I knew in my heart, I never forgot it, that I was not the same
as other Irish children. Like the daughter in a legend, I had been
somewhere else. I had eaten different foods. I had broken the
spell of place and family. By that logic alone, I could not return.

.   .   .

The issue between an artist and a nation is not a faith, but a self. The creative self must be complex and earned; the national self is ardent and singular, bent to the collective and determined to serve it.

At sixteen, once I had returned to Ireland, my life was both obedient and disordered. I stayed here and went there. I lived in a flat when I was not at boarding school. I was reading poetry and trying to write it. But when I took a piece of paper and began to write those first poems, even through the borrowed images and false gestures, I saw the existence and demand of a preliminary self. I had no language for it, and no wish for it. The vague sense of a future, where sexuality and memory, childhood and language would have to meet, was more a threat than a hope. The images of the nation were moving and compelling for that reason: they gathered the will into action; they turned the action into heroism.

I was beginning also to see the power of landscape, mostly, however, as cityscape. The relation of stone to water, and the way granite after dark or rain gave off a sort of streetlight, and the vivid streets and neighbourhoods of Dublin, all drew me in.

On Sunday afternoons, with time off school, or on Easter holidays, I would take a series of buses into the middle of the city. First from Killiney village, through Dun Laoghaire and along the coast for a while, with its strand and chimneys, leaning and turning to see the pinpoints of cantering ponies. Then another bus into Stephen's Green. Then I was free to walk around, looking at streets and back lanes. I had no coherent idea of where the town ended and the country began, of how the past inscribed itself in this place or that. I had no local history.

Even so I began to realize—although some of this is the work of hindsight—how hard it was to extricate place from nation. The names, the memories, even the inches of ground had become proof of pride and sacrifice. But these are not the thoughts or the words of a teenager. If I take an example now, I am arguing as a woman and not the girl who stood outside St Catherine's Church in Thomas Street one September afternoon and was told that Robert Emmet had been hanged here, in that month, in 1803.

EMMET. SEPTEMBER. The hero and the month of my birth. The beautiful opening act of winter when corners of Stephen's Green at dusk looked like a smoking room after midnight: a bluish haze, convivial and promising. The smell of leaves burning in crisp piles. The mulberry leaves drying out and the rowanberries turning scarlet. And a man hung by the neck until he died.

He was hanged on a September day. The executioner asked twice, three times on the scaffold, "Are you ready sir?" Then— after Emmet replied, "Not yet"— lost patience and opened the trapdoor. After half an hour his body was cut down, his head cut off and the hangman walked the wooden platform holding it and saying, "This is the head of Robert Emmet." Hard to believe that despite his end, he had been a real man. A young man. Hardly more than a boy in the winter of 1802, as he moved around Dublin, talking at dinner tables, over the salt cellars and crystal of a doomed and temporary Protestant nation, keeping his counsel. A flesh-and-blood man in the city where he would die.

AND THIS IS WHERE, outside St Catherine's Church, before my eyes and the eyes of that teenager, Robert Emmet disappears. He vanishes into soft words, garbled accounts of his speech from the dock. He becomes legend and excuse. He drifts, in a slow haze of half-truths, into memories that are neither clear nor accurate. He becomes romantic fable and nationalist invention. And in so doing, he describes the typical trajectory of the nationalist hero: from action to image. From event to invention.

In Emmet's case it was almost immediate. Within a few years of his death, his friend Tom Moore has turned him into a soft option. "O breathe not his name, let it sleep in the shade," he writes of him. The song was to be sung to the air of "The Red Fox." Moore reminisced happily about the sources of its inspiration: "How little did I then think in one of the most touching of the sweet airs I used to play to him, his own dying words would find an interpreter so worthy of their sad but proud feeling."

In the fastness of British drawing rooms, in the safe company of aristocrats and liberals, Moore knew exactly how much Irish patriotism was acceptable, and how little. Emmet became a fiction. Into that fiction was subsumed all the awkwardness, all the untidy events of conspiracy. Into it went the strained features of the young man who kept his hopes and seditions hidden in the winter of 1802. Into it went a hope for freedom. Out of it came the words of pre-Victorian sentiment—a strategy as effective in making rebellion safe as any spy or warrant from Dublin Castle.

AND SO THE CONTINUUM between poet and patriot, between language and action was not what I had thought. It was not a solid and useful bridge across which a history moved to safety. Instead, it was a soft and flawed connection, where words undid actions and actions could never be free of their consequences in language. For every death there would be a ballad. In every ballad the brokenhearted transactions between drawing room and street corner, and between English liberal and Irish rebel, would be stated and restated.

It is hard enough at fifteen and sixteen to know anything, and I knew less than most. I had lost the free speech of childhood. I was overintense and ready to seize on the wrong details. I found it hard to make my way from season to season, taking for granted the signposts that led to adulthood. My years away had given me a crooked respect for episodes. And here was a history rich in them. Here was an admixture of folly and locale and love of place. And it was hard to resist. Above all, it was hard to deny the force of this particular episode.

Outside a church on the north side of a city a scaffold had been built. Windows had shut and doors closed to the sound of that hammering. Autumn light had fallen on raw wood. A man had died there. I knew in my mind, in my intellect, through my reading of poetry, that place could be free of taint. Could be an imaginative design where freedom from exile and estrangement was found. And yet it was hard to look at the streets with their cowled streetlamps, to look at the hills at the end of them and to disentangle the idea of those stones and blues from the idea of a man who died. For this. And this. And this.

. . .

In my own way I understood the pageantry and tension behind the idea of a nation. The gibbets. The coffin ships. I saw it all through the glass of exile, by which the glamour of ownership was greatly magnified. But I was too young to understand that part of a nation which would come to challenge and exclude me as a woman and an artist: its sexual drama.

The teenage years, for any young person, have enough sexual drama. I was growing up, away from my parents, moving towards language and desire at the same time, but not at the same speed. I was awkward and dreamy. I looked in mirrors. I thought of a future with love and pleasure in it, but without location.

In the midst of those uncertainties, the nation, at least for a time, was a definite and sharp reality. It happened. It gathered. It was an irreducible part of an everyday life. I looked at the shamrocks, the wolfhounds, even the crude likenesses of the 1916 patriots with uncritical eyes. I listened to and used the dialect of patriotism. *Martyr. Sacrifice. Our own.* And if there was a hidden drama, to some extent it was concealed by the sheer eloquence of the cause and my own need for that eloquence. Viewed from a distance, the story of the nation was a narrative of destiny. A small island, next to a larger one, loses both territory and language. And, after centuries of oppression, recovers part of one and less of the other. Not a fortunate story, but a compelling one.

I NEED TO PAUSE HERE. I need to remember that at sixteen and seventeen I loved that narrative. A back street. The slime of cobbles near the river. A single shot undoing a century of humiliation. Or so it seemed. The individual act of courage drew me in. I carried the melody of patriotism with me as I came into the ordinary daylight of the city, as I passed Coca-Cola signs and advertisements for caricatures. I took books down from the shelves in libraries and the houses of friends. I read with wonder and enthusiasm.

I had, to accompany my discoveries, a powerful literature of protest and remembrance. Coming to my seventeenth birthday, I was reading the *Jail Journal* of John Mitchel. There in a black, staccato prose were the hinge and swing of the whole legend. Born in Derry, Mitchel had gone to Trinity College as I would. He had contributed to the *Nation* newspaper, founded by other patriots in 1842. In May of 1848, after the collapse of an ill-conceived rebellion, he was tried for sedition, found guilty and sentenced to fourteen years' transportation. And so here he was, in a beautiful early-summer twilight, steaming out of Dublin Bay on a prison ship. "Dublin city with its bay and pleasant villas," he wrote, "city of bellowing slaves, villas of genteel dastards— lies now behind us, and the sun has set behind the blue peaks of Wicklow, as we steam past Bray Head, where the vale of Shanganagh, sloping softly from the Golden Spears, sends its bright river murmuring to the sea. And I am on the first stage of my way, faring to what regions of unknown horror? And may never never—never more, O, Ireland—my mother and queen!—see vale or hill or murmuring stream of thine."

A dark violence blurred by Victorian sentiment. At first it was an irresistible mix. I read in starts and stops through the nineteenth century. The poems, speeches, ballads. Only gradually, and then only with a half awareness, did the sexual drama begin to unfold. Only in fractions and pieces of information and reflection did I begin to notice certain things: that the clairvoyance I needed to enter that theatre of action and danger demanded a troubling androgyny. If I wanted to be in those back streets, to speak in those conspiracies, I would have to be male. The male, after all, was an active principle, inviting admiration. And I was a teenage girl, looking not just to admire but to belong. Yet how could I belong to these actions, dreamed up by men and carried out by them? The fact is that teenage dreams of action and heroism are filled with exciting and impossible transpositions of sexuality. In those dreams, I would wear the green tailcoat, or crop my head or carry a revolver. If I wanted to feel the power of nation as well as its defeat, then I would take on the properties of the hero. I would raid a barracks for arms or write a note the night before my execution under the bluish sputter of a gas flame. I would crack my head against a pavement north of the Liffey as I fell, wounded to death by British bullets. And as soon as my head—a male, thick-necked head—touched the stone I would dissolve into refrains and stanzas. I would pass from hero to apotheosis.

But I was uneasy. Gradually, in inches not yards, I began to realize that this idea of a nation, for all its lore and invention, had ugly limits. For those empathies, those androgynies to exist, I had to make myself available for reconstruction. I could not be, for a start, quick or skeptical. I could not even be the untidy teenager that I was, moving between houses and schools and flats, looking for a home and unready to find one. I had to be prepared, with each encounter, to open my heart and close my mind.

And yet if you took the hero out of the story what was left? What female figure was there to identify with? There were no women in those back streets. None, at least, who were not lowly auxiliaries of the action. The heroine, as such, was utterly passive. She was Ireland or Hibernia. She was stamped, as a rubbed-away mark, on silver or gold; a compromised regal figure on a throne. Or she was a nineteenth-century image of girlhood, on a frontispiece or in a book of engravings. She was invoked, addressed, remembered, loved, regretted. And, most important, died for. She was a mother or a virgin. Her hair was swept or tied back, like the prow of a ship. Her flesh was wood or ink or marble. And she had no speaking part. If her harvests were spoiled, her mother tongue wiped out, her children killed, then it was for someone else to mark the reality. Her identity was as an image. Or was it a fiction?

Caught between these realities, I grew more and more unsettled. I had no exact words for how I felt. But after a while I was less free in my adventures. Gradually my re-creation of the back streets, my sense of the glamour of a single action were being undermined. I was having to see the story within the story. I was starting to notice the absence of my name in it. I was feeling the sexual opposites within the narrative. The intense passivity of the female; the fact that to the male principle was reserved the right, not simply of action but of expression as well. I was ready to weep or sing or recite in the cause of Ireland. To do any of that, however, I would have to change from the young girl who looked with increasing interest at the faces and shapes of boys. I would have to give up the body and spirit of a woman. If I chose to keep them, then my tears would dry out, my mouth would close, my words would disappear. I was restive and disappointed at the choices offered to me. And, in a certain sense, unclear. And there was something else: if the passive images of Ireland—the queen, the silver stamp—were so present in songs and remembrances, what had happened to the others? To the women who had survived. And those who had not.

· · ·

In a summer dusk, when I was seventeen, my mother told me a story. I was leaning across a chair, facing a window. Back out towards the river, which ran behind the house, the sky was still bright; everything else was darkening. The fruit trees were spare and dark—a child's drawing. The apples were black globes.

The story she told was about her mother. She had been

born into a family of millers, and had been one of thirteen children. She had married very young, a seaman who became a sea captain. She had died after the birth of her last child— my mother—at thirty-one in a Dublin hospital.

It was a short conversation. My mother spoke only rarely about the past. It was, in its way, a small piece of an oral tradition, told in a summer dusk and in a halting way. Of a woman she could not remember. Who had been deserted by good luck and had left five orphan daughters. There was nothing heroic in her account, and she offered no meanings. Instead, she did what innumerable human beings have done with their children: she told me what had happened.

. . .

My grandmother lived outside history. And she died there. A thirty-one-year-old woman, with five daughters, facing death in a hospital far from her home—I doubt that anything around her mattered then. Yet in her lifetime Ireland had gone from oppression to upheaval. A language had been reclaimed. Laws had changed. Conspiracies and explosions were everyday occurrences. And she had existed at the edge of it.

Did she find her nation? And does it matter? In one sense it does. Throughout the decade and a half in which she bore her children and moved nearer to her death, her country was restating itself in forceful and painful ways. One spring, twenty-five Fenians were sentenced to long terms of penal servitude. Among them was Tom Clarke, who would endure English prison and emerge to die before a British firing squad. In November 1884, the Congress of the Gaelic Athletic Association met in Thurles.

It was a stormy meeting. When a priest in Nenagh tried to

propose a different candidate for chairman of the meeting from the local Fenian, there was an immediate split between the clerical and Fenian members of the association. Imagine the scene. The tables bare and pushed aside. The flushed faces and scattered papers. The moon hanging outside, over a town, over a field. The man who raises a fist in the doorway and shouts about another man's betrayal.

Small events. Local frictions. And yet I wonder whether she turned in some corridor, looked up from some moment of play and heard the whispers and gossip which, by their force, suggested a wider truth. Did she hear in some muttered conversation the future of an armed struggle, the music of anger, the willingness to die? I doubt it. If she looked up at all, I believe that she was listening for her life—for some intonation in a voice which told her of simple love or downright annoyance.

And what was I listening for? Three-quarters of a century on, I lifted my head, I looked up. What troubled me, increasingly, was not whether she had included the nation in her short life. But whether that nation had included her.

. . .

What is this thing—a nation—that is so powerful it can make songs, attract sacrifice and so exclusive it drives into hiding the complex and skeptical ideas which would serve it best?

I would come to wonder in later years how a nation is made, how it continues to be made. Whether the whispers of an assassination, gathering force in back rooms and safe houses, guarantee it. Whether the ballad hummed after midnight in an empty street assists it. Whether its real energy lies in conspiracy or celebration. As I walked the streets, looking at green buses and letter boxes, at street names marked in Irish, I could see the visible signs of it. Its invisible life I was less sure of.

And here was the clue. The making of a nation—I would come to see this—lies not in codes or names but in its power to construct its unseen inner life from the minds and memories of those who live in it. To turn inhabitants into citizens and citizens into patriots.

For a season I was both. I have to look back and see a girl finding her way slowly in the outer world of a city yet relatively swiftly in the inner world which was its inference. My intelligence was a jumble of refrains and battles. I knew the names of men caught into obscure treasons; I knew the addresses of prisons in odd parts of the British Isles. I belonged to myself and to my country insofar as I could translate that self into that country. If I had continued in that moment, then the invisible nation would have continued its progress. An architecture of songs, roads, ambush sites and old graveyards would have built slowly. It would have taken over my ability to see landscape and my judgement of the last chapter of a book.

But it did not happen. I was reading other books. I was hearing other reminiscences. There were other lives—the lives, for instance, given over to language rather than action—which seemed to me exemplary. I was building within myself the hope that I could also live that life of language. I was starting to feel— although this may make it more conscious than it was—that the silent female imagery in the lore of the nation went badly with my active determination to be a poet.

It is not so hard to make a picture of one person's search for a nation. It is, after all, a subjective business. It is much harder to draw the map of the imaginative faculty which is threatened by that search. I wanted to find and belong to my country's power-

ful version of history. I found that the imagination I was beginning to sense in myself—perhaps only in a rudimentary feeling
for language—was limited and constrained by that version. To
understand the difficult oppositions between that version and
the life of the imagination, I would have to go further and look
harder. It would be lonely work.

FROM
IN SEARCH OF A LANGUAGE

T here is a defining moment which comes early in a poet's life. A moment full of danger. It happens at the very edge of becoming a poet, when behind there is nothing but the mute terrain where, until then, a life has been lived and felt without finding its formalization.

In my case, that mute backwards-reaching distance was my own childhood. It had been lived out of my country, away from the signals and clues by which a self, almost without knowing it, finds its way to adulthood. The moment of danger for me, as for other poets, came when it looked at last that the silence would yield to expression. At that split second—although, of course, it takes longer and is more gradual than that—all the rough surfaces give way to the polish and slip of language. Then it can easily seem that the force is in the language, not in the awkward experience it voices. In that initial excitement, when the stanza takes shape for the first time, when the rhyme fits or the cadence has a real music, more poets are lost than found. The temptation is to honor the power of poetry and forget that hinterland where you lived for so long, without a sound in your throat, without a syllable at your command.

I was now seventeen. There was a peculiar indignity for me in the silence of my childhood. Not only had it lacked words; it had lacked a name. When I stood on Hyde Park Corner on my way to school, there was nothing I could put my own idiom on. No slowness of a bus, or blunt corner teashop, or graveyard glimpsed from a train—none of the sights which become the shorthand of a place. Lacking an idiom, I had lacked a place. Therefore, in some strange way, although I talked too much and was a youngest child—I had been silent. Then slowly, in my early adolescence, came the consciousness of poetry. I remembered lines; I came on descriptions. Then I discovered Yeats and read him. Then, inching my way forward again, I began to make literary idioms, however self-conscious and artificial, for the color of the Liffey and the swans on it. It was awkward and sentimental, but it fitted words to the place for the first time.

Now, in my eighteenth year, I had gone forward again. I read more, I became more ambitious. The swans and the river were woven into something which reached further. All at once I became aware of a real power in form. The poems I wrote were still forced; but the act of writing them became less so.

At night I went up to the small dormitory above the bay. The evenings were less cold and growing longer. I could still see the eucalyptus tree in the last light. The sky stayed bright over the evergreens, and I could hear a bell from a church over to the east. The clarity of color and sound added to my feeling of power. And so without warning, and in that particular loneliness which is almost inseparable from the dangerous growth of understanding, I came to know the rewards and jubilance of control. I learned how to write a line with a ringing sound. I learned a small amount about the paragraph of the stanza. The river grew more elegant, the swans more important, and considerably less real. I sat there night after night writing—putting down words and crossing them out. Gradually I gained control. Gradually I erased Rilke's question: "Go inside yourself. Discover the motive that bids you write; examine whether it sends its roots down to the deepest places of your heart, confess to yourself whether you would have to die if writing were denied you. This before all: ask yourself in the quietest hour of your night: *must* I write?"

I wore a school uniform, which was dark green, with a flannel shirt and a heavy sweater. The dark woolen cuff of my right wrist was always under my eye as I turned the page. I came to know its threads, the weave and texture of the way the shirt cuff turned under it.

By now I was reading Latin literature. The Sixth Book of the *Aeneid*. Day by day the lines accumulated. It was a slow magic, an incantation of images and structures, a pounding syntax. The story line was clear and uncomplicated. Aeneas, Virgil's hero, has already travelled through other lands in other books. He has courted and betrayed Dido in Carthage. He has left her to commit suicide and sailed with the Trojan fleet to Libya and on to Sicily. Now the Sixth Book opens, and Aeneas visits the Cumaean sibyl in Italy. Once he has got the Golden Bough, she descends with him to the underworld and to the river Styx, and on the far shore of it they see the dead.

LET ME LOOK BACK AGAIN. The table is round and drab; the worn linen stays on the armrests, the sky is full of the light and danger of spring. The same gulls. The same pupils walking and laughing below the window, the same slight and irritating grinding where they walk on the gravel. The usual text is spread out, creased at the edges.

What my second sight shows me is not about the room, or the action, but about myself. I see, as I bend over the page, that everything which has defined my life up to that moment is something which has not happened. I have not had an Irish childhood. I have not found my sexuality. I feel no casual ownership about the distances behind me. My sense of language, therefore, is of something powerful enough to keep me sexless and stateless. In that realm, I feel my wants and absences least. In this language, most of all, with its syntax, its complete and structured perceptions, there are no small spaces for a childhood, an exile, to get through. These paragraphs are barricades against regret and anxiety. I can read them, day after day, as armories.

THE POET'S VOCATION—or, more precisely, the historical construction put upon it—is one of the single, most problematic areas for any woman who comes to the craft. Not only has it been defined by a tradition which could never foresee her, but it is construed by men about men, in ways which are poignant, compelling and exclusive.

For instance, I understood, even then, the charm of Gosse's description of Swinburne: "He sat back in the deep sofa in his sitting room, his little feet close together, his arms against his side, folded in his frock-coat like a grasshopper in its wing-covers, and fallen asleep apparently for the night before I could blow out the candles and steal forth from the door."

But charming as it was, the description was of a piece with

the exclusiveness. I looked with care and interest at the sketch of Keats in his death sweat, of Shelley with his shirt collar undone. They moved and interested me. I could feel the enticement to feel like that, to develop some precocious maleness which would carry me towards it.

And there was another tradition, encoded in the lost language of a nation I was just beginning to sense somewhere beyond that schoolroom. A land of wounds. Of scalded flesh and a single God. Where a complex and vital relation had existed between poetry and faith, between the vocation of the poet and the demands of a society. If the boy poet was the image of the British tradition, the Bardic poet was the shadow left on the Irish one.

"The Gaelic social order in Ireland," writes the scholar James Carney, "lasted from centuries before the beginnings of recorded history into the seventeenth century. It was in many ways an archaic society the origin of whose institutions are to be sought in the remote period of Indo-European unity. In this society the composing of poetry was not the occupation of the specially gifted, the aesthete or the dilettante. Poetry, even in Christian times, partook of the nature of a religious institution and was so closely woven into the fabric of political Gaeldom that without it that society could not continue to exist unless by changing its political essence."

The paradox of those traditions, with their sense of exclusiveness, was that I saw the power of language more clearly. I sensed a force that could heal wounds and soothe indecision. In the great systems of syntax I was just beginning to understand and in the faltering poems I wrote in the last light, I found a temptation to look for that place between the words themselves where I could forget girlhood and its longing, forget the dislocation of a childhood, clothe myself in an old and inherited sense of possession and so divide myself from the frailties which so far were all I knew of my self.

AT ONE LEVEL, I sat at a table with a spring tide behind me and learned a lesson. At another, the lessons I was learning were about powerlessness and not power. My body betrayed me into all the conventional dreams of girlhood. The Victorian hero glowed out of the novels I studied, signaling the peace of submission and belonging. But the country I belonged to offered no ready answers and no predictable destiny. By day I read Latin; at night I read Yeats and tried to write my own poetry. By day I touched the granite and marble of words. At nighttime I followed language into a land of hurt and disappointment.

My knowledge of Irish history was sketchy and still incomplete. But I understood enough to sense the rage and anxiety of a long nineteenth-century hunt for a place. What was harder to place was my own body and mind, caught in the sunny nowhere-ish morning of a schoolroom, learning the language of conquest in a country which had known nothing else. As I bent over the page, every one of those anomalies came with me.

THAT MOMENT OF DISCOVERY and power is so dangerous for the developing poet because it marks the point at which he or she stumbles on one of the family secrets of the tradition. That secret in turn was whispered throughout the nineteenth century, when, with the breakdown of faith and certainty, a new portrayal of the imagination became commonplace: the imagination as sacramental force, as a laying on of hands. The argument gained strength as organized religion declined. In his Oxford lectures on poetry Matthew Arnold said:

> There is not a creed which is not shaken, not an accredited dogma which is not shown to be questionable, not a received tradition which does not threaten to dissolve. Our religion has materialised itself in the fact, in the supposed fact; it has attached its emotion to the fact and now the fact is failing it. But for poetry the idea is everything; the rest is a world of illusion, of divine illusion. Poetry attaches its emotion to the idea; the idea is the fact. The strongest part of our religion today is its unconscious poetry.

I read his words as part of my studies. But they were beyond me. I was still a teenager in uniform, in the city where my childhood had not happened, feeling the first power and confusion of sexuality, dreading that the larger exiles would follow from the smaller one: that I would suffer the loss of self after the absence of self. The shaken creeds, the dissolving traditions, I knew were all the local and unimportant ones of my own history. For that reason, the piercing irony of his words was lost on me. I did not understand that to invest the imagination with sacramental powers restores to poetry not its religious force but its magical function. In the oldest societies they were part and parcel of each other. But magic is the search for control over an unruly environment; it is also the most inferior of the past associations of poetry. Yet it was what I rejoiced in as I sat at night, the bay in the distance, making artifice, making music. I did not know that the best such magic could achieve would be a simplification of life based on a dread of it.

FROM
TURNING AWAY

A t nineteen years of age I was a poet; I was sure of it. Now I look back I see the assurance itself as flawed and callow. But at the time it seemed enough. I lived in a small flat looking out on a busy road. I wore a skirt and a woolen jumper and a raincoat on wet days, and felt nothing about them. I had little enough interest in clothes. But the rooms of the flat had personalities. They welcomed or resisted me, and some part of me opened or closed in them. One faced north towards a convent balcony where a nun in a wimple and black habit walked slowly up and down at sunset. Another looked out on a garden with a crooked path. Occasionally a boy would come back with me, at the end of a college day, and we would lie on the floor or in the bed, caught in an odd unhappening dream of pleasure or hope. But rarely. It was language and not sex that happened there.

I had a soft and angry way of writing a poem. I would take a copy book and a biro, set it down on a table and make a jug of milky coffee. I would sit there, as if beside someone with a fever, waiting for the lines, the figures, the forms to take shape. I wrote it down and crossed it out; I read it out loud and wrote it again. I made it better. I made it worse.

I had a sense of language and a preliminary sense of form. I knew, in a poor sort of way, that this human action of sitting in a chair, taking a pen, writing lines on a page, was part of the history of the poem. In one way I was right. That action of closing the fingers of my right hand around a pen, of marking the page—there, alone in that small room—was indeed the central act; by this, the poem and its history happened at one and the same time. What I lacked was a clear and useful sense of how this central statement, by its very occurrence, touched and disordered all the other statements.

THE CITY I COULD REACH by a five- or six-minute bus ride was the location of an odd and powerful moment of European poetry. On the surface, such literary life as it had was limited to a few coffee houses and pubs. The pubs were crowded and badly lit. Sometimes they had old-fashioned and plumped-out seats, running against the wall, under mirrors engraved with the names of whiskeys or distilleries. Then it was possible to sit back in an atmosphere of noise and smoke, watching the glitter and crush of the evening happening in the mirrors.

It was not the substance of the conversation which drew me to those places—too much of it was gossip—but the shape of the conversation was different. At first, the literary surface was an ordinary mix of information and malice. As such, it was the replica of all such conversations which hover around the subject of success or failure. So-and-so had a book out. It was good; it was not good. He had been paid. Or much more likely, he had not been paid. More whiskeys. More details.

But if you listened carefully, as the night went on, you could hear an older historiography at work. The man—it was always a man—who was considered to have written good poetry was spoken of, if only for a bare moment, as exempt from the routine, scathing criticism. The poet described in that way was respected as a man who had put his fields, his enemies, his townlands into the poem. Who had brought his own reality to the poem and to whom the poem had yielded. For that moment he ceased to be described in terms of success and was talked about, although often so quickly you had to listen carefully, in terms of power.

The name I heard most often was that of Patrick Kavanagh. He had come to Dublin from a border farm a quarter century before, in the impossible aftermath of the Literary Revival. An awkward, sometimes fierce countryman, he had revealed the hypocrisies and costs of a national literature. In the fifties, sick and disaffected in the aftermath of a wounding libel case, he would sit on a bench beside the canal, the same ordinary piece of water that was near my flat. And there, with no word about nation or history, he had staked a claim to a new piece of ground. "O commemorate me where there is water."

For all this, apart from that elusive undertone of respect, there was nothing reverent in the talk about him; on the contrary. References to him were always familiar and sometimes, since he was not an easy man, exasperated. Yet from those conversations I took away a clear inference. Yeats had made a literature. Kavanagh had made the single, daring act of protest which pointed the way forward.

———

WHEN CLOSING TIME CAME, I was not far from home. I never drank, and so I came out clearheaded and on the edge of enchantment. I would walk home or take the last bus, my mind full of names and fragments of information. The cool, splashy darkness of a spring or autumn night would go by. Then I would turn the key and climb the stairs to my flat and find there the notebook still open on the oilskin tablecloth and the window with a few stars stuck to it.

I had no words for it, no way of structuring perception and no one to structure it for me. Yet I was beginning to understand that the marks on the page were a fraction of an inch high but reached a hundred miles deep into a country's past, its fears, superstitions, and memories.

The conversations I had heard were part of it. They were not elegant or well judged, those conversations. But in their way they were firsthand evidence that in this city two powerful histories of the European poem met and merged. The first was the history of the metropolitan poem, which had increasingly detached itself from powers and princes and had, with the romantic movement, become the commanding text of an interior life. Dublin with its Georgian squares, its fanlights and candle sconces, was no stranger to this poem which had crossed the sea to it in the nineteenth century and had been heard in drawing rooms and recited in vicarages. It proposed, at its weakest, only a fiction of inwardness. And as such it was a fashionable accessory for young women and the men who wished to please them. At its best it offered a rare and unsettling glimpse of an inner landscape.

But the other history, the other poem, was different. It was both sharper and more bitter, as well as more concerned with the external meaning of a poet's life. It was the history of the bard, the prince's friend, the honored singer. Who made his way from village to village, shifting from praise to invective as the occasion demanded. Who celebrated christenings and weddings, who flattered his patrons and excoriated their enemies. Who became, reluctantly, a witness to the totality of the British conquest and the loss of a vital language. After a childhood away, I did not speak that language. But I sensed that the poem it remembered was as deep in Irish life as the other was an outcome of British civilization. It was scarred by its origins and made loud by injustice. It gave a wider role to the poet and more credence to his prince.

FOR MANY YEARS I could make little sense of it—this remembered image of a girl in a jumper and skirt, leaving her flat, climbing onto the open, rocking platform of a bus and going into the heart of a city. For years, pieces of the journey and the destination would come back to me, like missing sections of a photograph. The curve and sway of the bus as it turned by Stephen's Green, and the trees to one side of the road. The smoky interior of a pub, a glass of stout on the table, with a broken creamy top and someone arguing about poetry. I remember the conversations with other poets and a growing estrangement from all kinds of assumptions which seemed easily or readily available to them. And then back to the flat. To the tablecloth. To the page.

It is there I now see myself. The window I am sitting against is an iron-framed square, small enough, and giving on a garden with an apple tree and a crooked path. The winter light is just sufficient to show me the marks which have been written. I know some things, even as I look back now. I know that my poem, poor as it looks on the page, has good intentions. It wants to say all the ambiguities, awkward regrets and distances of my childhood. It wants to say a country in which some strangeness of relation keeps happening, so that I am drawn in and unassimilated at the same time. It wants to unsay the cadences and certainties of one kind of Irishness. What the girl, whose face is absorbed and turned away, does not know yet, is that these are radical acts. They will not be enabled because of some grace of expression or a stumbled-over eloquence on a winter evening. They will require a series of engagements and assessments with the place and the time and the poem. They will require a sense of location in these, and then an act of leave-taking.

BUT FOR NOW THE CITY, with its twilights and meeting places, its conversations and memories, seemed made for poetry. There was even an enchantment about it. At night, after hours of rain, the pavements had the look of wet coal. The air in a café or a pub would be warm with the wrung-out smell of wet tea cloths. There was something about the impermanence of a table with empty glasses, or a cigarette turning itself into a sculpture of ash, which suggested the small melodrama of homelessness. On a given night everyone at that table, everyone with a glass or a cigarette—I was sure of it—secretly wanted to be a poet.

Here, if anywhere, I should be able to take up the poetic existence which was apparently on offer in this place. It was set out as a series of hopeful tensions: between bard and poète maudit. Between eighteenth-century mandarin and nineteenth-century romantic. It even seemed to me sometimes that I experienced one version or other of the poet according to which direction

I took in the morning. If I got off the bus and continued into Trinity College, I was back in the country of Goldsmith and Burke. On my way to lectures I could, if such a thing were possible, have reached out a hand and touched the preromantic scholarly poem. I could have climbed a stairway in any of the buildings in Front Square and walked back two centuries into a room as close and dark, as sheltered by cherry trees and quadrangles, as the one in which Thomas Gray wrote his "Elegy in a Country Churchyard." Everything reminded me that I was in a place of civility and reason. Even the cobblestones at the end of the day—small lumps of moonlight as I walked towards the city—recalled it.

But if I started out for Grafton Street, for a café or a pub, then sooner or later I would catch sight of something different: older and harder to see, but just as powerful. Not exactly a tradition. And nothing as formed as an aesthetic. But a living stream of talk, for all that, which recognized the poem in its time, which was angry and forceful and believing. On certain nights it was even possible to imagine its link to a lost world of Irish poetry, a place where the Irish bard Aogán Ó Rathaille had seen the Gaelic order collapse and his own patrons flee after the Treaty of Limerick failed at the end of the seventeenth century, and where he had been maddened by grief and pride into political poems, even when he was reduced to eating periwinkles on the Atlantic shore of Kerry.

Here in this city, itself caught between definitions, the concept of the poet should have been a rich and powerful one. There were even moments, such as those late-night conversations in the pubs, when a zone of grace opened for a moment and one tradition laid a hand on the other's shoulder.

In the eighteenth century, for instance, Oliver Goldsmith—a

young poet, struggling between medicine and literature—had moved around London, among the epigrams and coffee houses of a sophisticated city, in the age of science, of skepticism, of reason. For all the enclosure and self-regard of Augustan London, he had been able to recognize and salute the older and darker version of the poet.

"Their bards in particular," he wrote of the Irish, "are still held in great veneration among them: those traditionary heralds are invited to every funeral, in order to fill up the interval of the howls with their songs and harps. In these they rehearse the actions of the ancestors of the deceased, bewail the bondage of their country under the English government and generally conclude with advising the young men and maidens to make the best use of their time, for they will soon, for all their present bloom, be stretched under the table, like the dead body before them."

But I was still a teenager. Freckle-faced and bookish, anxious to take a protective coloring from this sharp-edged world I had found. In my struggle to find a life, I took for granted the wealth of ambiguity around me. And so I got up in the morning, put the silvery kettle on the gas ring and made a cup of instant coffee. Then took a bus to whichever station allowed me to look, half conscious and half aware, into the fierce countenance of Irish history.

I WAS DELIBERATELY LONELY. I liked the edgy solitude of nighttime walks which never took me far—perhaps only a round or so of the Green, under the streetlamps. Or the less than half mile from the Green to my flat. I liked spending time on my own over a cup of coffee, looking out on a street. I discovered there was something familiar and consoling about urban shapes: a vista of umbrellas or an infantry of feet moving towards a traffic light.

I look back now and I see that solitude as a forcing-house of perception, as nurturing a growing unease. I was still short of the exact words, the accurate perceptions. I still talked at night, and listened, with real excitement. And yet I was beginning to feel oddly stranded. Something was obstructing me, throwing me off course. I was between a poem—there, at home, on the tablecloth—and an idea of the poet. I could control the poem, even though it was with half-learned and hand-to-mouth techniques. I could listen for, and understand, the idea of the poet I picked up at night in the conversations I heard around me. But the space between them filled me with an odd malaise. Something about it seemed almost to have the force of an exclusion order.

Sometimes on my way to college, or making a detour to have a cup of coffee in the morning, I saw my reflection in a shop-window. I never liked what I saw. A redheaded girl, always self-conscious, never graceful enough. I saw the middle height, the untidiness, even the freckles if I went up close. I saw the student, the daughter, the girl friend, the bad-tempered fifth child. It was a measure of the confusion I felt, the increasing drain on my purpose and clearheadedness that I hardly ever thought I saw an Irish poet.

I MET PATRICK KAVANAGH in a café at the end of Grafton Street in Dublin. It was the middle sixties. He was within two years or so of his death. I sat at a small table, facing the door which opened out onto the street. I could see shop fronts and passersby. He sat with his back to the street: a man in early old age, wearing a coat and spectacles and a soft felt hat. I doubt if we talked for more than half an hour, forty minutes at the most.

In a simple sense, he was a man trying to eat his lunch in peace on a winter afternoon. I was callow enough to introduce myself; he was courteous enough to show no surprise and no irritation. I remember some details clearly; others have faded. I remember he wore a soft, felt hat at a rakish angle. But his coat will not come clear in my memory. It might have been a gaberdine raincoat. Then again I may have reinvented that from familiar photographs. I do remember that we ate hamburgers, which were then still new in Dublin. They were served on green plastic plates, on a dimpled paper napkin. As Kavanagh spoke—and he was short of breath from a lung operation—the paper fluttered under the hamburger.

His style of speech was shy and apocalyptic. He had a distinctive register of amazement, and impatience and dismissal. He spoke with real irritation about certain characters, "poetasters" as he would have called them. And shortly afterwards he told me with real pleasure that he had seen a golden eagle—in the States, I think—and that it was followed by "a retinue of little birds." But the connection is mine, not his.

By then Kavanagh had lived in Dublin for more than twenty years. I knew a little about him: that he had left Monaghan at the end of the thirties, that he had come to Dublin in search of literary fellowship. And that he regretted the decision. "No man," he once wrote of his townland "ever loved that landscape and even some of the people more than I." Dublin, however, was another matter. He had come to the city in the aftermath of the Literary Revival. He was scathing about its rhetoric and its preconceptions. "When I came to Dublin," he had written, "the

Irish Literary Affair was still booming. It was the notion that Dublin was a literary metropolis and Ireland as invented and patented by Yeats, Lady Gregory and Synge, a spiritual entity. It was full of writers and poets and I am afraid I thought their work had the Irish quality."

He finished lunch, drank a cup of tea and got up from the table. I stayed behind. The day still had big spaces in it. Nothing about it gave me an inkling—not at this point—that this had been important. Even so, I had touched something which would return to me later: an example of dissidence. Kavanagh was a countryman; I was a woman. Neither of those circumstances had much meaning for the other. But I had seen the witness of someone who had used the occasion of his life to rebuff the expectations and preconceptions of the Irish poem. I would remember it.

FOR ALL MY UNEASE, I was learning. It was a slow process, full of excitements. I was beginning to understand something about the poem on the page. Weekends and late at night I worked at line-lengths, stanza lengths, rhyme schemes.

I began to revel in it. The growth of control over language is one of the true—and one of the most deceptive—rewards for a young poet. There was less disappointment now as I sat at the table by the window. I was beginning also to connect my reading with my writing. The history of the stanza and the line was no longer abstract. At times, when something came out right on the page in front of me, or at least seemed to, a limitless adventure of language seemed to open backwards, like a map with trade routes offering access to only a few in every generation.

It was a solemn and self-conscious way of doing things, and yet the elements of form were still important in the Irish poem. They held it in place and pinned it down. It never occurred to me, at that point anyway, to question it. To that extent, I was working on the received version of a poem and my real achievement would be not a perfection of style or stanza but a growing doubt. In the meantime, on those dark, enclosed nights, in the odd loneliness and emptiness of a late girlhood, I laboured over someone else's poem. I was dogged about it. The telephone would ring. Friends would arrange a meeting. I would answer the phone and accept the invitation. But I always came back to the window, to the table, to the page. Once the young brother of a friend, a boy of about sixteen, called as I was finishing a poem that seemed important at the time. It was an afternoon in March. The garden outside was full of cold beginnings. The first blossoms. The last daffodils. A thrush calling. He looked at me, tongue-tied and round-cheeked, across the table. My copybook was open; the marks were on the page, waiting to be added to. For just a moment I felt the strangeness of it all. The stilted talk; the task that never ended. Then it passed and I was impatient for him to go.

It was an illusion—I learned that later—this sense of the enclosure and isolation of the work. But every young poet yields to it. It gives a glamour to the rented room and the painted blue dresser. It makes the window with its stars and leaves seem the edge and not the end of possibility. It turns an act of language into a sense of power.

POETRY AS MAGIC. Every young poet, struggling to find words, sooner or later touches that old and superstitious idea. Every apprentice, however clumsy with a piece of metre or a paragraph of music, has a sense—if only for a moment— that to name the lightning is to own it.

I felt it also. But in an oblique and surprising way. Because I was starting to locate myself in language, I was slowly, after so many disappointments, beginning to find myself in place. Gradually the city was catching my attention. Not far from my flat was the canal. At night the water glittered under streetlamps, the grass of the towpath took on a livid color and the wooden bulk of the locks turned into hunches of shadow.

Patrick Kavanagh had come here in the mid-fifties. He had sat by the water within sight of the bridge and the traffic. There was nothing particularly beautiful about the spot he had chosen. It was a noisy inch of city, shadowed by poplars and intruded on by passersby. He had been a sick man then, disillusioned and estranged. And, with his foot on that inch, he had written a visionary sonnet. I never passed the canal at that point without thinking of it. *O commemorate me where there is water.* There was something so downright and local about the poem that it opened out, for the first time, the idea of place as something language could claim even if ownership had been denied.

Language. Ownership. My childhood had been tormented by those fractions. The absence of my own place had led to the drying-up of my own language. The shorthand of possession, the inherited nicknames for a sweetshop or a dead tree or a public house on the site of a well—I understood now that they could not happen because the inheritance had not happened.

After midnight the city was quiet. I wore high heels, tipped with steel. I could hear them clicking and ringing as I set out for home. My flat was near enough to Stephen's Green to make it a short walk; and a safe one. It was not stone or water which moved me as I went along, nor light, nor even the combination of it all. It was the recurrences: the same granite rise of the bridge at Baggot Street, the same pear tree at the top of Waterloo Road. The same tree stump, waist-high, as you turned into Morehampton Road. A few more minutes and I came to the railed front gardens of the half street where I lived. My flat was at the top. I could see the window of my bedroom, the light I had forgotten to turn out, the shape of the roof which made the ceiling slope. By the time I reached the front door I would be fluent in streetlamps and the color of iron under them. I would know that copy book waited for me, and the pen. And I was full of the new knowledge that language can reclaim location.

My solitude was an illusion. No poet, however young or disaffected, writes alone. It is a connected act. The words on the page, however free and improvised, are on hire. They are owned by a complicated and interwoven past of language, history, happenstance.

The moment I was in was complicated enough. Ireland was emerging from two decades of airless self-reflection. I had been born in one of them, and not far from the flat I was writing in. I could have gone out of my door, turned left and walked for half a mile. I would have come to a broad street of set-back, well-built houses. They had railings at the front and a flight of steps to the front door. One of them—my old house—had a lilac bush right up against the railings. Even now I remembered the cloying, sweetish residue of lilac under my fingernails.

I never walked that half mile. It was, despite the actual nearness, an impossible distance. I had left there at five years of age. I was the sum of all the contradictions and interruptions which had divided me from the childhood I might have had. A clear line of identity had been broken. I had a flawed sense of the immediate past. I had spent the fifties, a crucial decade, outside the country. The religious festivals, the Irish dancing, the political meetings—they were missing from my vocabulary. I had not relearned them; I hardly knew they were missing. I sat down to write the Irish lyric with no sense of ownership, no automatic feeling of access.

The lyric I wrote had its own past and a stubborn series of contradictions which I discovered with my own. It had come with difficulty, that lyric, out of the claims and counterclaims made on it by the previous half century. Its currency represented both a survival and a compromise. Despite Yeats's example, the poetic model I encountered in Dublin was nearer to Joyce's quatrain, and its pre-Raphaelite influence, than the modernist paragraph, bristling with syntax and argument, which Yeats had used. The stanza I wrote, almost without thinking, was a hybrid: half British movement poem and half Irish lyric. Both had their roots in a Victorian romanticism, where the movement from stanza to stanza had a soft music about it.

Somewhere further back—I would sense this later—those poems split apart. The Irish poem continued travelling back into the rough angers of the street ballad, into the music and anxiety of a nationalist song. And further back again into the folk memory of bardic purpose and invective. The British poem tensed into the rearrangements of the true romantic movement, with its radical proposals about an inner and outer world.

IT IS LATE AT NIGHT. The room is airless and warm. The over-head light is on and the coffee jug is empty. I am just a few days short of my twentieth birthday. When I sit down to write I have an uncanny sense of spoiled identity and uncertain origin. I start to write about a swan. It is a legendary image at first, cloaked in the resonance of a myth. I try the stanzas, the structures. I write down nouns and adjectives, relishing the distance of this swan from the dirty, clustered birds I have seen at the foot of a bridge on the Liffey. Then the line falters. I try again. This time the swan in the poem is neither close to the birds at the foot of the bridge, nor part of a convincing myth. I try again.

Finally, only when most of what I write has been scrapped, I see the image for what it is. I see a swan who has never been imagined, only received. Who has never been part of an Irish myth or a true legend. That has come in fact, as one of the doubtful gifts of "The Victorian Gael"—an image from some declining part of a colonial tradition, smuggled from British drawing rooms into Irish poems. And so, on an ordinary evening in a city, bent over a copybook, and writing nothing of any importance, I have felt under my pen the flurry and corruption of divided language: a grammar of imagination split from top to bottom.

II

At first it was nothing. Just a dissonance glimpsed out of the corner of my eye, sensed in a solitude of coffee cups and mid-city mornings. Just one part of a larger unease. Then it grew wider and more puzzling: this sense of a gap between one part of me which wrote poetry and one part of me which did not.

There were times when I felt like a poet; and times when I did not. I felt like a poet in the kitchen of the flat. There, where no one could see me, I found parts of myself which only that strange working and reworking made visible. A lost mathematician in me saw the numbers in the words and heard the stresses in the line. I was less inclined now to take the inherited image file of the Literary Revival. I began to test the figures in the poem, to look for what was fresh and demanding in the arrangement of the lines.

I chose my skirts more carefully and looked at lipstick colors with interest. One day in a chemist's shop I heard someone talk about the blue tones in a certain shade of it. I waited behind, holding the lipstick up to a small mirror, looking for an elusive blue in the oily cyclamen color, failing to find it. I was twenty years of age now. Able to fall in love, and out again. Able to sit quarrelling with boyfriends, crying tears of temper and pride in the same cafés where a year ago I had talked about nothing but poetry.

The differences between myself and the male poets I knew were more obvious now. I felt less at ease, less equal in conversations with them, as if there had been a shift or a rebalancing. I began to notice certain things. If one of these male poets kissed a girl, the kiss would undergo a quick metamorphosis. It would be warm and impulsive one week. The next it would appear collected and purposeful, caught in a cold way between syntax and the metaphor and knowing its place in a sonnet or a villanelle.

My kisses did not appear in my poems. I did not feel like a poet when I kissed a boy. When I went home to my flat, where I did feel like one, the two fractions failed to connect. The part which had learned to be itself because it had found itself in form, which moved a stress back in a line, or split a caesura neatly, the way I had seen my mother split a chicken carcass right down the middle, held aloof from the other part. Obstinately, it remained sexless. It could not be heard in some region where a lipstick was held up to a mirror, or a boy caught me by surprise with a kiss. Increasingly it seemed that the power I felt when I wrote a poem came from an avoidance, and not a resolution, of the powerlessness I felt in other ways. No matter what I did, the gap widened.

I talked less about the past than other poets. The figures from it, in their Victorian coats and turned-up silk collars, were too whole and too male. Their lives, at least according to the legends which had survived them, never seemed to have broken apart in the small and ordinary ways mine did.

Yet I loved the poems of that past. Increasingly, I had a sense of their force and effect, of the figure they made in the time they were able to rearrange and heal. The more I wrote my own poems, the more I wondered at these other ones. And the more the isolation I felt deepened.

The first enchantment with the city—with its talk, with its casual assumption of a literary destiny—was fading. Once I had come back to the flat, from a day in the library or a night of heady talk, relishing the bus ride, the abrupt stop, the short walk to the gate. It had been enough for me to come up the short flight of steps, turn on the heater, make coffee and sit down at the table. Everything would be as I had left it. The ugly roses on the coffee jug. The cast-iron door of the stove. The red weave on the cover of the copybook. And there, as I had left it also, was the sense of power in a secret language, ready to be taken up again. Yet now I hesitated.

THE SEXUALITY OF ANY YOUNG POET is mysterious. It is not exactly the same thing as the longing for pleasure, or the forthright dreams and disappointments of everyday life. I had those as well. But this was different. It was something to do with a blurred text of names and customs rather than parts of the body or the way some boy turned around on a street corner.

In some complex way I felt—again I am making my ideas more sophisticated in retrospect than they could have been at the time—that the sexuality I could have as a poet was controlled in a way in which that day-to-day, ordinary sexuality was not. That it was allowed rather than spontaneous. It came to be a strange and awkward sense of not having the required permission. I had that sense most when I talked to male poets; I had it increasingly when I opened a book of poetry. Every day, in lectures and tutorials, and then later over coffee and conversation, the names whirled by: Chatterton. Keats. Byron. And the more they passed by me the less easy I became.

Gradually I began to feel that the poetic tradition itself was a house which held out an uncertain welcome to me. And when I entered it—I am carrying an image forward now as I never would have then—it was as if one room remained shut, locked against the air and intrusion of newness. When the door opened what was inside was the room of a boy child: everything kept still and poised to enact memory and reverence. His words, his toys all kept in the one place and the one order. Poetic tradition revered the boy child who had so often in its history given it glamour and purpose. It knew—if you can personify a body of opinion and grant it intelligent life—that poets are flawed and grow old, that they compromise with circumstance and are limited by dailyness. But in the intense light falling on a page of poetry, the confusion of those elements of youth and expression gave a venerable craft the poignance it required.

I understood the glamour. I saw the power in those lives which had been lived close to language. I also saw, again in a mute and unconfident way, the cost of such a hallowing of youth, promise, boyhood. The obvious gain was to a nineteenth-century myth of inspiration, a dearly held belief about the origins of poetry. The cost was to the poet like myself, whose mind was welcome in the tradition, but whose body was a strange and unrecorded part of it. Not strange and unrecorded, that is, if you were the object of the poem. Then you wore silks and listened to the cadences of the poem and became the silence they were addressed to. But unrecorded if, like me, the body you had was drawing you to the life you would lead.

Nothing I saw in the tradition—not the poems I read on the page or the conversations I heard from male contemporaries—encouraged me to follow my body with my mind and take myself to a place where they could heal in language: in new poems, in radical explorations. On the contrary. There was a deep suspicion of the ordinary life. It was assumed to be a narrow and antipoetic one.

There was a reason for this. For more than a century the poet's life had been edging away from the life lived in houses, parishes, settled communities. It had been fed on a strange and, finally, damaging self-regard. It was assumed—at least in the narrow world I knew—that in some way the poet's life was the highest expression of individuality. That it would treat only occasionally, and then high-handedly, with the collective systems of a particular time.

Increasingly, I doubted all this. The first delight of those conversations where the poet was exalted, and history made to sound like his accessory, was wearing off. I read more poetry now and not less. I noticed in it things no one spoke of. I saw, in the best of it, a perception of powerlessness and therefore a true understanding of the power of language. But I kept it to myself. If poetry was a kingdom where the boy child was the favored one, where the single human being was elevated to an emblem for all, then I could not live there. And that I hardly wanted to think about.

I walked more at night. The city was safe and almost empty

after eleven o'clock. I would come to Stephen's Green and begin a slow, purposeless round of the railings there. The streetlamps threw a yellowish glare on the pavements and benches. The overhanging leaves seemed six inches closer than in daylight. Overhead the sky was violet-colored and cloudy. I did not understand my life. It was, increasingly, a series of places and purposes I had failed to find. A childhood. A country. And now the suspicion was growing in my mind that I would not find a language either. Unformed as I was, anxious as I was to find a home, the ironies were clear me. Other poets in other countries—and several I knew in this one—had found their way. I had not. In the middle of an emblematic nation, at the heart of a formidable tradition of writing, I was lost.

OUTSIDE HISTORY

Years ago, I went to Achill for Easter. I was a student at Trinity then, and I had the loan of a friend's cottage. It was a one-story, stone building with two rooms and a view of sloping fields.

April was cold that year. The cottage was in sight of the Atlantic and at night a bitter, humid wind blew across the shore. By day there was heckling sunshine, but after dark a fire was necessary. The loneliness of the place suited me. My purposes in being there were purgatorial, and I had no intention of going out and about. I had done erratically, to say the least, in my first-year exams. In token of the need to do better, I had brought with me a small, accusing volume of the court poets of the silver age. In other words, those sixteenth-century English song writers, like Wyatt and Raleigh, whose lines appear so elegant, so off-hand yet whose poems smell of the gallows.

I was there less than a week. The cottage had no water, and every evening the caretaker, an old woman who shared a cottage with her brother at the bottom of the field, would carry water up to me. I can see her still. She has a tea towel round her waist—perhaps this is one image that has become all the images I have of her—she wears an old cardigan and her hands are blushing with cold as she puts down the bucket. Sometimes we talk inside the door of the cottage. Once, I remember, we stood there as the dark grew all around us and I could see stars beginning to curve in the stream behind us.

She was the first person to talk to me about the famine. The first person, in fact, to speak to me with any force about the terrible parish of survival and death which the event had been in those regions. She kept repeating to me that they were great people, the people in the famine. *Great people.* I had never heard that before. She pointed out the beauties of the place. But they themselves, I see now, were a subtext. On the eastern side of Keel, the cliffs of Menawn rose sheer out of the water. And here was Keel itself, with its blonde strand and broken stone, where the villagers in the famine, she told me, had moved closer to the shore, the better to eat the seaweed.

Memory is treacherous. It confers meanings which are not apparent at the time. I want to say that I understood this woman as emblem and instance of everything I am about to propose. Of course I did not. Yet even then I sensed a power in the encounter. I knew, without having words for it, that she came from a past which affected me. When she pointed out Keel to me that evening when the wind was brisk and cold and the light was going, when she gestured towards that shore which had stones as outlines and monuments of a desperate people, what was she pointing at? A history? A nation? Her memories or mine?

Those questions, once I began to write my own poetry, came back to haunt me. "I have been amazed, more than once," writes Hélène Cixous, "by a description a woman gave me of a world all her own, which she had been secretly haunting since early childhood." As the years passed, my amazement grew. I would see again the spring evening, the woman talking to me. Above all, I would remember how, when I finished speaking to her I went in, lit a fire, took out my book of English court poetry and memorized all over again—with no sense of irony or omission—the cadences of power and despair.

II

I have written this to probe the virulence and necessity of the idea of a nation. Not on its own and not in a vacuum, but as it intersects with a specific poetic inheritance and as that inheritance, in turn, cut across me as woman and poet. Some of these intersections are personal. Some of them may be painful to remember. Nearly all of them are elusive and difficult to describe with any degree of precision. Nevertheless, I believe these intersections, if I can observe them at all properly, reveal something about poetry, about nationalism, about the difficulties for a woman poet within a constraining national tradition. Perhaps the argument itself is nothing more than a way of revisiting the cold lights of that western evening and the force of that woman's conversation. In any case, the questions inherent in that encounter remain with me. It could well be that they might appear, even to a sympathetic reader, too complex to admit of an answer. In other words, that an argument like mine must contain too many imponderables to admit of any practical focus.

Yet I have no difficulty in stating the central premise of my argument. It is that over a relatively short time—certainly no more than a generation or so—women have moved from being the objects of Irish poems to being the authors of them. It is a momentous transit. It is also a disruptive one. It raises questions of identity, issues of poetic motive and ethical direction which can seem almost impossibly complex. What is more, such a transit—like the slow course of a star or the shifts in a constellation—is almost invisible to the naked eye. Critics may well miss it or map it inaccurately. Yet such a transit inevitably changes our idea of measurement, of distance, of the past as well as the future. And as it does so, it changes our idea of the Irish poem, of its composition and authority, of its right to appropriate certain themes and make certain fiats. And since poetry is never local for long, that in turn widens out into further implications.

Everything I am about to argue here could be taken as local and personal, rooted in one country and one poetic inheritance, and both of them mine. Yet if the names were changed, if situations and places were transposed, the issues might well be revealed as less parochial. This is not, after all, an essay on the craft of the art. I am not writing about aesthetics but about the ethics which are altogether less visible in a poetic tradition. Who the poet is, what he or she nominates as a proper theme for poetry, what selves poets discover and confirm through this subject matter—all of this involves an ethical choice. The more volatile the material—and a wounded history, public or private, is always volatile—the more intensely ethical the choice. Poetic ethics are evident and urgent in any culture where tensions between a poet and his or her birthplace are inherited and established. Poets from such cultures might well recognize some of the issues raised here. After all, this is not the only country or the only politic where the previously passive objects of a work of art have, in a relatively short time, become the authors of it.

So it was with me. For this very reason, early on as a poet, certainly in my twenties, I realized that the Irish nation as an existing construct in Irish poetry was not available to me. I would not have been able to articulate it at that point, but at some preliminary level I already knew that the anguish and power of that woman's gesture on Achill, with its suggestive hinterland of pain, was not something I could predict or rely on in Irish poetry. There were glimpses here and there; sometimes more than that. But all too often, when I was searching for such an inclusion, what I found was a rhetoric of imagery which alienated me: a fusion of the national and the feminine which seemed to simplify both.

It was not a comfortable realization. There was nothing clear-cut about my feelings. I had tribal ambivalences and doubts, and even then I had an uneasy sense of the conflict which awaited me. On the one hand, I knew that as a poet I could not easily do without the idea of a nation. Poetry in every time draws on that reserve. On the other, I could not as a woman accept the nation formulated for me by Irish poetry and its traditions. At one point it even looked to me as if the whole thing might be made up of irreconcilable differences. At the very least, it seemed to me that I was likely to remain an outsider in my own national literature, cut off from its archive, at a distance from its energy. Unless, that is, I could re-possess it. This proposal is about that conflict and that repossession and about the fact that re-possession itself is not a static or single act. Indeed the argument which describes it may itself be no more than a part of it.

III

A nation. It is, in some ways, the most fragile and improbable of concepts. Yet the idea of an Ireland, resolved and healed of its wounds, is an irreducible presence in the Irish past and its literature. In one sense, of course, both the concept and its realization resist definition. It is certainly nothing conceived in what Edmund Burke calls "the spirit of rational liberty." When a people have been so dispossessed by event as the Irish in the eighteenth and nineteenth centuries, an extra burden falls on the very idea of a nation. What should be a political aspiration becomes a collective fantasy. The dream itself becomes freighted with invention. The Irish nation, materializing in the songs and ballads of these centuries, is a sequence of improvised images. These songs, these images, wonderful and terrible and memorable as they are, propose for a nation an impossible task: to be at once an archive of defeat and a diagram of victory.

As a child I loved these songs. As a teenager I had sought them out for some meaning, some definition. Even now, in some moods and at certain times, I can find it difficult to resist their makeshift angers. And no wonder. The best of them are written—like lyrics of Wyatt and Raleigh—within sight of the gibbet. They breathe just free of the noose.

In one sense I was a captive audience. My childhood was spent in London. My image makers as a child, therefore, were refractions of my exile: conversations overheard, memories and visitors. I listened and absorbed. For me, as for many another exile, Ireland was my nation long before it was once again my country. That nation, then and later, was a session of images: of defeats and sacrifices, of individual defiances happening offstage. The songs enhanced the images; the images reinforced the songs. To me they were the soundings of the place I had lost: drowned treasure.

It took me years to shake off those presences. In the end, though, I did escape. My escape was assisted by the realization that these songs were effect, not cause. They were only the curators of the dream, not the inventors. In retrospect I could accuse both them and the dream of certain crucial simplifications. I made then, as I make now, a moral division between what those songs sought to accomplish and what Irish poetry must seek to achieve. The songs, with their postures and their angers, glamourized resistance, action. But the Irish experience, certainly for the purposes of poetry, was only incidentally about action and resistance. At a far deeper level—and here the Achill woman returns—it was about defeat. The coffin ships, the soup queues, those desperate villagers at the shoreline—these things had actually happened. The songs, persuasive, hypnotic, could wish them away. Poetry could not. Of course, the relation between a poem and a past is never that simple. When I met the Achill woman, I was already a poet, I thought of myself as a poet. Yet nothing that I understood about poetry enabled me to understand her better. Quite the reverse. I turned my back on her in that cold twilight and went to commit to memory the songs and artifices of the very power systems which had made her own memory such an archive of loss.

If I understand her better now, and my relation to her, it is not just because my sense of irony or history has developed over the years, although I hope they have. It is more likely because of my own experience as a poet. Inevitably, any account of this carries the risk of subjective codes and impressions. Yet in poetry in particular and women's writing in general, the private witness is often all there is to go on. Since my personal experience as a poet is part of my source material, it is to that I now turn.

IV

I entered Trinity to study English and Latin. Those were the early sixties, and Dublin was another world—a place for which I can still feel Henry James's "tiger-pounce of homesickness." In a very real sense, it was a city of images and anachronisms. There were still brewery horses on Grafton Street, their rumps draped and smoking under sackcloth. In the coffee bars eggs were poached in a rolling boil and I spooned them onto thick, crustless toast. The lights went on at twilight; by midnight the city was full of echoes.

After the day's lectures, I took a bus home from college. It was a short journey. Home was an attic flat on the near edge of a town that was just beginning to sprawl. There in the kitchen, on an oilskin tablecloth, I wrote my first real poems: derivative, formalist, gesturing poems. I was a very long way from Adrienne Rich's realization that "instead of poems about experience, I am getting poems that are experiences." If anything, my poems were other people's experiences. This, after all, was the heyday of the movement in Britain, and the neat stanza, the well-broken line were the very stuff of poetic identity.

Now I wonder how many young women poets taught themselves—in rooms like that, with a blank discipline—to write the poem that was in the air, rather than the one within their experience. How many faltered, as I did, not for lack of answers but for lack of questions. "It will be a long time still, I think," wrote Virginia Woolf, "before a woman can sit down to write a book without finding a phantom to be slain, a rock to be dashed against."

But for now let me invent a shift of time. I am turning down those streets which echo after midnight. I am climbing the stairs of a coffee bar which stays open late. I know what I will find. Here is the salt-glazed mug on a table-top which is as scarred as a desk in a country school. Here is the window with its view of an empty street, of lamplight and iron. And there, in the corner, is my younger self.

I draw up a chair, I sit down opposite her. I begin to talk— no, to harangue her. Why, I say, do you do it? Why do you go back to that attic flat, night after night, to write in forms explored and sealed by Englishmen hundreds of years ago? You are Irish. You are a woman. Why do you keep these things at the periphery of the poem? Why do you not move them to the center, where they belong?

But the woman who looks back at me is uncomprehending. If she answers at all it will be with the rhetoric of a callow apprenticeship: that the poem is pure process, that the technical encounter is the one which guarantees all others. She will speak about the dissonance of the line and the necessity for the stanza. And so on. And so on.

"For what is the poet responsible?" asks Allen Tate. "He is responsible for the virtue proper to him as a poet, for his special *arete*: for the mastery of a disciplined language which will not shun the full report of the reality conveyed to him by his awareness."

She is a long way, that young woman—with her gleaming cup and her movement jargon—from the full report of anything. In her lack of any sense of implication or complication, she might as well be a scientist in the thirties, bombarding uranium with neutrons.

If I try now to analyze why such a dialogue would be a waste of time, I come up with several reasons. One of them is that it would take years for me to see, let alone comprehend, certain realities. Not until the oilskin tablecloth was well folded and the sprawling town had become a rapacious city, and the attic flat was a house in the suburbs, could I accept the fact that I was a woman and a poet in a culture which had the greatest difficulty associating the two ideas. "A woman must often take a critical stance towards her social, historical and cultural position in order to experience her own quest," writes the American poet and feminist, Rachel Blau DuPlessis. "Poems of the self's growth, or of self-knowledge, may often include or be preceded by a questioning of major social prescriptions about the shape women's experience should take." In years to come I would never be sure whether my poems had generated the questions or the questions had facilitated the poems. All that lay ahead. "No poet," says T. S. Eliot, "no artist of any kind has his complete meaning alone." In the meantime, I existed whether I liked it or not in a mesh, a web, a labyrinth of associations. Of poems past and present. Contemporary poems. Irish poems.

V

Irish poetry was predominantly male. Here or there you found a small eloquence, like "After Aughrim" by Emily Lawless. Now and again, in discussion, you heard a woman's name. But the lived vocation, the craft witnessed by a human life—that was missing. And I missed it. Not in the beginning, perhaps. But later, when perceptions of womanhood began to redirect my own work, what I regretted was the absence of an expressed poetic life which would have dignified and revealed mine. The influence of absences should not be underestimated. Isolation itself can have a powerful effect in the life of a young writer. "I'm talking about real influence now," says Raymond Carver. "I'm talking about the moon and the tide."

I turned to the work of Irish male poets. After all, I thought of myself as an Irish poet. I wanted to locate myself within the Irish poetic tradition. The dangers and stresses in my own themes gave me an added incentive to discover a context for them. But what I found dismayed me.

The majority of Irish male poets depended on women as motifs in their poetry. They moved easily, deftly, as if by right among images of women in which I did not believe and of which I could not approve. The women in their poems were often passive, decorative, raised to emblematic status. This was especially true where the woman and the idea of the nation were mixed: where the nation became a woman and the woman took on a national posture.

The trouble was these images did good service as ornaments. In fact, they had a wide acceptance as ornaments by readers of Irish poetry. Women in such poems were frequently referred to approvingly as mythic, emblematic. But to me these passive and simplified women seemed a corruption. Moreover, the transaction they urged on the reader, to accept them as mere decoration, seemed to compound the corruption. For they were not decorations, they were not ornaments. However distorted these images, they had their roots in a suffered truth.

What had happened? How had the women of our past—the women of a long struggle and a terrible survival—undergone such a transformation? How had they suffered Irish history and inscribed themselves in the speech and memory of the Achill woman, only to re-emerge in Irish poetry as fictive queens and national sibyls?

The more I thought about it, the more uneasy I became. The

wrath and grief of Irish history seemed to me, as it did to many, one of our true possessions. Women were part of that wrath, had endured that grief. It seemed to me a species of human insult that at the end of it all, in certain Irish poems, they should become elements of style rather than aspects of truth.

The association of the feminine and the national—and the consequent simplification of both—are not, of course, a monopoly of Irish poetry. "All my life," writes Charles de Gaulle, "I have thought about France in a certain way. The emotional side of me tends to imagine France like the princess in the fairytale, or the Madonna of the Frescoes." De Gaulle's words point up the power of nationhood to edit the reality of womanhood. Once the idea of a nation influences the perception of a woman, then that woman is suddenly and inevitably simplified. She can no longer have complex feelings and aspirations. She becomes the passive projection of a national idea.

Irish poems simplified women most at the point of intersection between womanhood and Irishness. The further the Irish poem drew away from the idea of Ireland, the more real and persuasive became the images of women. Once the pendulum swung back, the simplifications started again. The idea of the defeated nation's being reborn as a triumphant woman was central to a certain kind of Irish poem. Dark Rosaleen. Cathleen ni Houlihan. The nation as woman; the woman as national muse.

The more I looked at it, the more it seemed to me that in relation to the idea of a nation many, if not most, Irish male poets had taken the soft option. The irony was that few Irish poets were nationalists. By and large, they had eschewed the fervor and crudity of that ideal. But long after they had rejected the politics of Irish nationalism, they continued to deploy the emblems and enchantments of its culture. It was the culture, not the politics, which informed Irish poetry: not the harsh awakenings, but the old dreams.

In all of this I did not blame nationalism. Nationalism seemed to me inevitable in the Irish context, a necessary hallucination within Joyce's nightmare of history. I did blame Irish poets. Long after it was necessary, Irish poetry had continued to trade in the exhausted fictions of the nation, had allowed those fictions to edit ideas of womanhood and modes of remembrance. Some of the poetry produced by such simplifications was, of course, difficult to argue with. It was difficult to deny that something was gained by poems which used the imagery and emblem of the national muse. Something was gained, certainly, but only at an aesthetic level. While what was lost occurred at the deepest, most ethical level, and what was lost was what I valued. Not just the details of a past. Not just the hungers, the angers. These, however terrible, remain local. But the truth these details witness—human truths of survival and humiliation—these also were suppressed along with the details. Gone was the suggestion of any complicated human suffering. Instead you had the hollow victories, the passive images, the rhyming queens.

I knew that the women of the Irish past were defeated. I knew it instinctively long before the Achill woman pointed down the hill to the Keel shoreline. What I objected to was that Irish poetry should defeat them twice.

"I have not written day after day," says Camus, "because I desire the world to be covered with Greek statues and masterpieces. The man who has such a desire does exist in me. But I have written so much because I cannot keep from being drawn toward everyday life, toward those, whoever they may be, who are humiliated. They need to hope and, if all keep silent, they will be forever deprived of hope and we with them."

This argument originates in some part from my own need to locate myself in a powerful literary tradition in which until then, or so it seemed to me, I had been an element of design rather than an agent of change. But even as a young poet, and certainly by the time my work confronted me with some of these questions, I had already had a vivid, human witness of the stresses which a national literature can impose on a poet. I had already seen the damage it could do.

VI

I remember the Dublin of the sixties almost more vividly than the city which usurped it. I remember its grace and emptiness and the old hotels with their chintzes and Sheffield trays. In one of these I had tea with Padraic Colum. I find it hard to be exact about the year, somewhere around the middle sixties. But I have no difficulty at all about the season. It was winter. We sat on a sofa by the window overlooking the street. The lamps were on and a fine rain was being glamourized as it fell past their cowls.

Colum was then in his eighties. He had come from his native Longford in the early years of the century to a Dublin fermenting with political and literary change. Yeats admired his 1907 volume of poetry, *Wild Earth*. He felt the Ireland Colum proposed fitted neatly into his own ideas. "It is unbeautiful Ireland," Yeats writes, "he will contrast finely with our Western dialect-makers."

In old photographs Colum looks the part: curly-headed, dark, winsome. In every way he was a godsend to the Irish Revival. Nobody would actually have used the term *peasant poet*. But then nobody would have needed to. Such things were understood.

The devil, they say, casts no shadow. But that folk-image

applies to more than evil. There are writers in every country who begin in the morning of promise but by the evening, mysteriously, have cast no shadow and left no mark. Colum is one of them. For some reason, although he was eminently placed to deal with the energies of his own culture, he failed to do so. His musical, tender, hopeful imagination glanced off the barbaric griefs of the nineteenth century. It is no good fudging the issue. Very few of his poems now look persuasive on the page. All that heritage which should have been his—rage robbed of language, suffering denied its dignity—somehow eluded him. When he met it at all, it was with a borrowed sophistication.

Now in old age he struggled for a living. He transited stoically between Dublin and New York, giving readings, writing articles. He remained open and approachable. No doubt for this reason, I asked him what he really thought of Yeats. He paused for a moment. His voice had a distinctive, treble resonance. When he answered, it was high and emphatic. "Yeats hurt me," he said, "he expected too much of me."

I have never been quite sure what Colum meant. What I understand by his words may be different from their intent. But I see his relation with the Irish Revival as governed by corrupt laws of supply and demand. He could only be tolerated if he read the signals right and acquiesced in his role as a peasant poet. He did not and he could not. To be an accomplice in such a distortion required a calculation he never possessed. But the fact that he was screen-tested for it suggests how relentless the idea of Irishness in Irish poetry has been.

Colum exemplified something else to me. Here also was a poet who had been asked to make the journey, in one working lifetime, from being the object of Irish poems to being their author. He too, as an image, had been unacceptably simplified in all those poems about the land and the tenantry. So that—if he was to realize his identity—not only must he move from image to image-maker, he must also undo the simplifications of the first by his force and command of the second. I suspect he found the imaginative stresses of that transit beyond his comprehension, let alone his strength. And so something terrible happened to him. He wrote Irish poetry as if he were still the object of it. He wrote with the passivity and simplification of his own reflection looking back at him from poems, plays and novels in which the so-called Irish peasant was a son of the earth, a cipher of the national cause. He had the worst of both worlds.

VII

Like Colum, Francis Ledwidge was born at the sharp end of history. He was an Irish poet who fought as a British soldier, a writer in a radical situation who used a conservative idiom to support it, and Ledwidge's short life was full of contradiction. He was in his early twenties when he died in the First World War.

Despite his own marginal and pressured position, Ledwidge used the conventional language of romantic nationalism. Not always; perhaps not often. But his poem on the death of the leaders of the Easter Rising, "The Blackbirds," is a case in point. It is, in a small way, a celebrated poem, and I have certainly not chosen it because it represents careless or shoddy work. Far from it. It is a skillful poem, adroit and quick in its rhythms, with an underlying sweetness of tone. For all that, it provides an example of a gifted poet who did not resist the contemporary orthodoxy. Perhaps he might have had he lived longer and learned more. As it was, Ledwidge surrendered easily to the idioms of the Irish Revival. This in turn meant that he could avail himself of a number of approved stereotypes and, chief among them, the easy blend of feminine and national. Even here he could exercise a choice although, it must be said, a limited one. He could have had the Young Queen or The Old Mother. As it happens, he chose the Poor Old Woman. But we are in no doubt what he means:

THE BLACKBIRDS

I heard the Poor Old Woman say
"At break of day the fowler came,
And took my blackbirds from their songs
Who loved me well through shame and blame.

"No more from lovely distances
Their songs shall bless me mile from mile,
Nor to white Ashbourne call me down
To wear my crown another while.

"With bended flowers the angels mark
For the skylark the place they lie.
From there its little family
Shall dip their wings first in the sky.

"And when the first surprise of flight
Sweet songs excite, from the far dawn
Shall there come blackbirds, loud with love,
Sweet echoes of the singers gone.

"But in the lonely hush of eve
Weeping I grieve the silent bills"
I heard the Poor Old Woman say
In Derry of the little hills.

I am not sure this poem would pass muster now. There are too many sugary phrases—"loud with love" and "shame and blame"—evoking the very worst of Georgian poetry. But Ledwidge was young and the impulse for the poem was historical. The 1916 leaders were dead. He was at a foreign front. The poem takes on an extra resonance if it is read as a concealed elegy for his own loyalties.

What is more interesting is how, in his attempt to make the feminine stand in for the national, he has simplified the woman in the poem almost out of existence. She is in no sense the poor old woman of the colloquial expression. There are no vulnerabilities here, no human complexities. She is a Poor Old Woman in capital letters. A mouthpiece. A sign.

Therefore, the poem divides into two parts; one vital, one inert. The subject of the poem appears to be the woman. But appearances deceive. She is merely the object, the pretext. The real subject is the blackbirds. They are the animated substance of the piece. They call from "lovely distances"; their "sweet songs" "excite" and "bless." Whatever imaginative power the lyric has, it comes from these birds. Like all effective images, the blackbirds have a life outside the poem. They take their literal shape from the birds we know and to these they return an emblematic force. They continue to be vital once the poem is over.

The woman, on the other hand, is a diagram. By the time the poem is over, she has become a dehumanized ornament. When her speaking part finishes, she goes out of the piece and out of our memory. At best she has been the engine of the action, a convenient frame for the proposition.

The question worth asking is whether this fusion of national and feminine, this interpretation of one by the other is inevitable. It was after all common practice in Irish poetry: Mangan's "Dark Rosaleen" comes immediately to mind. In fact, the custom and the practice reached back, past the songs and simplifications of the nineteenth century, into the bardic tradition itself. Daniel Corkery refers to this in his analysis of the Aisling convention in *The Hidden Ireland*. "The vision the poet sees," he writes there, "is always the spirit of Ireland as a majestic and radiant maiden."

So many male Irish poets—the later Yeats seems to me a rare exception—have feminized the national and nationalized the feminine that from time to time it has seemed there is no other option. But an Irish writer who turned away from such usages suggests that there was, in fact, another and more subversive choice.

In the opening pages of *Ulysses* Joyce describes an old woman. She climbs the steps to the Martello tower, darkening its doorway. She is, in fact, the daily milkwoman. But no sooner has she started to pour a quart of milk into Stephen's measure than she begins to shimmer and dissolve into legendary images: "Silk of the kine and poor old woman, names given her in old times. A wandering crone, lowly form of an immortal serving her conqueror and her gay betrayer, their common cuckquean, a messenger from the secret morning. To serve or to upbraid, whether he could not tell: but scorned to beg her favour."

The same phrase as Ledwidge uses—poor old woman—is included here. But whereas Ledwidge uses it with a straight face, Joyce dazzles it with irony. By reference and inference, he

shows himself to be intent on breaking the traditional association of Ireland with ideas of womanhood and tragic motherhood.
After all, these simplifications are part and parcel of what he,
Joyce, has painfully rejected. They are some of the reason he is
in exile from the mythos of his own country. Now by cunning
inflations, by disproportions of language, he takes his revenge.
He holds at a glittering, manageable distance a whole tendency
in national thought and expression; and dismisses it. But then
Joyce is a poetic moralist. Much of *Ulysses*, after all, is invested
in Dedalus's search for the ethical shadow of his own aesthetic
longings. He has a difficult journey ahead of him. And Joyce has
no intention of letting him be waylaid, so early in the book, by
the very self-deceptions he has created him to resolve.

VIII

It is easy, and intellectually seductive, for a woman artist to
walk away from the idea of a nation. There has been, and there
must continue to be, a great deal of debate about the energies
and myths women writers should bring with them into a new
age. "Start again," has been the cry of some of the best feminist
poets. "Wipe clean the slate, start afresh." It is a cry with force
and justice behind it. And it is a potent idea: to begin in a new
world, clearing the desert as it were, making it blossom; even
making the rain.

In any new dispensation the idea of a nation must seem an
expendable construct. After all, it has never admitted of women.
Its flags and songs and battle cries, even its poetry, as I've suggested, make use of feminine imagery. But that is all. The true
voice and vision of women are routinely excluded.

Then why did I not walk away? Simply because I was not free to. For all my quarrels with the concept, and no doubt partly because of them, I needed to find and repossess that idea at some level of repose. Like the swimmer in Adrienne Rich's poem "Diving into The Wreck," I needed to find out "the damage that was done and the treasures that prevail." I knew the idea was flawed. But if it was flawed, it was also one of the vital human constructs of a place in which, like Leopold Bloom, I was born. More important, as a friend and feminist scholar said to me, we ourselves are constructed by the construct. I might be the author of my poems; I was not the author of my past. However crude the diagram, the idea of a nation remained the rough graphic of an ordeal. In some subterranean way I felt myself to be part of that ordeal; its fragmentations extended into mine.

"I am invisible," begins the Prologue of Ralph Ellison's *Invisible Man.* "I am invisible, understand, because people refuse to see me. Like the bodiless heads you see sometimes in circus side shows it is as though I have been surrounded by mirrors of hard, distorting glass. When they approach me they see only my surroundings, themselves, or figments of their imagination—indeed, everything and anything except me."

In an important sense, Ellison's words applied to the sort of Irish poem which availed of that old, potent blurring of feminine and national. In such poems, the real woman behind the image was not explored, she was never even seen. It was a subtle mechanism, subtle and corrupt. And it was linked, I believed, to a wider sequence of things not seen.

A society, a nation, a literary heritage are always in danger of making up their communicable heritage from their visible elements. Women, as it happens, are not especially visible in Ireland. This came to me early and with personal force. I realized when I published a poem that what was seen of me, what drew approval, if it was forthcoming at all, was the poet. The woman, by and large, was invisible. It was an unsettling discovery. Yet I came to believe that my invisibility as a woman was a disguised grace. It had the power to draw me, I sensed, towards realities like the Achill woman. It made clear to me that what she and I shared, apart from those fragile moments of talk, was the danger of being edited out of our own literature by conventional tribalisms.

Marginality within a tradition, however painful, confers certain advantages. It allows the writer clear eyes and a quick critical sense. Above all, the years of marginality suggest to such a writer—and I am speaking of myself now—the real potential of subversion. I wanted to relocate myself within the Irish poetic tradition. I felt the need to do so. I thought of myself as an Irish poet, although I was fairly sure it was not a category that readily suggested itself in connection with my work. A woman poet is rarely regarded as an automatic part of a national poetic tradition, and for the reasons I have already stated. She is too deeply woven into the passive texture of that tradition, too intimate a part of its imagery, to be allowed her freedom. She may know, as an artist, that she is now the maker of the poems and not merely the subject of them. The critique is slow to catch up. There has been a growing tendency in the last few years for academics and critics in this country to discuss women's poetry as a subculture, to keep it quarantined from the main body of poetry. I thought it vital that women poets such as myself should establish a discourse with the idea of the nation. I felt sure that the most effective way to do this was by subverting the previous terms of that discourse. Rather than accept the nation as it appeared in Irish poetry, with its queens and muses, I felt the time had

come to rework those images by exploring the emblematic relation between my own feminine experience and a national past.

The truths of womanhood and the defeats of a nation? An
improbable intersection? At first sight perhaps. Yet the idea of it
opened doors in my mind which had hitherto been closed fast. I
began to think there was indeed a connection, that my womanhood and my nationhood were meshed and linked at some root.
It was not just that I had a womanly feeling for those women who
waited with handcarts, went into the sour stomach of ships and
even—according to terrible legend—eyed their baby's haunches
speculatively in the hungers of the 1840s. It was more than that.
I was excited by the idea that if there really was an emblematic
relation between the defeats of womanhood and the suffering
of a nation, I need only prove the first in order to reveal the
second. If so, then Irishness and womanhood, those tormenting
fragments of my youth, could at last stand in for one another.
Out of a painful apprenticeship and an ethical dusk, the laws of
metaphor beckoned me.

I was not alone. "Where women write strongly as women,"
says Alicia Ostriker, the American poet and critic, in her seminal
book *Stealing the Language*, "it is clear their intention is to subvert the life and literature they inherit." This was not only true
of contemporary women poets. In the terrible years between
1935 and 1940, the Russian poet Anna Akhmatova composed
"Requiem." It was written for her only son, Lev Gumilev, who
at the start of the Stalinist Terror had been arrested, released,
rearrested. Then, like so many others, he disappeared into the
silence of a Leningrad prison. For days, months, Akhmatova
queued outside. The epilogue to "Requiem" refers to that experience. What is compelling and instructive is the connection it
makes between her womanhood and her sense of a nation as a

community of grief. The country she wishes to belong to, the monument she would be commemorated by, is the one revealed to her by her suffering.

> The hideous clanging gate, the old
> Woman wailing like a wounded beast.
> (Translation D. M. Thomas)

IX

I want to summarize this argument. At the same time I am concerned that in the process it may take on a false symmetry. I have, after all, been describing ideas and impressions as if they were events. I have been proposing thoughts and perceptions in a way they did not and could not occur. I have given hard shapes and definite outlines to feelings which were far more hesitant.

The reality was different. Exact definitions do not happen in the real life of a poet; and certainly not in mine. I have written here about the need to repossess the idea of a nation. But there was nothing assured or automatic about it. "It is not in the darkness of belief that I desire you," says Richard Rowan at the end of Joyce's *Exiles*, "but in restless, living, wounding doubt." I had the additional doubts of a writer who knows that a great deal of their literary tradition has been made up in ignorance of their very existence, that its momentum has been predicated on simplifications of its complexity. Yet I still wished to enter that tradition, although I knew my angle of entry must be oblique. None of it was easy. I reached tentative havens after figurative storms. I came to understand what Mallarmé meant when he wrote: "Each newly acquired truth was born only at the expense of an impression that flamed up and then burned itself out, so that its particular darkness could be isolated."

My particular darkness as an Irish poet has been the subject of this piece. But there were checks and balances. I was, as I have said, a woman in a literary tradition which simplified them. I was also a poet lacking the precedent and example of previous Irish women poets. These were the givens of my working life. But if these circumstances displaced my sense of relation to the Irish past in Irish poetry, they also forced me into a perception of the advantages of being able to move, with almost surreal inevitability, from being within the poem to being its maker. A hundred years ago I might have been a motif in a poem. Now I could have a complex self within my own poem. Part of that process entailed being a privileged witness to forces of reaction in Irish poetry.

Some of these I have named. The tendency to fuse the national and the feminine, to make the image of the woman the pretext of a romantic nationalism—these have been weaknesses in Irish poetry. These simplifications isolated and estranged me as a young poet. They also made it clearer to me that my own discourse must be subversive. In other words, that I must be vigilant to write of my own womanhood—whether it was revealed to me in the shape of a child or a woman from Achill—in such a way that I never colluded with the simplified images of women in Irish poetry.

When I was young, all this was comfortless. I took to heart the responsibility of making my own critique, even if for years it consisted of little more than accusing Irish poetry in my own mind of deficient ethics. Even now I make no apology for such a critique. I believe it is still necessary. Those simplified women, those conventional reflexes and reflexive feminizations of the national experience, those static, passive, ornamental figures do no credit to a poetic tradition which has been, in other respects, radical and innovative, capable of both latitude and compassion.

But there is more to it. As a young poet I would not have felt so threatened and estranged if the issue had merely been the demands a national program makes on a country's poetry. The real issue went deeper. When I read those simplifications of women, I felt there was an underlying fault in Irish poetry, almost a geological weakness. All good poetry depends on an ethical relation between imagination and image. Images are not ornaments; they are truths. When I read about Cathleen ni Houlihan or the Old Woman of the Roads or Dark Rosaleen, I felt that a necessary ethical relation was in danger of being violated over and over again, that a merely ornamental relation between imagination and image was being handed on from poet to poet, from generation to generation, was becoming orthodox poetic practice. It was the violation, even more than the simplification, which alienated me.

No poetic imagination can afford to regard an image as a temporary aesthetic maneuver. Once the image is distorted, the truth is demeaned. That was the heart of it all as far as I was concerned. In availing themselves of the old convention, in using and reusing women as icons and figments, Irish poets were not just dealing with emblems. They were also evading the real women of an actual past, women whose silence their poetry should have broken. In so doing, they ran the risk of turning a terrible witness into an empty decoration.

Writers, if they are wise, do not make their home in any comfort within a national tradition. However vigilant the writer, however enlightened the climate, the dangers persist. So too do the obligations. There is a recurring temptation for any nation, and for any writer who operates within its field of force, to make an ornament of the past, to turn the losses to victories and to restate humiliations as triumphs. In every age language holds out narcosis and amnesia for this purpose. But such triumphs in the end are unsustaining and may, in fact, be corrupt.

If a poet does not tell the truth about time, his or her work will not survive it. Past or present, there is a human dimension to time, human voices within it and human griefs ordained by it. Our present will become the past of other men and women. We depend on them to remember it with the complexity with which it was suffered. As others, once, depended on us.

THE WOMAN, THE PLACE,
THE POET

Clonmel is the county town of Tipperary. Its name comes from the Irish—*cluain meala*—meadow of honey. This is a storied part of Ireland. The Danes visited it in the eighth century. Cromwell fixed his batteries here on rising ground to the north of the town and received one of the worst reverses of his Irish campaign.

In the first decades of the nineteenth century Clonmel prospered. Travellers praised its regular streets, its well-built houses "the greater part of which are rough cast, and are either cream-coloured or white, save here and there one of neat appearance, whose front is often curiously ornamented with blue slates." The rows of thatched cabins had been cleared from the outskirts of the town. Corn stores were hoarded by the river; the quays were embanked with limestone ashlar. "Mr Banfield," simpers one contemporary account, "has added much to the appearance of the town by the erection of a row of very genteel houses."

It was a garrison town. Two militia regiments of the Tipperary Artillery were quartered there. Sometime after the Crimean War my great-grandfather took up a position on this headquarters staff as a sergeant-major. He could read and write, that much is certain. Otherwise, he could not have kept accounts or made a note of provisions. And he was something of a dandy. "He had a head of thick nut-brown hair the colour of your own," wrote my grandfather to his son. "My mother used to tell us how, on parade days when his toilet was of special care, he used to curse the waves in his hair that prevented him getting it to lie as he wanted."

A peacock. A soldier. A literate Irishman in a dark century. But I had not come to find him. I turned out past the town center and took the Old Western Road. After a hundred yards or so it takes a broad, bluish turn—those shrubs again—and becomes a gradual hill. To the right there is a sudden crest with a straggle of buildings.

I walked up the hill. It was steep, the path winding and edged by trees. They had a dark, inappropriate presence. I would not have recognized cypress or yew, but these I thought deserved their legend. The higher I went, the more the valley—the old meadow of honey—scrolled beneath me.

The buildings were grim. One ran the length of the hill, an institutional ramble of granite and drainpipes. Below it, further down, was a smaller building. Over to one side were a separate house and, further down again, at road level, a small church and a deserted school.

I needed to see all this. Sometime in 1874, with a growing family to maintain, my great-grandfather cast around for a secure position. He took the only one vacant—"the only one," as my grandfather put it—"to which a Catholic could hope for appointment." Sometime in the autumn of that year, with the approval of the Board of Guardians, he became the Master of that most dreaded Irish institution the workhouse.

Now, more than a hundred years later, it was hard enough to distinguish from that scatter of granite, which building was which. The largest one now served as the local hospital. I went inside. Two women, one elderly, both dressed as nurses, came over. The older one was sweet-faced and vague. The younger one was definite. Yes, this had been the poorhouse—she gave it its folk name—this building overlooking the hill.

I came out into sunshine. Poetic license is an age-old concept. Traditionally poets have been free to invoke place as a territory between invention and creation. I myself might once have proposed it as an act of imagination or an article of faith. But here, on a blue summer morning, I could feel it to be what it has been for so many: brute, choiceless fact.

WE YIELD TO OUR PRESENT, but we choose our past. In a defeated country like Ireland we choose it over and over again, relentlessly, obsessively. Standing there looking back at the bleak length of the building, I refused to imagine him—my ancestor, with his shock of nut-brown hair. The truth was I was ashamed of his adroit compliance, the skillful opportunism by which he had ensured our family's survival.

Instead, I imagined a woman. A woman like myself, with two small children, who must have come to this place as I came to the suburb. She would have come here in her twenties or thirties. But whereas my arrival in the suburb marked a homecoming, hers in the workhouse would have initiated a final and, almost certainly fatal, homelessness. At an age when I was observing the healings of place, she would have been a scholar of its violations.

There were several reasons why she might have been there. The most obvious, unmarried motherhood, remains the most likely. But she could as easily have been a survivor of an eviction. Hundreds of them—complete with bailiff and battering ram—took place in Ireland every year of that century. British cartoons and a few old photographs tell the story: wretched homemade tables strewn on the road, the cabin door barred, the windows boarded up. She may even have married a soldier. Clonmel after all was a garrison town. Two regiments were quartered there. Hadn't my own great-grandfather fallen for the stagy glitter of the uniforms? Didn't his wife fear that her children might do the same?

Whatever her reasons for being there, her sufferings would have been terrible. When I looked up the hill I could see how the main length of the building ended in a kitchen garden. There was a small house with blunt gables and an outhouse. Was this where my great-grandfather lived? Where he stabled his pony, collected his ration, sheltered his children in the security of his position as overseer of other people's tragedies? At least, by these visible survivals, I could guess at his existence. There was no trace of hers.

The Clonmel workhouse—or, to give it its more respectable title, the Clonmel Union—was founded in 1838. In that year, and against all informed advice, the English Poor Law of 1834 was extended to Ireland. Until then this building had served as a catchall: asylum, orphanage, geriatric ward. *The Survey of Clonmel*, for instance, published in 1813, clothes its account of it in the chilly language of nineteenth-century altruism:

"A very extensive House of Industry was finished two years ago in the west end of the town, both at the public expense of the county and by private subscription. It is a common receptacle for all descriptions of mals fortunes, serving at the same time as a place of confinement for vagrants and lunatics, as well as an asylum for the poor and helpless."

When the Poor Law was introduced, Ireland stood at the edge of its greatest ordeal: the famine. In the next few years the workhouses would fill to overflowing with the children of emigrants, the orphans of typhus, the debris of a preventable tragedy.

Most of the buildings which accommodated them were themselves casualties of bad planning and hasty decision making. The walls and ceilings were not plastered. Limestone was burned on the site and then used as a crude whitewash. Maintenance was scanty. Contemporary accounts tell of sparrows nesting in the downpipes and water leaking through the mortar. Subsistence was deliberately harsh. The diet consisted of oatmeal, bread, milk at times, but by no means always or in every workhouse. In many, the children got gruel instead. In the 1860s a radical improvement consisted in putting ox heads in the soup: three ox heads for each hundred inmates. There were small, carefully planned degradations to go with the larger ones. Children, for instance, were refused footwear whatever the weather. The Guardians believed it unwise to get them accustomed to shoes.

By the 1870s, when my great-grandfather became master of the Clonmel Union, there were some improvements. But of what interest are historical modifications to the person—to this woman—for whom suffering is fresh, first time, without memory or hope? She would have felt no hope at 6:00 A.M. when she rose; no hope at 9:00 P.M. when she finished a day of carefully planned monotony.

Yet she also would have seen the coming and going of the seasons. She also, like me, must have seen them in her children's faces. The meadow would have glittered beneath her on fine days; on wet ones the Comeraghs would have loomed in heathery colors. She may not, however, have seen them for long. Statistics argue persuasively that more than likely, she would have died—still of childbearing age—in the fever hospital a hundred yards down the hill. Clonmel was low-lying. The river Suir ran behind its streets with an ornamental sluggishness. Drainage was poor. Every few years typhus swept through the town. Its first victims must have been the inmates of the workhouse. It would have been my great-grandfather's decision where to bury them. He would have consulted the Board of Guardians. There were rules for such things.

II

And where does poetry come in? Here, as in so many other instances, it enters at the point where myth touches history. Let me explain. At one level, I could have said that there were summer dusks and clear, vacant winter mornings when I was certain the suburb nurtured my poetry. I might have found it hard to say how or why. In every season the neighbourhood gathered around me and filled my immediate distance. At times it could be a shelter; it was never a cloister. Everywhere you looked there were reminders—a child's bicycle thrown sideways on the grass, a single roller skate, a tree in its first April of blossom—that lives were not lived here in any sort of static pageant, but that they thrived, waned, changed, began and ended here.

Inevitably this sense of growth could not remain just at the edge of things. Apart from anything else, time was passing. Roads were laid. Houses were finished. The builders moved out. Summers came and went, and trees began to define the road. Garden walls were put up, and soon enough the voices calling over them on long, bright evenings, the bicycle thrown on its side and the single roller skate belonged to my children. Somewhat to my surprise, I had done what most human beings have done. I had found a world and I had populated it. In so doing, my imagination had been radically stirred and redirected. It was not, of course, a simple process. In poetry, let alone in life, it never is. It would be wrong, even now, to say that my poetry expressed the suburb. The more accurate version is that my poetry allowed me to experience it.

Yet there remained a sense of unease, as if some part of me could not assent to the reassurance of patterning. On bright days, for no apparent reason, my mind would swerve. Then I could sense, below the levels of my own conscious perception, something different, as if I could still remember—indeed had never forgotten—that place is never so powerful as when it is suffered in silence.

AT WHAT POINT does an actual, exact landscape—those details which are recurrent and predictable—begin to blur and soften? Sometimes on a summer evening, walking between my house and a neighbour's, past the whitebeam trees and the bicycles left glinting in the dusk, I could imagine that I myself was a surreal and changing outline, that there was something almost profound in these reliable shadows, that such lives as mine and my neighbours' were mythic, not because of their strangeness but because of their powerful ordinariness. When I reached a point in the road where I could see the children at the end of it, milling around and shrieking in the consciousness that they would have to come in soon, I would stand there with my hand held sickle-shaped to my eyes. Almost always I was just trying to remember which cotton T-shirt one child of mine or the other was wearing so I could pick it out in the summer twilight and go and scoop them up and bring them in. But just occasionally, standing there and breathing in the heavy musks of rose beds and buddleias, I would feel an older and less temporary connection to the moment. Then I would feel all the sweet, unliterate melancholy of women who must have stood as I did, throughout continents and centuries, feeling the timelessness of that particular instant and the cruel time underneath its surface. They must have measured their children, as I did, against the seasons and looked at the hedges and rowan trees, their height and the color of their berries, as an index of the coming loss.

Is it true, as Patrick Kavanagh says in his beautiful poem "Epic," that "gods make their own importance"? Is the origin, in other words, so restless in the outcome that the parish, the homestead, the place are powerful sources as well as a practical location? On those summer evenings, if my thoughts had not been full of details and children, I could have wondered where myth begins. Is it in the fears for harvest and the need for rain? Are its roots in the desire to make the strange familiar, to domesticate the thunder and give a shape to the frost? Or does it have, as Kavanagh argues, a more local and ritual source? Is there something about the repeated action—about lifting a child, clearing a dish, watching the seasons return to a tree and depart from a vista—which reveals a deeper meaning to existence and heals some of the worst abrasions of time?

Not suddenly then, but definitely and gradually, a place I

lived became a country of the mind. Perhaps anywhere I had grown used to, raised my children in, written my poetry about would have become this. But a suburb by its very nature—by its hand-to-mouth compromises between town and country—was particularly well suited to the transformation. Looking out my window at familiar things, I could realize that there had always been something compromised in my own relation to places. They had never been permanent. Therefore I had never developed a permanent perception about them.

Now here at last was permanence: an illusory permanence, of course, but enough stability to make me realize that the deepest sustenances are not in the new or surprising. And with that realization came the surrender of any prospect of loving new things: a prospect so vital when I was younger. Instead, many of the things I now did—from the casual gesture of looking out a window to the writing of poems—became an act of possessing the old things in a new way. I watched for the return of the magpies every February to their nest in the poplars just beyond my garden. I took an almost concert hall pleasure, in an August twilight, in listening to the sound of my neighbours' garden shears as she cut and pruned and made things ready for another season.

None of this was purely instinctive; none of it involved an intellectual suppression or simplification. I had a clearer and clearer sense, as time went on, of the meaning of all this to me as a poet. I knew what repetitions meant in poetry. I understood those values in language and restraint.

When Coleridge wrote, in the *Biographia Literaria*, of metrical units as "at first the offspring of passion and then the adopted children of power," I felt I understood a concept of linguistic patterning which both lulled the mind and facilitated the meaning.

Now here, in front of me every day, were repetitions which had almost exactly the same effect. The crocuses under the rowan tree, the same child wheeled down to the shops at the same time every day. A car that returned home, with the same dinge on its bumper, every night. And the lamps which sprang into symmetries across our hills at dusk in November.

What were all these if not—as language and music in poetry were—a sequence and repetition which allowed the deeper meanings to emerge: a sense of belonging, of sustenance, of a life revealed, and not restrained, by ritual and patterning?

NOW LET ME REWRITE that scenario. Let me darken the evening and harden the detail. The road is no longer paved; there are no streetlamps. My own outline is no longer surreal. It is the harsh shape of that woman, that client of my ancestor. My lips now are as blue as hers, the shallow blue of those shrubs. I have no house, no room in which I write, no books. My children are not healthy and noisy. They are the fractions of my own grief which cling at my skirt, their expressions scarred with hunger and doubt. Instead of bright cotton and denim—clothes they pick out and array themselves in—they wear fustian and the hated flannel. And they, like me, are ripe for the fevers which come in off the marshes and stagnate in the water of the town.

Of course this is impossible. The most awkward memory is known to be a figment, not a ghost. Yet even as a figment this woman was important. She cast her shadow across the suburb. She made me doubt the pastoral renewals of day-to-day life. And whenever I tried to find the quick meanings of my day in the deeper ones of the past, she interposed a fierce presence in case the transaction should be too comfortable, too lyric.

It would be wrong to say her presence changed my idea of poetry. But it changed my idea of place. Then again, it would also be true to say that my most optimistic view of place had never excluded her. Familiar, compound ghosts such as she—paragons of dispossession—haunt the Irish present. She is a part of all our histories. The cadences I learned to see in that suburb, those melodies of renewal, had their roots in her silence. There is a hard, unglamourous suffering in such a silence. And I imagined it often, imagined the mute hatred with which she must have looked at my great-grandfather as he descended from his trap, unharnessed his pony.

In thinking about her at all I was exercising a peculiar, perhaps even a dangerous freedom. It is a freedom inherent in the shifting outlines of a defeated history. Such a history is full of silences. Hers is only one of them. And those silences in turn are the quicksand on which any stable or expressive view of place will forever after be built. The more I thought of her, the more it seemed to me that a sense of place can happen at the very borders of myth and history. In the first instance there are the healing repetitions, the technology of propitiation. In the second there is the consciousness of violent and random event. In the zone between them something happens. Ideas of belonging take on the fluidity of sleep. Here is a nose, an eye, a mouth, but they may belong to different people. And here, on the edge of dream, is a place in which I locate myself as a poet: not exactly the suburb, not entirely the hill colored with blue shrubs. But somewhere composed of both.

I could put it another way. A suburb is all about futures. Trees grow; a small car becomes a bigger one to accommodate new arrivals. Then again, there is little enough history, almost no appeal to memory. The children learn the names of the sweet shop and the bike repair shop. They talk about the sixty-foot tree in the grounds of an old castle. The fact that the castle is a Norman keep and may cover Norman remains is of no interest.

A workhouse, on the other hand—to adapt Yeats's phrase—is the fiery shorthand of a history. Fever, eviction, the statistics of poverty—it infers them all. The immediate past of a nation sleeps in its cots and eats its coarse rations. But what a workhouse lacks is a future.

WHAT I HAVE TRIED to write about here is neither metaphorical nor emblematic but something which is, in fact, the common source of both. There is a quality about the minute changes, the gradations of a hedge, the small growth of a small boy which makes a potent image out of an ordinary day in a suburb. Nothing I have described here can catch the simple force for me of looking out my window on one of those mornings at the end of winter, when a few, small burgundy rags would be on the wild cherry tree but otherwise everything was bare and possessed a muted sort of expectancy. The hills would have the staring blues which signaled rain. A car would pass by. A neighbour's dog would bark, then be silent. Maybe the daffodils which had been closed the week before would now be open, after an afternoon of that quick, buttery sunshine which is the best part of an Irish spring.

But all of this constitutes the present tense. And the present tense, surely, is instructed by the past. And perhaps I want to say that women poets—Akhmatova and Adrienne Rich come to mind—are witnesses to the fact that myth is instructed by history, although the tradition is full of poets who argue the opposite with force and eloquence. In my case, to paraphrase the myth, I gradually came to know at what price my seasons—my suburb—had been bought. My underworld was a hundred miles southwest. But there, too, the bargains had been harsh, the outcome a terrible compromise. The woman I imagined—if the statistics are anything to go by—must have lost her children in that underworld, just as I came to possess mine through the seasons of my neighbourhood. This account has been about how that past, those images, her compromised life came to find me in the midst of my incomparably easier one. And how I wanted to be found.

SUBJECT MATTERS

I t was the early seventies, a time of violence in Northern Ireland. Our front room was a cold rectangle with white walls, hardly any furniture and a small television chanting deaths and statistics at teatime.

It was also our first winter in the suburb. The weather was cold; the road was half finished. Each morning the fields on the Dublin hills appeared as slates of frost. At night the streetlamps were too few. And the road itself ran out in a gloom of icy mud and builders' huts.

One evening, at the time of the news, I came into the front room with a cup of coffee in my hand. I heard something at the front door. I set down the coffee, switched on the light and went to open the door.

A large, dappled head—a surreal dismemberment in the dusk—swayed low on the doorstep, then attached itself back to a clumsy horse and clattered away. I went out and stood under the streetlamp. I saw its hindquarters retreating, smudged by mist and darkness. I watched it disappear around a corner. The lamp above me hissed and flickered and finally came on fully.

There was an explanation. It was almost certainly a traveller's horse with some memory of our road as a travelling site and our gardens as fields where it had grazed only recently. The memory withstood the surprises of its return, but not for long. It came back four or five times. Each time, as it was startled into retreat, its huge hooves did damage. Crocus bulbs were uprooted. Hedge seedlings were dragged up. Grass seeds were churned out of their place.

Some months later I began to write a poem. I called it "The War Horse." Its argument was gathered around the oppositions of force and formality. Of an intrusion of nature—the horse—menacing the decorous reductions of nature which were the gardens. And of the failure of language to describe such violence and resist it.

I wrote the poem slowly, adding each couplet with care. I was twenty-six years of age. At first, when it was finished, I looked at it with pleasure and wonder. It encompassed a real event. It entered a place in my life and moved beyond it. I was young enough in the craft to want nothing more.

Gradually I changed my mind, although I never disowned the poem. In fact, my doubts were less about it than my own first sense of its completeness. The poem had drawn me easily into the charm and strength of an apparently public stance. It had dramatized for me what I already suspected: that one part of the poem in every generation is ready to be communally written. To put it another way, there is a poem in each time that waits to be set down and is therefore instantly recognizable once it has been. It may contain sentiments of outrage or details of an occasion. It may invite a general reaction to some particular circumstance. It may appeal to anger or invite a common purpose.

It hardly matters. The point is that to write in that cursive and approved script can seem, for the unwary poet, a blessed lifting of the solitude and skepticism of the poet's life. Images are easily set down; a music of argument is suddenly revealed. A difficult pursuit becomes a swift movement. The poem takes on a glamour of meaning against a background of public interest.

Historically—in the epic, in the elegy—this has been an enrichment. But in a country like Ireland, with a nationalist tradition, there are real dangers. In my poem, the horse, the hills behind it—these were private emblems which almost immediately took on a communal reference against a background of communal suffering. In a time of violence it would be all too easy to write another poem, and another. To make a construct where the difficult "I" of perception became the easier "we" of a subtle claim. Where an unearned power would be allowed by a public engagement.

In such a poem the poet would be the subject. The object might be a horse, a distance, a human suffering. It hardly mattered. The public authorization would give such sanction to the poet that the object would not just be silent. It would be silenced. The subject would be all-powerful.

At that point I saw that in Ireland, with its national tradition, its bardic past, the confusion between the political poem and the public poem was a dangerous and inviting motif. It encouraged the subject of the poem to be a representative and the object to be ornamental. In such a relation, the dangerous and private registers of feeling of the true political poem would be truly lost. At the very moment when they were most needed.

And yet I had come out of the Irish tradition as a poet. I had opened the books, read the poems, believed the rhetoric when I was young. Writing the political poem seemed to me almost a franchise of the Irish poet, an inherited privilege. I would come to see that it was more and less than that, that like other parts of the poet's life, it would involve more of a solitary scruple than a communal eloquence. And yet one thing remained steady: I continued to believe that a reading of the energy and virtue of any tradition can be made by looking at the political poem in its time. And who writes it and why. At who can speak in the half-light between event and perception without their voices becoming shadows as Aeneas's rivals did in the underworld of the Sixth Book.

In that winter twilight, seeing the large, unruly horse scrape the crocus bulbs up in his hooves, making my own connections between power and order, I had ventured on my first political poem. I had seen my first political image. I had even understood the difficulties of writing it. What I had not realized was that I myself was a politic within the Irish poem: a young woman who had left the assured identity of the city and its poetic customs and who had started on a life which had no place in them. I had seen and weighed and struggled with the meaning of the horse, the dark night, the sounds of death from the television. I had been far less able to evaluate my own hand on a light switch, my own form backlit under the spluttering streetlight against the raw neighbourhood of a suburb. And yet without one evaluation the other was incomplete.

I would learn that it was far more difficult to make myself the political subject of my own poems than to see the metaphoric possibilities in front of me in a suburban dusk. The difficulty was a disguised blessing. It warned me away from facile definitions. The more I looked at the political poem, the more I saw how easy it was to make the claim and miss the connections. And I wanted to find them.

II

I could start with the spring of 1843. In that season Ireland faced both ways. In one direction was a hopeful past: Daniel O'Connell's populist oratory and the bill of Catholic emancipation. In the other direction lay the future and catastrophe: the coming famine and the failure of the 1848 Rising.

Early in that year a volume of poetry appeared. It was called *The Spirit of the Nation* and was sold as a sixpenny booklet. It consisted of poems published in *The Nation*, a tabloid newspaper which had started up the previous October.

The founders of *The Nation* were a group of young middle-class men—Thomas Davis, Charles Gavan Duffy and John Blake Dillon—who advocated a new style of Irish nationalism. Their rhetoric was often abstract and intellectual, but their methods were populist and journalistic. They advocated the Irish language, a self-reflective literature and a new self-reliance. They became known as Young Ireland—to distinguish them from O'Connell's older strategies—and in some respects they were indeed different. Irish nationalism, since the passing of the Act of Union in 1800, had undertaken some awkward engagements which it needed to rid itself of if it was to become an effective and persuasive politic. Not the least of these was with British drawing rooms. The songs, letters and speeches of Irish patriots of the twenties and thirties—O'Connell was not innocent of this and neither was Tom Moore—have the occasional look of a souvenir shop. Wolfhounds, harps and shamrocks appear with suspicious frequency.

The Nation turned its back on British drawing rooms and commended the spiritual intactness of the Irish nation through its articles, poems and polemics. Its natural constituency was the engaged and doomed generation of Irish Catholics who had listened to O'Connell and would die by their hundreds and thousands in the famine. The newspaper cost sixpence and sold widely: at the height of its popularity its sales were ten thousand—an enormous figure in the circumstance. It is hard to judge how widely it reached the landless Catholic class. There are stories of it being read out to listeners in the cabins and cottages. According to Gavan Duffy, it outsold the local newspaper in some provincial towns where "it passed from hand to hand till it was worn to fragments." But it also sought out the young Protestant middle class who, since 1800, had held aloof from the Irish cause. "Gentlemen," Davis reminded the students of Trinity College, "you have a country."

The poems in the *Nation* were often written by Davis but they also included work by James Clarence Mangan and other gifted writers. The titles reveal the themes: "Lament for the Death of Owen Roe O'Neill," "Dark Rosaleen," "Nationality," "The West's Asleep." In the main—James Clarence Mangan was a notable exception—they were crude and memorable: a strange mix of florid imagery and martial invective. This stanza from "Nationality" by Davis gives a fair sampling:

> *A nation's voice, a nation's voice—*
> *It is a solemn thing*
> *It bids the bondage-sick rejoice—*
> *'Tis stronger than a king.*
> *'Tis like the light of many stars,*
> *The sound of many waves;*
> *Which brightly look through prison bars;*
> *And sweetly sound through caves*
> *Yet is it noblest, godliest known*
> *When righteous triumph swells its tone.*

The mixing of the national and the feminine is also a recurrent usage in the rhetoric of the newspaper. As Davis himself said, referring to Ireland in an address to the Historical Society at Trinity College, "I have thought I saw her spirit from her dwelling, her sorrowing place among the tombs, rising, not without melancholy, yet with a purity and brightness beyond other nations." Added to this, was the view of the political poem Davis proposed. "National poetry," he wrote, "presents the most dramatic events, the largest characters, the most impressive scenes and the deepest passions in the language most familiar to us. It magnifies and ennobles our hearts, our intellects, our country and our countrymen; binds us to the land by its condensed and gem-like history. It solaces us in travel, fires us in action . . . is the recognized envoy of our minds among all mankind and to all time."

The *Nation* was influential for several reasons. In the poems it chose and published, it paid an obvious homage to the ballads of the street. In giving an intellectual legitimacy to those cadences, the *Nation* drew them into the mainstream of the nationalist enterprise, and made a vital and lasting connection in Irish poetry. More important, in its pages, the public poem and the political poem were confused at the very moment when the national tradition was making a claim on Irish poetry which would color its themes and purposes for a century.

III

No life was less public or apparently political than mine when I first became conscious of all this. I lived in a world familiar to many women. I had a husband, young children and a home. I did the same things over and over again. At night I watched water sluice the milk bottles to a bluish gleam before I put them out on the step. By day I went to collect my children under whitebeam trees and in different weathers.

Yet merely by the act of going upstairs in a winter dusk, merely by starting to write a poem at a window that looked out on the Dublin hills, I was entering a place of force. Just by trying to record the life I lived in the poem I wrote, I had become a political poet.

Part of the reason for this was that my material was already politicized. The image of the woman which I was dealing with had already been allotted a place in the Irish poem. But as object, not subject. Therefore, the life I lived was at variance, in the poetic tradition, with the power and activity of the poet's voice. I not only experienced that life but expressed it. I gave it a speaking part in the previous drama of its silence. But I was aware of resistances and difficulties in doing so. In a fine essay called "What Foremothers?" the wonderful Irish-language poet Nuala Ní Dhomhnaill writes "how the image of woman in the national tradition is a very real dragon that every Irish woman poet has to fight every time she opens her door."

There was an odd isolation about those years; but an impersonal one. What comes back to me now is not the pain but the paradox. One part of the poem I wrote was in light, the other in shadow. As a woman the life I lived—its dailyness, its complexity—had been given a place of passivity and silence in the very tradition that had given me my voice as a poet.

It seemed I had a choice. I could write my life into the Irish poem in the way tradition dictated—as mythic distaff of the national tradition—or I could confront the fact that in order to write the Irish poem I would have to alter, for myself, the powerful relations between subject and object which were established there. That in turn involved disrupting the other values encoded in those relations: the authority of the poet. Its place in the historic legend. And the allegory of nationhood which had customarily been shadowed and enmeshed in the image of the woman.

But in reality I had no choice. I was that image come to life. I had walked out of the pages of the *Nation*, the cadences of protest, the regret of emigrant ballads. But I spoke with the ordinary and fractured speech of a woman living in a Dublin suburb, whose claims to the visionary experience would be sooner made on behalf of a child or a tree than a century of struggle. I was a long way from what Davis thought of as a national poet. And yet my relation to the national poem—as its object, its past—was integral and forceful and ominous.

In that was the clue. It seemed to me that the connection between my life and that poem, while private and obsessive, was simultaneously political. Even in the fastness of the suburb I saw the intensity of witness which the previous silent object of a poetic tradition could give as its articulate present.

The more I thought of it, the more it seemed to me that, in Ireland, the political poem and the public poem should not be one and the same. On the contrary, given the force of the national tradition and the claim it had made on Irish literature, the political poem stood in urgent need of a subversive private experience to lend it true perspective and authority. An authority which, in my view, could be guaranteed only by an identity—and this included a sexual identity—which the poetic tradition, and the structure of the Irish poem, had almost stifled.

IV

I do not believe the political poem can be written with truth and effect unless the self who writes that poem—a self in which sexuality must be a factor—is seen to be in a radical relation to the ratio of power to powerlessness with which the political poem is so concerned.

This relation, and the way it is construed, is now visibly altered in the Irish poem. One of the characteristics of the political poem—the accruing of power by the speaker in the poem in the face of a perceived powerlessness outside it—has been subverted. At a downright and sensible level, the sense of power a woman speaker might have in an Irish poem today will not just be political; it must also be politicized. In other words, her sense of power inside the poem must be flawed and tempered, not just by a perception of powerlessness outside it but also by the memory of her traditional and objectified silence within it.

The final effect of the political poem depends on whether it is viewed by the reader as an act of freedom or an act of power. This in turn has everything to do with the authority of the speaker. Paradoxically, that authority grows the more the speaker is weakened and made vulnerable by the tensions he or she creates. By the same logic, it is diminished if the speaker protects themselves by the powers of language he or she can generate.

The political poem, in other words, proves in a single genre what is true of all poetry. The mover of the poem's action—the voice, the speaker—must be at the same risk from that action as every other component in the poem. If that voice is exempt, then the reader will hear it as omniscient; if it is omniscient, it can still commend the ratio of power to powerlessness—but with the reduced authority of an observer.

It is impossible to be abstract about these things. You cannot prove a change in poetry by diagrams and numbers. You cannot swear to it or set your clock by it. It is something which has to be deduced by instinct and practice, by reading and writing, often against the grain, often without certainty.

V

I was certain of one thing: the confusion of the public and the political—although the cause of some real eloquence—could also make the genuinely radical poem less visible than it ought to be. And this frustrated me. I wanted to see the powerful public history of my own country joined by the private lives and solitary perspectives, including my own, which the Irish poetic tradition had not yet admitted to authorship. I wanted to see the effect of an unrecorded life—a woman in a suburban twilight under a hissing streetlight—on the prescribed themes of public importance.

Without this, I felt that the argument of the political poem might be limited to the public event and the communal interpretation of it. That was not the poem I wanted to write; it was not even the poem I wanted to read. Besides, I had a sense of an alternative. The eloquent and destabilizing effect of the private voice was already something I had observed in the best Irish poetry. And I was sure—if only the tradition would admit it as subject matter—that this could throw the conventional Irish political poem off balance, offering it fresh perspectives and different alignments.

I already knew of a beautiful example. It came in a poem by Yeats called "Meditations in Time of Civil War." I had read it first as a teenager, just returned to boarding school after a visit to Galway. I could still see the stone walls and feel the roads rising and winding under the wheels of the car as I opened the book. Yeats had written his poem in Thoor Ballylee, his stone tower near the village of Gort, with the Slieve Aughty Mountains rising to the east and the stopped-up green water of a stream in front of it. The poem describes desolation, both within and without. It sets an ominous breakdown of public order—"that young soldier in his blood"—against the poet's own darkening perceptions. Throughout the first four sections of the poem these different realities seek each other out. Then in the fifth section they come together wonderfully:

> An affable Irregular,
> A heavily-built Falstaffian man,
> Comes cracking jokes of civil war
> As though to die by gunshot were
> The finest play under the sun.
>
> A brown Lieutenant and his men,
> Half dressed in national uniform,
> Stand at my door, and I complain
> Of the foul weather, hail and rain,
> A pear tree broken by the storm.
>
> I count those feathered balls of soot
> The moor-hen guides upon the stream,
> To silence the envy in my thought;
> And turn towards my chamber, caught
> In the cold snows of a dream.

The effect of this poem is wonderful and surprising. It takes a public reality of fixed meaning—a civil war fought in a rural setting—and destabilizes it through the intensity of a private world. Yeats meets the irregular at his front door and hears him cracking jokes about violence and death. Then he meets his opposite number, a lieutenant in the newly constituted national army, and complains to him, but this time about the natural violence of the weather.

At the end of the poem he is a pastoral poet, counting the moorhen's ducklings to suppress his own ambiguous feelings about the world of action, to silence "the envy in my thought." And at the end of the poem also there is no doubt which is the paramount adventure: it is not the uniformed man or his opponent. Nor is it the natural world with its renewals and catastrophes. It is the vivid and divided world of the subject. Yeats had done what I had not realized needed to be done that winter evening in the suburb. He had proposed a private world in a political poem—a world so volatile that it had collapsed and refreshed all the other apparently stable meanings in the poem.

To me this was the Irish political poem as it should be: fresh and startling, a lyric that could not be predicted or arranged. It made an encouraging sign about the real ability of an inner world to suffer the outer world so powerfully that history itself faltered before that gaze.

VI

I have never felt I owned Irish history; I have never felt entitled to the Irish experience. There have been Irish poets who have written the political poem with exactly this sense of ownership and entitlement. I doubt those credentials. It is a weakness and not a strength of the Irish poetic tradition that it encourages its poets to act as envoys of dispossession. The political poem is not the report of a privileged witness. It is a continuing action which revises, in some decisive way, the perceived relation of power between an inner and outer world. In the great dramas of language and vision these worlds are rebalanced so that one can comment on the other rather than crush it, so that the fracture in one annotates the wound in the other.

During my twenties and thirties my interest in the political poem increased as my apparent access to it declined. I sensed resistances around me. I was married; I lived in a suburb; I had small children. Permissions are neither spoken nor conceded in a poetic discourse. Yet I knew that the permission for a suburban woman to write the Irish political poem was neither allowed nor foreseen.

Irish poetry was male and bardic in formation. Its secrets and inheritances divided it, even from the historical radical-isms of the romantic movement. I had a deep suspicion of those secrets. It was not just that having read American poets like Elizabeth Bishop, my sense of the value and possibility of being a guest editor at the historical process had been confirmed. It was something more.

I was skeptical of the very structure of the Irish poem. Its inherited voice, its authoritative stance, its automatic reflex of elegy—these given qualities, from a technical perspective, accrued too much power to the speaker to allow that speaker to be himself a plausible critic of power. And the power he had was a sweet and venerable one, with its roots deep in the flattery of princes and a bardic outrage at losing protected status for poets. It gave to Irish poets an authority long taken from or renounced by their British counterparts. The romantic poet was so suspicious of power that, by 1820, he was safely on the road to a suspicion of poetry. The crisis of modernism was part of that outcome. The bardic poet, in his Irish manifestation, remained shuttered in an older faith: where poetry and privilege were inflexibly associated. Where, whatever the dispossession and humiliation of an outer world, maleness remained a caste system within the poem.

The shadow of bardic privilege still fell on the Irish poem when I was young. It was hard to question and harder to shift. Yet I knew I would have to do both if I wanted access to the political poem in Ireland. Nor did I simplify it into a question of gender and prejudice. It went far beyond that, to raise the whole issue of poetic authority: women had for so long been a natural object relation for the Irish poem that women poets seemed less a new arrival in the literary tradition than a species of insubordination. It was as though a fixed part of the Irish poem had broken free and become volatile.

VII

From the top windows at dusk I could see the steady lamps at the base of those hills and the flickering spiral of car headlights moving down it.

My children were born. I entered a world of routine out of which, slowly and mysteriously, a world of vision manifested itself. For all that, it was a commonsense and familiar world, a stretch of road with whitebeam trees and driveways where cars—the same, for all I knew, which had just moved down the hillside—returned at dusk and left first thing in the morning.

It was not just that I lived there. I learned to do that, and with full attention. Nor that I wrote poems there. I learned to do that too. The challenge was in making the connection, was in the care with which I perceived that the same tree and the daylight frost were not just recurrences but had the power to alter my view of the elegy, the pastoral and the nature poem.

One of the problems in making that connection was that all this was at a contradictory angle from the Irish poem as I first encountered it and had learned to write it. The Dublin I entered and published in as an undergraduate poet honored—in a small circle—its own view of the life of the poet. It was still, although this was less visible, recovering from the claim which the Literary Revival—and through it the national tradition—had laid on poetry. This claim dictated a certain sequence of importances and permissions for the Irish poem: for its themes, its language and purpose. The political poem in Ireland, by this definition, proved its Irishness by a subtle series of referential gestures. It was still weighed, as many post-colonial instruments are, by a burden of proof: so that the oppression could be further disproved, the oppressed must be proved worthy over and over again. A stultifying series of themes and tones lay heavily on the poem. And it offered, and considered, no name for a poet who was about to live a life it did not recognize as suitable for the Irish poem.

"The poetic image," writes Muriel Rukeyser, "is not a static thing. It lives in time as does the poem." I wanted the Irish poem to live in my time. The dial of a washing machine, the expression in a child's face—these things were at eye level as I bent down to them during the day. I wanted them to enter my poems. I wanted the poems they entered to be Irish poems. I was about to find that the poem in its time is a register of resistances and difficulties which go well beyond the intention and determination of any one poet. I was about to find also that the politic of the poem—and also the political poem—is a subtle and risky negotiation not only between perceptions of power but between what is included in the poem and what remains outside it. That relation between the excluded and the included is the dominant politic of the poem.

In my mid-twenties I had left an established literary world for a neighbourhood—real and figurative—where such arguments and evaluations had no reality. If I had stayed, there is at least a chance I might have renamed my life to comply with a forceful absence of any other name for it. Instead, to use Adrienne Rich's words, "I did begin to resist the apparent splitting of poet from woman, thinker from woman and to write what I feared was political poetry."

VIII

My sense of the private life as a politic of its own was not fanciful. It had its source in my own sense of certain actions, certain commentaries as radical in context. In my twenties I had failed to see the connection between a young woman under a streetlamp and a horse blundering away in the dusk. I was determined it would not happen again.

The Irish poem, as it came from the nineteenth century, was marked and shaped by public perceptions. Its substance was eloquent and poignant. It canvassed the death of heroes and triumph against the odds. It ranged all the way from the street ballad about an execution to Samuel Ferguson's lament for Thomas Davis. It was the poem I heard as a child, the poetic decorum I inherited.

The problem was that this substance predicted a speaker. And the speaker of the poem—of the political poem, that is—was too often in sympathy with the substance, almost to the point where his viewpoint seemed to be created by it. Therefore, the planes and angles of the poem became flattened out. Where they should have jutted against a horizon, defining it by a sharp and challenging shape, they made a continuum with it. Or in other words, they fitted smoothly into the context of public opinion and assumption.

Even as I was debating this with myself, Irishwomen were writing poems where the public world was indeed a radical commentary. In her beautiful first book, *The Flower Master*, Medbh McGuckian, a poet from Belfast, had included a poem called "The Flitting." Its astonishing swerves and recoveries, its kaleidoscopic imagery created a perception of the exterior world which once again, as in Yeats's poem, testified to the power of the inner one, as its speaker "postpone[d] my immortality for my children" and a train

> *Ploughed like an emperor living out a myth*
> *Through the cambered flesh of clover and wild carrot.*

In the same way Eiléan Ní Chuilleanáin could write in her first book, *Site of Ambush*, about "Light, weathered filterings / That shift under her feet" in a poem called "Darkening All the Strand" which infers the complex layerings of Irish culture. And in an eloquent poem called "The Pattern" a younger Dublin poet, Paula Meehan, in a poem which summons the life of her mother, at the mercy of history, inflects a world well beyond it:

> *And as she buffed the wax to a high shine*
> *did she catch her own face coming clear?*

Of course, women poets in Ireland also inherited a powerful history and a persuasive construct. It would be foolish to deny it. The Irish nineteenth century reached out to them also, with its cause and its cadences. But there was a difference. Within a poetry inflected by its national tradition, women had often been double-exposed, like a flawed photograph, over the image and identity of the nation. The nationalization of the feminine, the feminization of the national, had become a powerful and customary inscription in the poetry of that very nineteenth-century Ireland. "Cathleen ni Houlihan!" exclaimed MacNeice. "Why / must a country like a ship or a car, be always / female?" A poetic landscape which had once been politicized through women was not politicized by them. The obstinate and articulate privacy of their lives was now writing the poem, rather than simply being written by it. If this did not make a new political poem, it at least constituted a powerful revision of the old one. As more and more poems by Irishwomen were written, it was obvious that something was happening to the Irish poem. It was what happens to any tradition when previously mute images within it come to awkward and vivid life, when the icons return to haunt the icon makers. That these disruptions had been necessary at all, that they were awkward and painful when they happened, had something to do with the force of the national tradition.

IX

Nationalism has an ironic effect on literature. In Irish poetry, at the end of the colonial nineteenth century, the national tradition operated as a powerful colonizer. It marked out value systems; it politicized certain realities and devalued others. To those it recognized and approved, it offered major roles in the story. To others, bit parts only.

Patrick Kavanagh got a bit part. And he knew it. Born in 1904 into a hard-pressed rural family, he represented a class which was falsely depicted and inaccurately politicized, both in Yeats's poetry and in the Literary Revival as a whole. He was acerbic about that misrepresentation. "When I came to Dublin," he writes in his *Self-Portrait*, "the Irish Literary Affair was still booming. It was the notion that Dublin was a literary metropolis and Ireland as invented and patented by Yeats, Lady Gregory and Synge, a spiritual entity. It was full of writers and poets and I am afraid I thought their work had the Irish quality."

Kavanagh was an obstinate lyric poet. His interests were not in social history but in the effects of language on vision—a concern which was disallowed by the expectations of the Literary Revival. Poets like Kavanagh were intended to exemplify the oppressions of Irish history by being oppressed. Kavanagh resisted. He rejected a public role in favor of a private vision. It was a costly and valuable resistance—exemplary to poets like myself who have come later, and with different purposes, into that tradition.

Kavanagh was especially sensitive to the politicization of his own experience in previous Irish poetry. The Literary Revival was invested in a false pastoral. Against a heroic background, the rural experience was both glamourized and distorted. Therefore, a poet such as Kavanagh was screen-tested in much the same way that Padraic Colum had been. They were meant to exemplify the oppressions of Irish history by being oppressed. "In those days in Dublin," Kavanagh writes, "the big thing besides being Irish was peasant quality. They were all trying to be peasants. They had been at it for years but I hadn't heard."

To be politicized in a poetic tradition, without having powers of expression or intervention to change the interpretation, is an experience Irish woman poets share with Kavanagh. Like them, he was part of the iconic structure of the Irish poem long before he became its author. Like them, his authorship involved him in iconic reversals and important shifts of emphasis. Like them, his previous objectification in the poem made him an important witness not just to his own themes but to the structure of a poetic tradition which had, in effect, silenced him. His poem "The Great Hunger" is an antipastoral. It sets out to explore and comment on a relation between man and nature which is neither the soft elegy of the British pastoral nor the social protest of the Irish one but marks out a painful and achieved connection between private suffering and all the complex references of local faith and sexual anguish and undependable vision.

> *The twisting sod rolls over on her back—*
> *The virgin screams before the irresistible sock.*

X

I wrote the political poem in Ireland because I was once politicized within it. By the same token, my womanhood—once its object and icon—became part of its authorship. These are difficult and awkward transitions. They in no way guarantee good poetry, but they have allowed me to take a different perspective on an old and hallowed craft. I am slow, for instance, to believe that the political poem can be written by a self that is not politicized, even radicalized. Once again, I find it hard to accept that a radical self can function authoritatively in the political poem if the sexual self, which is part of it, remains conservative, exclusive and unquestioning of inherited authority.

In Ireland a paradox exists. A country with a wealth of themes encourages its poets, through a bardic past and a national tradition, to diminish them from political complexity to public statement. The best Irish poets have resisted this, and it needs to be resisted. Political poetry operates in the corridor between rhetoric and reality. It is an ineffective presence there if the poet provides the rhetoric while the reality remains outside the poem. How to draw the reality into the poem, and therefore into a subversive relation with the rhetoric, is the crucial question. But there are political poems written in Ireland, even today, where the question is not even asked, let alone answered. This in turn prompts an even more central question: how can you subvert that relation if you have failed to subvert the tradition of expression with which you approach it?

The emergence of women poets in Ireland guarantees nothing. I want to be clear about that. They also use language; their language is open to scrutiny. But I have argued here, and I truly believe, that where icons walk out of the poem to become authors of it, their speculative energy is directed not just to the iconography which held them hostage but to the poem itself. This gives the woman poet such as myself the unique chance to fold language and history in on itself, to write a political poem which canvasses Irish history by questioning the poetic structures it shadowed. To dismantle, in other words, the rhetorical relationship by dismantling the poetic persona which supported it. And to seek the authority to do this not from a privileged or historic stance within the Irish poem but from the silences it created and sustained.

There is nothing restrictive in this. Nothing in my argument dishonors, or intends to dishonor, the good work done by male poets in Ireland. But I do intend to challenge the assumption, which is without intellectual rigor, that public poetry—whether it is about a scandal or a death or the situation in Northern Ireland—is necessarily political poetry. The two may overlap, but they are not the same. I also intend to challenge the central tenet of their confusion: the voice at the center of too many Irish poems which assumes that an inherited stance can stand in for an achieved poetic authority.

The confusion of the two has been damaging. It has created false acceptance and exclusions. It has opened the way for poems which are glibly concerned with violence, while on the other hand proposing that the life of a woman, as a theme, was incompatible with the purpose and seriousness of the political poem. Both these views owe something—even obliquely—to the shadowing of a poetic tradition by a national program which has sought, since the nineteenth century, to generate and recruit the political poem in Ireland. At its best the political poem can be an illuminating form. But in Ireland, above all, there is a need to remember that it is not exempt, by any virtue of contemporary reference, from the rules of vigilance and necessity which govern all poetic expression.

MAKING THE DIFFERENCE

I t is an evening in summer. The suburb is quiet. The Dublin hills are the last color they will be in the succession of colors they have been all day: a sort of charcoal violet. The trellises and sidewalls are well hidden with clematis and sweet pea. A neighbour's rectangle of rose garden is full of pastels, with one or two scarlets. A bicycle lies sideways on the ground. A child's plastic mug, with an orange beak on the lid of it, is thrown at the bottom of a step. Everywhere you look there is evidence that this is a landscape of rapid change and ordinary survivals.

I am talking to a woman in the last light. I have just finished cutting the grass at the front, and we are outside, between her house and mine. We make that temporary shape which conversing neighbours often assume: not exactly settled into a discussion, yet not ready to leave it either. She lives across the road from me. Her children are teenagers. Mine are still infants, asleep behind the drawn curtains in the rooms upstairs.

As we talk, I feel the shadow of some other meaning across our conversation, which is otherwise entirely about surface things. That it is high summer in my life, not in hers. That hers is the life mine will become, while mine is the life she has lost. Then the conversation ends. I turn to go in. I lift the bicycle and the mug.

That night something strange happens. I begin to make notes for a poem. I try to write it. As I do, I am aware of that split screen, that half-in-half perspective which is so connected with the act of writing. I am at a table at an open window. Outside the poem, I can smell the sweet cut grass of the evening's task. Through the open doors of two rooms I can hear my children breathing. I see the poplars with their shadow-colored leaves. The connection between this world outside the poem and something it might become inside it is at first exciting, then difficult, then impossible to make. At some point I do what I have rarely done—at least not at such a preliminary stage of writing. I put down the pen. I leave my notes. I set aside the poem in the certainty that it will never be written.

Now let me stand back, from this distance, as I never could in the act of composition. Let me return to that night, to the page on the table, so as to look more closely at what it is I am trying to write, that I have not written, this poem that has failed to run what Frost called "a lucky course of events." Let me say, for the sake of argument, that the notes for the poem—although in fact they were nothing as coherent as this—involved three different elements: a suburb; the Dublin hills behind it; two women talking under a window where the children of one of them are asleep. Again, let me ask a question which is more self-conscious than any which could have proposed itself at that point: which of these elements has given me so much difficulty that not only do I not write the poem but I know in a very short time that it will not be written?

It is not the suburb, that much is certain. By now I have come to terms with the fact that a suburb is an awkward and unlikely theatre for a poem. It is certainly true that this ordinary street, of young trees and younger children, has provided me with one of the most challenging components in a poetic theme: a devalued subject matter. It has given me an insight into the flawed permissions which surround the inherited Irish poem: in which you could have a political murder, but not a baby, and a line of hills, but not the suburbs under them. Nevertheless, I think of these as problems rather than obstructions. They test me; they do not silence me. They make it clear that the tense relation between the suburb and a societal perception of it is only a restatement of the connection between the complexity of any theme and its caricature.

Then there are the Dublin hills. All through that conversation, they have been collecting shadows. By now it must be obvious that I am making a deliberate artifice: arguing as though the elements of a poem were separable and clear units, some of which may be inspected for obstructive tendencies, others of which can be considered free of them. Of course they cannot. But allowing for the artifice, let me look more closely at these hills.

Outside the poem, they make a half circle on the southwest of our horizon. Their low curve is marked by soft colors. Their contour hides the rising of the river Liffey—a trickle among ling and bracken and heather—which made the city. Inside the poem, the two blunt syllables of the word *Dublin* and the poignant signaling which the local makes to the national are presences and inferences which must be reckoned with. But by now, as an Irish poet and a woman, I have come face-to-face with these things. The truths of womanhood and the defeats of a nation have drawn nearer to one another in my work; they make an improbable intersection. Nevertheless, I sense they may yet inform one another. I already know that for me anyway, the only possible dialogue with the idea of a nation will be a subversive one. And even this will not be easy.

The suburb. The Dublin hills. They are not the problem. They offer challenges not silences. And the challenges simply serve to illustrate that a place should find its poem, a time its expression—things which most poets know anyway. For all the difficulties, they hold out the possibility of such discoveries—of that glamour of meaning which Pasternak describes happening in the Petersburg poems of Blok: "Adjectives without a noun, predicates without a subject, alarm, excitement, hide-and-seek, abruptness, whisking shadows—how well this style accorded with the spirit of a time, itself secretive, hermetic, underground, only just out of the cellars, and still using the language of conspiracy, the spirit of a time and of a tale in which the chief character was the town and the street was the chief event."

It is in the foreground of the poem that the difficulties exist. That the poem falters. Where the women stand and talk—deep within that image is, I know, another image. The deeper image is that shadow, the aging woman, the argument that the body of one woman is a prophecy of the body of the other. Here, at the very point where I am looking for what Calvino calls "that natural rhythm, as of the sea or the wind, that festive light impulse," the exact opposite happens. I cannot make her real; I cannot make myself real. I cannot make the time we are happening in real, so that the time I fear can also happen.

But why? The answer to that question, which was hardly formulated then, is part of the reason for my argument. Then I was merely confused; even now I may not be clear. And yet I sensed, hidden in the narrative distance between myself and this theme of aging women, some restriction; some thickening and stumbling. Writing a poem is so instinctive that it can be almost impossible, in the actual moment, to separate an aesthetic difficulty from a personal limitation. But this was different. I could not write these women. I could not write the misadventure of time which was happening to them in an ordinary Dublin twilight. That I could not write it was nothing new. What unsettled me was that—at some level I barely understood— neither did I feel free to imagine it.

Why does the page lie on the table by the window? Why are the table deserted and the pen to one side of it? Why am I about to make an unwritten poem into this small biography of the silences it retreated into? The answer is as complicated and elusive as anything I know and understand about poetry. I could say that, through a failed poem, I stumbled on a field of force. Even then I will have given only part of the answer. As the poem hesitated, as I failed to make those women real, two things happened: I lost the poem I might have written, and I found—although this was not clear until later—a place of fixities and resistances where the lineaments of a tradition meet the intention of an individual poet. Something had shifted. Something had brought me to a place of change. I thought of Adrienne Rich's words about her own revision of her working methods: "Like the novelist who finds that his characters begin to have a life of their own and to demand certain experiences, I find that I can no longer go to write a poem with a neat handful of materials and express those materials according to a prior plan."

Plans. Materials. These are not words readily associated with poetry. Then again, what I felt that summer night was outside my experience as a poet. I needed to analyze my failure. Was it technical? Or imaginative? Related to the tradition? Or merely part of my circumstance? The more I thought about it, the more drawn I was towards the interior of the poem—

that structure which, for every generation of poets, is a new mystery. Changes to it are rarely visible; fixities within it are hard to describe. Enormous questions loomed up. Was it possible that the precedents and customs of the poetic tradition were fixed in such a way—like signs facing south on a road due west—that they could mark the interior of the poem with some inbuilt resistance to a woman aging in it? No sooner did I ask the question than I had a sense of its vastness. No sooner did I try to answer it than I had an equivalent sense of how frail and makeshift the language of poetic practice has become in our generation, in contrast to the formidable extrapoetic definitions of it that exist beyond the poem. Then again, a working poet, struggling to make sense of a complex tradition in a time of change, cannot be a theorist or an ideologue. The questions I asked and the answers I attempted, and everything that follows from them in this account, did not come from any such source. They came simply and inevitably—to use Stevens's words— from "my desire to add my own definitions to poetry's many existing definitions."

II

I want a poem I can grow old in. I want a poem I can die in. It is a human wish, meeting language and precedent at the point of crisis. What is there to stop me? What prevents me taking up a pen and recording in a poem the accurate detail of time passing, which might then become a wider exploration of its meaning? My daughters' shadows in the garden, for instance, now grown longer than my own.

It is not so simple. The assumption is still made, is a sort of leftover from romanticism, that a poem is a free space within which the poet exercises options comparable to those outside. The reality is different. Outside the poem the poet is indeed free, does indeed have choices. Once he or she is inside it, these choices are altered and limited in several specific ways. Let me say, for the sake of argument, that a woman poet is writing at a window, that she is trying to formalize something that has happened to her, that she writes words on the page, crosses them out and begins again. She has now entered the poem and is absorbed by the difficulties and possibilities within it. By these various actions she has made an important alteration in the fixity or freedom of her position: she is now not only the author of the action, but an image within it. This changes things. Image systems within poetry—of which she is now a part—are complex, referential and historic. Within them are stored not simply the practices of a tradition but the precedent which years of acquaintance with, and illumination by, that tradition offers to the poet at that moment of absorption in the poem.

Let me now put this abstraction back into the narrative I began with. I believe the unwritten poem of that summer night prompted me to continue—I had already begun to move in that direction—a journey of doubt and discovery which would bring me to the heart of poetry, as I understood it. There I found, as all poets do, the treasurable inscriptions and fixities which are the powerful outcome of tradition and precedent. There again, as all poets do, I struggled to make sense of them, and, as all poets must, I determined to make some transaction with them which would recognize their wisdom, while still allowing me to experiment in my work. Increasingly—I am now greatly simplifying these processes of doubt and discovery—I came to understand that one of these signs would not yield to such a transaction, could not easily be made an informative part of my work and might even be part of the reason I had felt such a resistance within theme and language that summer evening.

If I had to name this inscription, I would say that the sexual and erotic were joined in a powerful sign which marked the very center of poetry. I knew without yet being able to reason it out that this was one of the oldest, most commanding fixities in poetry, responsible for the beauty of the erotic object in the poem. But also, for its silence and agelessness. And I sensed—but this is getting well ahead of the argument—that this sign might be the very one which was responsible for those resistances deep within the tradition which I was certain I had encountered that summer night. In its mixture of image and emblem, of desire and expression, it took a mortal woman and fixed her in a certain relation within the poem. By so doing, it emphasized her ornamental qualities and disallowed her mortality. And I knew two other things as well—instinctively, and without hesitation: that I could not make this sign and that I would have to define it. And it is this last which I will make some attempt at now.

I am well aware that words such as *sexual* and *erotic* have—in the world outside the poem—daunting engagements with the social, the psychological, the sociological. These are not my concern and are, in any case, well outside my competence. Nevertheless, in order to get to their meaning in the poem, I will attempt some makeshift definition of their meaning outside it. For most people, if the sexual act is the unambiguous physical union, the erotic is something different. While the *Oxford English Dictionary* describes it merely as something "tending to arouse sexual love or desire," its existence in culture and reference is both more oblique and more mysterious. Even its common caricature as a shoe or a silk garment or a piece of leather cannot hide its poignant complexity: that it is the outcome of an imaginative sexual world—in which fear and awe are powerful presences—which may remain unexpressed, or even rebuffed, by the act itself. That it comes into focus in that hinterland of perception where sense and spirit are wounded and fractured. That it is at once the object of desire and the reminder of such a fracture.

These definitions are replaceable with a hundred more, and even then they will be contentious. But in the day-to-day world of poetic practice I believe these broad terms sharpen and narrow and gather a more precise meaning. They cease to be merely a dialect of our malaise. They acquire references to, and engagements with, forceful and customary parts of poetic expression. For all that, an exact definition remains thoroughly elusive. I could start by proposing the functions of these words, rather than their meaning. The erotic object, for instance, is most often part of the image system of the poem, while the sexualization of it is integral to the poet's perspective and stance; it therefore becomes part of voice and argument. In a poem about the silks a woman is wearing, written by her lover, the silks become the mute erotic object, while the perception of them as beautiful and exciting becomes part of the poet's perspective in the poem.

The problem with this neat and blunt way of looking at things is that it sweeps away, in a few words, the crucial fact about the sexual and the erotic in poetry: that their fusion is so powerful not simply because the erotic object, as an image, is distanced and controlled by the sexual perspective of the poet, although it is. Nor that we see in this fusion the appropriation of the powerless by the powerful, although we do. The crucial aspect of the relation between the sexual and the erotic in this context is that the erotic object is possessed not by the power of sexuality but by the power of expression. The erotic object therefore becomes a beautiful mime of those forces of expression which have silenced it. Its reason for being there may seem to be that it is both beautiful and yearned for, but at a deeper level it becomes a trophy of the forces which created it, not simply because it is sexualized but because it is sexualized within a triumphant and complex act of poetry.

III

Where did I find this fusion of the sexual and the erotic proposed, and how did I decipher it? The answer is clear enough. I read poems. I thought about them. I tried to define their meaning as I came to write my own. The light on the page and the poem was a variable: it could be my interest in a particular form, or a sense of time passing, or pleasure in another poet's use of language. The landscape around me as I read was a summer darkness or a hill frost or a child crying my name or a telephone ringing.

The things I found as I read and wrote intrigued and excited me. But when I came to describe them—then as now—my definitions were halting and unscientific and incomplete. And not only halting but fallible and idiosyncratic as well. I read poems other people might not have read. I read them in contexts which were private rather than communal. And so I have no exact words of explanation for how charmed and troubled I was by a poem like "Upon Julia's Clothes" by Robert Herrick:

> *Whenas in silks my Julia goes,*
> *Then, then (methinks) how sweetly flows*
> *That liquefaction of her clothes.*

Next, when I cast mine eyes and see
That brave vibration each way free;
O how that glittering taketh me.

Who could deny it? Robert Herrick, the goldsmith's apprentice and vicar—whose life-span reached from the Armada to the Restoration—could put together a seamless music. His six-liner is eloquent and forceful. It is also a diagram of the appropriation of the erotic by the sexual and of both by a power of expression which is self-aware and triumphant and whose assertion is a prime mover in the poem, a shape changer shifting pronouns and disassembling metaphor before our eyes. The erotic object—those silks turning to water and light—is fixed in a relation to the more volatile parts of the poem. The outcry of the final line, where the possessor is possessed, is at once a bright irony and a coded pastoral. The impression the poem leaves is of power and possession, rendered as delight by the decorum of language. It is an impression made more vivid by the use—in a tiny workspace—of *me* and *my*; the ascribing of vision and perception to the speaker and only movement to the spoken-of; the perfect, rapid cadence and the final solipsistic cry. And all the while Julia and the silks are silent and still.

There are problems with all this. To start with, I am using a language which is itself a construct of hindsight. It may serve to highlight the text, but it does no justice to the way I first read a poem such as this. It implies sharp practice, a sort of loitering with intent in books and anthologies, keeping a sharp eye out for unwary images and references. Almost the opposite is true. I came on these poems with delight. I read them. I remembered them. Only later did I reconsider them in the light of my own work and my own hesitant progress towards a voice that was mine. And once I began to reconsider, I could see these tropes and figures as both persuasive and unsettling. And then I read more and with a growing sense of their recurrence in the traditional poem. And once again this was the tradition as I had known it, both as a young woman and a scholar. The works of the British canon. The poems read by the poets who wrote poems which were read by other poets. In such downright ways traditions are made. In such clear and yet complex ways their legislation is enacted:

> *Fair youth, beneath the trees, thou canst not leave*
> *Thy song, nor ever can those trees be bare;*
> *Bold Lover, never, never canst thou kiss*
> *Though winning near the goal—yet, do not grieve;*
> *She cannot fade though thou hast not thy bliss,*
> *Forever wilt thou love, and she be fair!*

At first sight Keats's lines from "Ode on a Grecian Urn" seem to contradict the fusion of the erotic and the sexual. A closer look reveals an astonishing and intense poise of these elements and a candid appraisal of both as creatures of the expressive. It is simply that the parts are dismantled and put together in a fresh and strange way. The young man in decorative chase on the side of the urn has the sexual perspective which seeks to possess; the maiden has the erotic task of being simply mute and beautiful. The poet has assumed the expressive power which controls the act of desire, the intent to possess, which can leave both in that timeless posture of seeking and restraining, while the true possession of either is assumed by art rather than sexuality. And thus—through a wonderful elliptical syntax, and the musical vocative of the last line—the elements of the sexualized erotic are revealed to be what they truly are in the poem of the tradition: not a drama of desire but a drama of expression.

IV

What if those components were taken apart and reworked? What if the elements which made up a narrow and intense convention were disassembled and changed and put back into the poem? The very reason I wrote this piece is to give an account of how I came on those questions. Of how I tried to answer them. And yet the arguments involved are so difficult that to put them forward at all is to feel at times like a physicist searching for black vacuums in outer space which can only be deduced by equations which rule out other possibilities. And so to turn the difficulties into some kind of accessible drama, I intend to propose them for a moment as surrealisms, as a series of what-ifs and whether-nots.

Suppose it were possible to encounter the poems of the past not as finished forms but as actions we could reverse. Suppose I could gather these objects from those poems: the light in the jewel, the silk of the skirt, the skin of the shepherdess and the hair of the nymph. What would I have collected? I would have—I have entered the surreal now—a series of fixed and glittering objects. Which could not age. Which could not suffer.

Now let me extend the fabulous element of this argument. What if their age-old poetic connection with the sexualized were broken? What if the silk reverted to honest cloth rather than his mistress's skirt? What if I took them up and set them down in poems I wrote—in a landscape which was sensory and not erotic. The answer must be that they would no longer be erotic objects. And I would be a woman poet in a poignant place: a magnetic field where the created returns as creator. A place I already knew.

V

My mid-thirties were a time of delay and puzzlement and reflection. A time when I stood talking to a neighbour on a summer evening and went upstairs to write a poem that was never written. Unspoken subjects deep within ordinary conversation. Unwritten poems on a table by the window. All poets have testing times. This was mine.

The apprenticeship of any poet—the years of learning and discouragement and skill—is a mystery. Not because of its importance, but because so much gets lost. What remains the same is the struggle with language and the encounter with precedent. What changes is the detail of the encounter: Keats putting on a white shirt to write. Akhmatova's friend memorizing her work in a back garden in Leningrad. Plath turning on the Pifco coffee pot at 4:00 A.M. in the last month of her life.

I began to write poetry, in a serious way, in my late teens. I knew I was Irish. I knew I was a woman. But at the oilskin tablecloth where I laid out my books to work in the evening it sometimes seems to me, looking back, that I was sexless, Victorian, a product of nineteenth-century ideas. I worked for the clear line, the pure stanza. Certainly at first I had no idea how to include the awkward, jagged reality in the decorums I admired.

As I wrote more, as I discovered the sensory world, as I saw the power of language to edit it, I changed. It was not so much, at first, that I wrote differently. But when I read it was as if I saw something out of the corner of my eye, which disappeared, which I caught sight of again. A shepherdess in Spenser. The rustling silks in "The Eve of St Agnes." A nymph. These mute objects stayed at the edges of my vision. As my life did.

And in the poems of my youth—this must be true of the majority of young poets—my sexual sense was conventional. My erotic sense lay beneath it like a reef beneath water. And however radical my hopes as a poet, they could have remained trapped in that conventional sexuality had it not been for one thing: I married. I moved to the suburbs. I made a home in a place where the writ of poetry did not run. I was now a suburban woman and although I might find myself as a minor character in a novel, I would not find myself in a poem unless I wrote it. And then my children were born and suddenly those objects which had caught my eyes and disappeared, and yet remained on the edges of my vision when I was as a young poet, came to the center of my world.

As my children woke, as they slept, a visionary landscape scrolled around me. It was not made by my children, although the bright digits of their gloves and their plastic mugs littered it. It was made by my body. As I moved through a world of small tasks and almost endless routines, the red mug and the blue glove crept out of their skins. They were not erotic objects; almost the reverse. They were not emblems of the power of the body or the triumph of expression. They were annunciations of what my body had created and what, with every hour, and every day, it was losing. When I stood on my front doorstep on a summer night the buddleia and the lamplight glossing the hedge were not just visible to me. I saw them with my body. And the sight of my body was clear and different and intense. What was seen by it was both made more clear and more ominous because I could not see it that way forever.

And for some reason, although it was a radical difference in my life, I trusted this way of seeing. I believed what was seen. It was—at certain definable moments in that ordinary world—that I felt I stood in the place of myth and lyric and vision. "It is," says Eliade, "the irruption of the sacred into the world, an irruption narrated in myths, that establishes the world as a reality."

I have tried to create here a diagram of one adventure in perception. In doing so, I am making conscious and schematic what lay under the surface of that perception. I am putting a chronology, a shape, a dialectic on what was never so exact. And yet there is accuracy in it. My children grew. Tennis rackets replaced mugs and toys. Gradually the visionary world hid itself in the world of detail which only occasionally gives way to it. But I had learned something. I knew—like a traveller who returns from a land that is not yet on the map—that I had lived in a sensory world so intense that it had marked me. From then on I was conscious of an ill-defined but important relation between the erotic object of the male poem and the sensory world I had lived in, with its colors and edges and enticements. And it seemed to me, in terms of my own poetry, that whereas the erotic object inflected the power of expression and was fixed by the senses, these sensory objects revealed a world suffered by the senses but not owned by them. And yet my line of reasoning at this stage was so halting and uncertain that to follow it further would be to see it disappear. I was faltering between perceptions. Building an argument then losing the line of it. Coming to conclusions then backing away. Only slowly did a story begin to emerge. Only gradually did I come to believe I could tell it.

VI

I want to look briefly at four poems by women—one of them my own—so as to illustrate and press these points. I intend them as quickly taken snapshots of the ways women poets are rewriting the old fixities of the sexual and erotic, are reassembling a landscape where subject and object are differently politicized, where expression, far from being an agent of power, may be an index of powerlessness. I intend them to suggest, however sketchily, the distances and differences which open up when these traditional elements are disassembled.

In the last month of her life Sylvia Plath was living in a flat in Fitzroy Road in London. I remember that winter. I shared a garden flat in South Dublin with my sister. It was my first winter out of school and I was eighteen years of age, a student at Trinity College. The house in which we had the flat was on a leafy road, hardly five minutes by bus from the center of town. It backed onto a narrow garden which led, by a makeshift path, to the Dodder River, a tributary of the Liffey. Dublin was still a town. There was something uncityish still about these outlying roads, which were only slowly turning into suburbs. That January I studied Keats and Byron. I wrote poems, but in a faltering way. What I remember most clearly is the stone windowsill at garden level, smoking with frost in an early dark. It was cold in a way I had never known before in Ireland: a relentless, killing cold.

Sylvia Plath's flat was minimalist, put together in the pre-Christmas haste and fragmentation of that time. The young woman who had once written about wanting a house with "spreading apple trees, fields, a cow and a vegetable garden" was now older and lived in the heart of a city. Al Alvarez described her in that setting: "She had deliberately kept the place bare: rush matting on the floor, a few books, bits of Victoriana and cloudy blue glass on the shelves."

Against that background she set a poem called "Balloons." It is dated February 6, the same day on which she wrote "Edge," her lovely, scalding farewell to life, with its funerary images and odd lilt of peace. Five days later she was dead. "Balloons" occurs in an original and powerful sensory world, poised somewhere between treasure and danger.

> *Such queer moons we live with*
> *Instead of dead furniture!*

Obviously—since they are unconnected to a sexual perspective—the balloons are not erotic. Yet as images they operate in that territory where the strongest love poems also take hold: in a place where spirit and sense are seeking one another out. And in some ways, by being intensely sensory—highly colored, richly perceived, and presences in the world of the body which children evoke—the balloons are pre-erotic. What distinguishes them so powerfully from the erotic object of the traditional poem is that they signify not the desire of the body or the triumph of expression but the fragility of the one and the intense vulnerability of the other. And far from being possessed by the perspective which creates them, the balloons are set free within the poem as they might be outside it: to ride out a current of association and surrealism which ends in their destruction and the end of the poem. And the balloon which ends up as "a red shred" has had, by the end, a joyous, rapid mutation: has been a cat head and a globe, has been held by a child and has squeaked like a cat. Above all, it has not been fixed. The dominant impression left by the poem is of an imagination which has surrendered generously to the peril and adventure of the sensory moment, whose powers of expression have not been confirmed by it and whose bodily vulnerability has been increased by it. Most intriguingly of all, the poem glances over a reference which—with its resonance of ornament and myth—could easily be part of the erotic signposting of the traditional poem. But instead of that, the poem inflects the peacock differently. It becomes the beautiful, lucky emblem of a free heart and a blessed place. "[W]ith a feather beaten in starry metals." As we drown in the image, a pastoral convention flashes before our eyes, but in reverse: instead of a natural world artificialized and regretted from the vantage point of the court, the artifice of the peacock is glimpsed through the beautiful lens of a natural and sensory world.

When Keats wrote "The Eve of St Agnes," he assembled an elaborate series of word pictures, against which a cardboard-thin dramatic action unfolds. The characters are stock characters; the fable is a predictable mix of medieval nostalgia and Regency romance. The great beauty and force of the piece lie in the skilled distances and vowel melodies, the true stanzaic dramas and the clairvoyant sense of the erotic moment as a still life:

> . . . *her vespers done,*
> *Of all its wreathèd pearls her hair she frees*
> *Unclasps her warmèd jewels one by one;*
> *Loosens her fragrant bodice; by degrees*
> *Her rich attire creeps rustling to her knees.*

The wonderful, drawn-out vowels—wreathèd/ frees/ degrees/ creeps/ knees—create a static and delayed mood. They make a pageant of the stanza. Against that background the pearls are erotic objects, an integral part of the drama which unfolds.

How different are the pearls of another poem by the marvelous British poet Carol Ann Duffy. The poem "Warming Her Pearls" is an unsparing evocation of power and desire between women, the servant dressing her mistress:

> *In her looking-glass*
> *my red lips part as though I want to speak.*

"Warming Her Pearls" is a bold subversion of the sexualized erotic, a lyric which reassembles the love poem so that it becomes, like handwriting in a mirror, a menacing reversed message: the speaker is powerless, while the object of her affections has a power which puts her well beyond possession by either desire or expression. The pearls are not the fixed object of Keats's poem. They are the flawed, wounded and ironized erotic object of the traditional poem, but this time held in common between the women, rather than perceived as a fixed object, distanced from the speaker. In addition, they have a human warmth—they are milky, heated—which removes them once again from the glittering and unmortal objects of the traditional love poem. Just as this poem disassembles elements of the traditional love poem, so the subject–object relations come apart as well. The pearls are part of the disassembling. Where Keats's pearls happen at a great distance, these are heated, dangerous, ambiguous. Where the erotic object of the traditional love poem—such as Julia's silks—witnesses the orderly progression of power between poet and perception, the pearls restate the fixed decorum of that relation by deliberately suggesting a breakdown of power within the poem. Far from signaling controlled distance, they inflect the anguish and ugliness of control itself.

The erotic object defied nature. Timeless and ageless, it lay in the amber of the poem. If it were disassembled, a question might arise which said: What exactly is the nature poem? Certainly it has progressed and changed, evolved and revolved around the powerful disruptions which define poetry in its time. The romantic movement, being one of these, reworked the idea that the nature poem stated a series of moral recognitions between the inner and outer world. Wordsworth's midnight cliff. Shelley's west wind.

One of the exciting outcomes of women disassembling the sexual and erotic in poetry is a different nature poem. Different, above all, in its interpretation of what nature is. "Mock Orange" by Louise Glück is a new kind of nature poem. Once again its starting point is a disassembly of familiar elements of the sexualized erotic. A woman speaks in the poem. A woman who might once—like the pearls—have been spoken of. She does not consider nature an outward sign of an inward grace. Quite the opposite. She considers the wound between spirit and sense almost intolerable, and that nature, far from healing it, has actually authorized it. She speaks bitterly of the betrayals of the sexual act, of the deceptions of nature in the scent and grace of the mock orange. As she deploys deceptive ecstasy as a metaphor for deceiving nature, age-old stabilities of poetic convention—nymphs, dryads, obedient Muses—seem to take flight, like wood spirits evicted from a forest. As the action develops, a superb and radical restatement of the nature poem forms before our eyes.

One of the fascinations of this poem is that its voice is not simply the achieved voice of the narrator; it can also be heard as the cry of the erotic object—that silenced, paralyzed, gagged object—finding air and expression and dissent from its age-long role as servant of desire and trophy of the power of poetry. The narrator of this poem does not flinch from the volatile mix of the sexual and erotic, "*the man's mouth / sealing my mouth*," but once again they are radically disassembled. The erotic object is now the speaker. The sexualizing perspective is now the substance of the rebuke. The powers of nature so often celebrated and invoked in the traditional love poem are accused and reproached.

By the end of my thirties I had reached some peace with my work. The fragments and contradictions which had tormented my youth as a poet—issues of Irishness and of womanhood and the more subtle issues of an ethical identity—were beginning to find some repose. Yet in some area of my mind that failure remained: that inability to write the aging body. And in some part of my memory remained also those glowing, broken images of the first years of the children's lives: the luminous glove, the bright mug.

And yet stating it like this gives an ingenuity and symmetry to what was barely recognized. There were yearnings and false starts. Starings out of the window. A sense of a theme just out of sight. Barely more than that. To bring all this to the light of day now and present it as argument and answer runs the risk of falsifying it. And yet I need some construct to explain how—slowly and unsurely—I began to move towards that theme.

I make these remarks as a preliminary to a poem I wrote about a black lace fan my mother had given me, which my father had given her in a heatwave in Paris in the thirties. It would be wrong to say I was clear, when I wrote this poem, about disassembling an erotic politic. I was not. But I was aware of my own sense of the traditional erotic object—in this case the black fan—as a sign not for triumph and acquisition but for suffering itself. And without having words for it, I was conscious of trying to divide it from its usual source of generation: the sexualized perspective of the poet. To that extent I was writing a sign which might bring me closer to those emblems of the body I had seen in those visionary years, when ordinary objects seemed to warn me that the body might share the world but could not own it. And if I was not conscious of taking apart something I had been taught to leave well alone, nevertheless, I had a clear sense of—at last—writing the poem away from the traditional erotic object towards something which spoke of the violations of love, while still shadowing the old context of its power. In other words, a back-to-front love poem.

THE BLACK LACE FAN MY MOTHER GAVE ME

It was the first gift he ever gave her
buying it for five francs in the Galeries
in pre-war Paris. It was stifling.
A starless drought made the nights stormy.

They stayed in the city for the summer.
They met in cafés. She was always early.
He was late. That evening he was later.
They wrapped the fan. He looked at his watch.

She looked down the Boulevard des Capucines.
She ordered more coffee. She stood up.
The streets were emptying. The heat was killing.
She thought the distance smelled of rain
        and lightning.

These are wild roses appliquéd on silk by hand,
darkly picked, stitched boldly, quickly.
The rest is tortoiseshell and has the reticent
clear patience of its element. It is

a worn-out underwater bullion and it keeps,
even now, an inference of its violation.
The lace is overcast as if the weather
it opened for and offset had entered it.

The past is an empty café terrace.
An airless dusk before thunder. A man running.
And no way now to know what happened then—
none at all—unless of course you improvise:

The blackbird on this first sultry morning
in summer, finding buds, worms, fruit
feels the heat. Suddenly she puts out her wing.
The whole, full, flirtatious span of it.

VII

It stands to reason that the project of the woman poet—
connected as it is by dark bonds to the object she once was—
cannot make a continuum with the sexualized erotic of the
male poem. The true difference women poets make as authors
of the poem is in sharp contrast to the part they were assigned
as objects in it. As objects they were once images. As images
they were eroticized and distanced. A beautiful and compel-

ling language arose around them. In pastorals, lyrics, elegies, odes they were shepherdesses, mermaids, nymphs. The accoutrements of their persons became images within images; their jewels, silks, skin, eyes became tropes and figures, at once celebrated and silenced.

It has been my argument that in a real and immediate sense, when she does enter upon this old territory where the erotic and sexual came together to inflect the tradition, the woman poet is in that poignant place I spoke of, where the subject cannot forget her previous position as object. There are aesthetic implications to this, but they are not separable from the ethical ones. And the chief ethical implication it seems to me is that when a woman poet deals with these issues of the sexual and the erotic, the poem she writes is likely to have a new dimension. It can be an act of rescue rather than a strategy of possession. And the object she returns to rescue, with her newly made Orphic power and intelligence, would be herself: a fixed presence in the underworld of the traditional poem. It is easy enough to see that her dual relation to the object she makes—both as created and rescuer—shifts the balance of subject and object, lessens the control and alters perspectives within the poem.

I have also argued here that far from making a continuum, the contemporary poem as written by women can actually separate the sexual and erotic, and separate, also, the sexual motif from that of poetic expression. And that when a woman poet does this, a circuit of power represented by their fusion is disrupted. The erotic object can be rescued and restored: from silence to expression, from the erotic to the sensory. When this happens, beautiful, disturbing tones are free to enter the poem.

Poetry itself comes to the threshold of changes which need not exclude or diminish the past but are bound to reinterpret it.

Above all—and this was what chiefly drew me towards the whole complex process of argument and exploration—this disassembling of a traditional fusion offered a radical and exciting chance to restate time in the poem. If the erotic object was indeed part of a drama of expression rather than a drama of desire, then it was also a signal of powers which were expressive and poetic more than they were sexual. As such, the erotic object had to do justice to the powers it reflected. It had to be a perfect moon to that sun. It could not be afflicted by time or made vulnerable by decay. It could not age. If this object—whether it was silk or pearls or a tree or a fan—were reclaimed by the woman poet and set down in a sensory world which inflected the mortality of the body, rather than the strength of the expressive mind, then, by just such an inflection, it would be restored to the flaws of time.

And here at last, it seemed to me, right across my path lay the shadow that had fallen across my poem that summer night. In the poem of the tradition the erotic object was a concealed boast, a hidden brag about the powers of poetry itself: that it could stop time. That it could fend off decay. Therefore, I—and other women poets—as we entered our own poems found an injunction already posted there. Inasmuch as we had once been objects—or objectified—in those poems, we had been perfect and timeless. Now, as authors of poems ourselves, if we were to age or fail or be simply mortal, we would have to do more than simply write down those things as themes or images. We would have to enter the interior of the poem and reinscribe certain powerful and customary relations between object and subject. And be responsible for what we did.

VIII

I have come to believe that the woman poet is an emblematic figure in poetry now in the same way the modernist and romantic poets once were. And for the same reasons. Not because she is awkward and daring and disruptive but because—like the modernist and romantic poets in their time—she internalizes the stresses and truths of poetry at a particular moment. Her project therefore is neither marginal nor specialist. It is a project which concerns all of poetry, all that leads into it in the past and everywhere it is going in the future.

But it cuts both ways. Unlike a poet such as Adrienne Rich, to whom I feel so much indebtedness, I believe the past is the profound responsibility of the woman poet, as it was of the romantic and modernist poets in their time. She did not make it, and Adrienne Rich, more than any poet in my lifetime, has had the courage to address this. Nevertheless, if the woman poet makes a new custom and a different sign, she is not, by that process alone, free of her engagement with the old signs. She must renegotiate a position with the poetic past which is appropriate to her project and faithful to her imaginative freedoms. But which also is generous to that past and delicate in manner to the spirit of a tradition which sustained her.

This is intensely problematic. The sign I have written about here, which concerns eroticism and aging, is only one of several which women poets are remaking. The remaking is often done under difficult circumstances, and often consists in marking a text from which she was erased or where she was fixed and silenced. And yet she must try to balance the elements of innovation and justice, as other poets did before her. Even if she is unclear, unsettled, uncertain. As indeed I was. And may still be.

Ideology is unambiguous; poetry is not. As a younger poet I had discovered that feminism had wonderful strengths as a critique; and almost none as an aesthetic. Had I followed the clear line of feminism, which had so sustained me in other ways, I would have found poems which fused the sexual and erotic either oppressive or disaffecting. And I did not. On the contrary, I found many of them beautiful and persuasive. It added both complexity and enrichment that these poems which I needed to reconsider as a woman had shaped and delighted me as a poet.

The contradictions did not stop there. As an Irish poet who was also a woman I had been increasingly aware—at times it was almost a malaise—that Irish women poets had gone from being the objects of the Irish poem to being its authors in a relatively short space of time. It was a rapid and disruptive process. It encountered resistances, some of which were interdictions within the tradition rather than a shortage of permissions outside it. The Irish poetic tradition wove images of women into images of the nation, simplifying both in the process. I had struggled with it and defined myself against it. But this iconography of the Irish poem was a local ordinance. The fusion of the sexual and the erotic was not; it appeared as a customary and enduring feature of poetry rather than of a single place or tradition.

Then why did I not find it still more oppressive? The reason was complex and ambiguous. The more I thought about it, the more the poetic relation between the erotic and sexual seemed to play out a drama of expression rather than a drama of desire. It was a relation between the expressive and the silenced, between the subject and the object. As such it could not just have an aesthetic dimension; it had an ethical one as well. But the ethical dimension—unlike the intercutting of feminine and national in the Irish poem—was extraordinarily complex. The erotic and sexual met in the poem of the tradition in the very place where poetry canvassed one of its great themes: the fracture of sense and spirit. I found it extraordinarily hard to be sure at times whether that beautiful appropriation of the erotic by the sexual, and both by the expressive, was an act of healing or an exercise of power. As I read the poems of the tradition, it could often seem to me that I was entering a beautiful and perilous world filled with my own silence, where I was accorded the unfree status of an object. And yet there was paradox. As I struggled to become my own subject—in poems I could hardly write and in a literary tradition which blurred the feminine and the national—these poems were enabling and illuminating. As a woman I felt some mute and anxious kinship with those erotic objects which were appropriated; as a poet I felt confirmed by the very powers of expression which appropriated them.

IX

It is a February night. The suburb is dark, and rain is spilling noisily from our gutter onto the garage roof. The garden is black and soaking. The streetlamps are on. My children are teenagers now. Their shoes, clothes, letters and diaries litter every room in the house.

That moment has come to me which was prophesied by another woman's body in a summer twilight years ago. I am older, less hopeful, more acquainted with the craft, more instructed by my failures in it. And once again there is a notebook open on the table by the window. The window looks out to dark roofs and the dripping twigs of the laburnum and the shapes of the garden. If I stood in that garden and looked southwest I would see the Dublin hills. If I looked east, I would see the suburbs that led to the city. And high in those hills is the river which had made the city: the Liffey, now being refilled by rain. Its source and mouth, its definition and loss seem to me at that moment close to the realizations and dissolutions my body had known in this very house. I walk to the table. I sit down and take up my pen. I begin to write about a river and a woman, about the destiny of water and my sense of growing older. The page fills easily and quickly.

THE WOMAN POET:
HER DILEMMA

I believe that the woman poet today inherits a dilemma. That she does so inevitably, no matter what cause she espouses and whatever ideology she advocates or shuns. That when she sits down to work, when she moves away from her work, when she tries to be what she is struggling to express, at these moments the dilemma is present, waiting and inescapable.

The dilemma I speak of is inherent in a shadowy but real convergence between new experience and an established aesthetic. What this means in practical terms is that the woman poet today is caught in a field of force. Powerful, persuasive voices are in her ear as she writes. Distorting and simplifying ideas of womanhood and poetry fall as shadows between her and the courage of her own experience. If she listens to these voices, yields to these ideas, her work will be obstructed. If, however, she evades the issue, runs for cover and pretends there is no pressure, then she is likely to lose the resolution she needs to encompass the critical distance between writing poems and being a poet. A distance which for women is fraught in any case, as I hope to show, with psychosexual fear and doubt.

"Dramatize, dramatize," said Henry James. And so I will. Imagine, then, that a woman is going into the garden. She is youngish; her apron is on, and there is flour on her hands. It is early afternoon. She is going there to lift a child who for the third time is about to put laburnum pods into its mouth. This is what she does. But what I have omitted to say in this small sketch is that the woman is a poet. And once she is in the garden, once the child, hot and small and needy, is in her arms, once the frills of shadow around the laburnum and the freakish gold light from it are in her eyes, then her poetic sense is awakened. She comes back through the garden door. She cleans her hands, takes off her apron, sets her child down for an afternoon sleep. Then she sits down to work.

Now it begins. The first of these powerful distracting voices comes to her. For argument's sake, I will call it the Romantic Heresy. It comes to her as a whisper, an insinuation. What she wants to do is write about the laburnum, the heat of the child, common human love—the mesh of these things. But where, says the voice in her ear, is the interest in all this? How are you going to write a poem out of these plain Janes, these snips and threads of an ordinary day? Now, the voice continues, listen to me, and I will show you how to make all this poetic. A shade here, a nuance there, a degree of distance, the lilt of complaint, and all will be well. The woman hesitates. Suddenly the moment that seemed to her potent and emblematic and true appears commonplace, beyond the pale of art. She is shaken. And there I will leave her, with her doubts and fears, so as to look more closely at what it is that has come between her and the courage of that moment.

THE ROMANTIC HERESY, as I have chosen to call it, is not romanticism proper, although it is related to it. "Before Wordsworth," writes Lionel Trilling, "poetry had a subject. After Wordsworth its prevalent subject was the poet's own subjectivity." This shift in perception was responsible for much that was fresh and revitalizing in nineteenth-century poetry. But it was also responsible for the declension of poetry into self-consciousness, self-invention.

This type of debased romanticism is rooted in a powerful, subliminal suggestion that poets are distinctive not so much because they write poetry as because in order to do so, they have poetic feelings about poetic experiences. That there is a category of experience and expression which is poetic and all the rest is ordinary and therefore inadmissible. In this way a damaging division is made between the perception of what a poetics is on one hand and, on the other, what is merely human. Out of this emerges an aesthetic which suggests that in order to convert the second into the first, you must romanticize it. This idea gradually became an article of faith in nineteenth-century postromantic English poetry. When Matthew Arnold said at Oxford, "the strongest part of our religion is in its unconscious poetry," he was blurring a fine line. He was himself one of the initiators of a sequence of propositions by which the poetry of religion became the religion of poetry.

There are obvious pitfalls in all of this for any poet. But the dangers for a woman poet in particular must be immediately obvious. Women are a minority within the expressive poetic tradition. Much of their actual experience lacks even the most rudimentary poetic precedent. "No poet," says Eliot, "no artist of any kind has his complete meaning alone." The woman poet is more alone with her meaning than most. The ordinary routine day that many women live—must live—to take just one instance, does not figure largely in poetry. Nor the feelings that go with it. The temptations are considerable, therefore, for a woman poet to romanticize these routines and these feelings so as to align them with what is considered poetic.

Now let us go back to the woman at her desk. Let us suppose that she has recovered her nerve and her purpose. She remembers what is true: the heat, the fear that her child will eat the pods. She feels again the womanly power of the instant. She puts aside the distortions of romanticism. She starts to write again, and once again she is assailed. But this time by another and equally persuasive idea.

And this is feminist ideology or at least one part of it. In recent years feminism has begun to lay powerful prescriptions on writing by women. The most exacting of these comes from that part of feminist thinking which is separatist. Separatist prescriptions demand that women be true to historical angers which underwrite the women's movement, that they cast aside preexisting literary traditions, that they evolve not only their own writing but the criteria by which to judge it. I think I understand some of these prescriptions. I recognize that they stem from the fact that many feminists—and I partly share the view—perceive a great deal in preexisting literary expression and tradition which is patriarchal, not to say oppressive. I certainly have no wish to be apologetic about the separatist tendency because it offends or threatens or bores—and it does all three—the prevailing male literary establishments. That does not concern me for the moment. There is still prejudice—the Irish poetic community is among the most chauvinist—but as it happens, that is not part of the equation.

What does concern me is that the gradual emphasis on the appropriate subject matter and the correct feelings has become as constricting and corrupt within feminism as within romanticism. In the grip of romanticism and its distortions, women can be argued out of the truth of their feelings, can be marginalized, simplified and devalued by what is, after all, a patriarchal tendency. But does the separatist prescription offer more? I have to say—painful as it may be to dissent from a section of a movement I cherish—that I see no redemption whatsoever in moving from one simplification to the other.

So here again is the woman at her desk. Let us say she is feminist. What is she to make of the suggestion by a poet like Adrienne Rich that "to be a female human being, trying to fulfill female functions in a traditional way, is in direct conflict with the subversive function of the imagination"?

Yet the woman knows that whether or not going into the garden and lifting her child are part of the "traditional way," they have also been an agent and instrument of subversive poetic perception. What is she to do? Should she contrive an anger, invent a disaffection? How is she to separate one obligation from the other, one truth from the other? And what is she to make of the same writer's statement that "to the eye of the feminist, the work of Western male poets now writing reveals a deep, fatalistic pessimism as to the possibilities of change . . . and a new tide of phallocentric sadism." It is no good to say she need not read these remarks. Adrienne Rich is a wonderful poet and her essay—"When We Dead Awaken"— from which these statements are quoted is a central statement in contemporary poetry. It should be read by every poet. So there is no escape. The force or power of this stance, which I would call separatist, but may more accurately be called anti-traditional, must be confronted.

Separatist thinking is a persuasive and dangerous influence on any woman writing today. It tempts her to disregard the whole poetic past as patriarchal betrayal. It pleads with her to discard the complexity of true feeling for the relative simplicity of anger. It promises to ease her technical problems with the solvent of polemic. It whispers to her that to be feminine in poetry is easier, quicker and more eloquent than the infinitely more difficult task of being human. Above all, it encourages her to feminize her perceptions rather than humanize her femininity.

But women have a birthright in poetry. I believe, though an antitraditional poet might not agree, that when a woman poet begins to write, she very quickly becomes conscious of the silences which have preceded her, which still surround her. These silences will become an indefinable part of her purpose as a poet. Yet as a working poet she will also—if she is honest—recognize that these silences have been at least partly redeemed within the past expressions of other poets, most of them male. And these expressions also will become part of her purpose. But for that to happen, she must have the fullest possible dialogue with them. She needs it; she is entitled to it. And in order to have that dialogue, she must have the fullest dialogue also with her own experience, her own present as a poet. I do not believe that separatism allows for this.

Very well. Let us say that after all this inner turmoil the woman is still writing. That she has taken her courage with both hands and has resisted the prescriptions both of romanticism and separatism. Yet for all that, something is still not right. Once again she hesitates. But why? "Outwardly," says Virginia Woolf, "what is simpler than to write books? Outwardly, what obstacles are there for a woman rather than for a man? Inwardly I think the case is very different. She still has many ghosts to fight, many prejudices to overcome." Ghosts and prejudices. Maybe it is time we took a look at these.

II

I am going to move away from the exploratory and the theoretical into something more practical. Let us say, for argument's sake, that it is a wet Novemberish day in a country town in Ireland. Now, for the sake of going a bit further, let us say that a workshop or the makings of one have gathered in an upstairs room in a school perhaps or an adult education center. The surroundings will—they always are on these occasions—be just a bit surreal. There will be old metal furniture, solid oak tables, the surprising gleam of a new video in the corner. And finally, let us say that among these women gathered here is a woman named Judith. I will call her that, a nod in the direction of Virginia Woolf's great essay *A Room of One's Own*. And when I—for it is I who am leading the workshop—get off the train or out of the car and climb the stairs and enter that room, it is Judith—her poems already in her hand—who catches my eye and holds my attention.

"History," says Butterfield, "is not the study of origins; rather it is the analysis of all the mediations by which the past has turned into our present." As I walk into that room, as Judith hands me her poems, our past becomes for a moment a single present. I may know, she may acknowledge, that she will never publish, never evolve. But equally I know we have been in the same place and have inherited the same dilemma.

She will show me her work diffidently. It will lack almost any technical finish—lineation is almost always the chief problem—but that will not concern me in the least. What will concern me, will continue to haunt me, is that it will be saying to me—not verbally but articulately nonetheless—I write poetry, but I am not a poet. And I will realize, without too much being said, that the distance between writing poetry and being a poet is one that she has found in her life and her time just too difficult, too far and too dangerous to travel. I will also feel—whether or not I am being just in the matter—that the distance will have been more impassable for her than for any male poet of her generation. Because it is a preordained distance, composed of what Butterfield might call the unmediated past. On the surface that distance seems to be made up of details: lack of money, lack of like minds and so on. But this is deceptive. In essence the distance is psychosexual, made so by a profound fracture between her sense of the obligations of her womanhood and the shadowy demands of her gift.

In his essay on Juana de Asbaje, Robert Graves sets out to define that fracture. "Though the burden of poetry," he writes, "is difficult enough for a man to bear, he can always humble himself before an incarnate Muse and seek instruction from her . . . The case of a woman poet is a thousand times worse: since she is herself the Muse, a Goddess without an external power to guide or comfort her, and if she strays even a finger's breadth from the path of divine instinct, must take a violent self-vengeance."

I may think there is a certain melodrama in Graves's commentary. Yet in a subterranean way this is exactly what women fear. That the role of the poet, added to that of woman, may well involve them in unacceptable conflict. The outcome of that fear is constant psychosexual pressure. And the result of that pressure is a final reluctance to have the courage of her own experience. All of which adds up to that distance between writing poems and being a poet, a distance which Judith—even as she hands me her work—is telling me she cannot and must not travel.

I will leave that room angered and convinced. Every poet carries within them a silent constituency, made of suffering and failed expression. Judith and the "compound ghost" that she is—for she is, of course, an amalgam of many women—is mine. It is difficult, if not impossible, to explain to men who are poets—writing as they are with centuries of expression behind them—how emblematic are the unexpressed lives of other women to the woman poet, how intimately they are her own. And how, in many ways, that silence is as much part of her tradition as the troubadours are of theirs. "You who maintain that some animals sob sorrowfully, that the dead have dreams," writes Rimbaud, "try to tell the story of my downfall and my slumber. I no longer know how to speak."

How to speak. I believe that if a woman poet survives, if she sets out on that distance and arrives at the other end, then she has an obligation to tell as much as she knows of the ghosts within her, for they make up, in essence, her story as well. And that is what I intend to do now.

III

I began writing poetry in the Dublin of the early sixties. Perhaps *began* is not the right word. I had been there or thereabouts for years: scribbling poems in boarding school, reading Yeats after lights out, reveling in the poetry on the course.

Then I left school and went to Trinity. Dublin was a coherent space then, a small circumference in which to be and become a poet. A single bus journey took you into college for the day. Twilights over Stephen's Green were breathable and lilac-colored. Coffee beans turned and gritted off the blades in the windows of Roberts' and Bewleys. A single cup of it, moreover, cost ninepence in old money and could be spun out for hours of conversation. The last European city. The last literary smallholding.

Or maybe not. "Until we can understand the assumptions in which we are drenched," writes Adrienne Rich, "we cannot know ourselves." I entered that city and that climate knowing neither myself nor the assumptions around me. And into the bargain, I was priggish, callow, enchanted by the powers of the intellect.

If I had been less of any of these things, I might have looked more about me. I might have taken note of my surroundings. If history is the fable agreed upon, then literary traditions are surely the agreed fiction. Things are put in and left out, are preselected and can be manipulated. If I had looked closely, I might have seen some of the omissions. Among other things, I might have noticed that there were no women poets, old or young, past or present in my immediate environment. Sylvia Plath, it is true, detonated in my consciousness, but not until years later. Adrienne Rich was to follow, and Bishop later still. As it was, I accepted what I found almost without question. And soon enough, without realizing it, without enquiring into it, I had inherited more than a set of assumptions. I had inherited a poem.

This poem was a mixture really, a hybrid of the Irish lyric and the British movement piece. It had identifiable moving parts. It usually rhymed, was almost always stanzaic, had a beginning, middle and end. The relation of music to image, of metaphor to idea was safe, repetitive and derivative. "Ladies, I am tame, you may stroke me," said Samuel Johnson to assorted fashionable women. If this poem could have spoken, it might have said something of the sort. I suppose it was no worse, if certainly no better, than the model most young poets have thrust upon them. The American workshop poem at the moment is just as pervasive and probably no more encouraging of scrutiny. Perhaps this was a bit more anodyne; the "bien-fait poem," as it has since been called; the well-made compromise.

This, then, was the poem I learned to write, laboured to write. I will not say it was a damaging model because it was a patriarchal poem. As it happens it was, but that matters less than that I had derived it from my surroundings, not from my life. It was not my own. That was the main thing. "Almost any young gentleman with a sweet tooth," wrote Jane Carlyle of Keats's "Isabella," "might be expected to write such things." The comment is apt.

In due course I married, moved out of the city and into the suburbs—I am telescoping several years here—and had a baby daughter. In so doing I had, without realizing it, altered my whole situation.

When a woman writer leaves the center of a society, becomes a wife, mother and housewife, she ceases automatically to be a member of that dominant class which she belonged to when she was visible chiefly as a writer. As a student, perhaps, or otherwise as an apprentice. Whatever her writing abilities, henceforth she ceases to be defined by them and becomes defined instead by subsidiary female roles. Jean Baker Miller, an American psychoanalyst, has written about the relegation to women of certain attitudes which a society is uneasy with. "Women," she says, "become the carriers for society of certain aspects of the total human experience, those aspects which remain unsolved." Suddenly, in my early thirties, I found myself a "carrier" of these unsolved areas of experience. Yet I was still a writer, still a poet. Obviously something had to give.

What gave, of course, was the aesthetic. The poem I had been writing no longer seemed necessary or true. On rainy winter afternoons, with the dusk drawn in, the fire lighted and a child asleep upstairs, I felt assailed and renewed by contradictions. I could have said with Éluard, "there is another world, but it is in this one." To a degree I felt that, yet I hesitated.

"That story I cannot write," says Conrad, "weaves itself into all I see, into all I speak, into all I think." So it was with me. And yet I remained uncertain of my ground.

On the one hand poetic convention—conventions, moreover, which I had breathed in as a young poet—whispered to me that the daily things I did, things which seemed to me important and human, were not fit material for poetry. That is, they were not sanctioned by poetic tradition. But, the whisper went on, they could become so. If I wished to integrate these devalued areas into my poetry, I had only to change them slightly. And so on. And in my other ear feminist ideology—to which I have never been immune—argued that the life I lived was a fit subject for anger and the anger itself the proper subject for poetry.

Yet in my mind and in the work I was starting to do a completely different and opposed conviction was growing: that I stood at the center of the lyric moment itself, in a mesh of colors, sensualities and emotions that were equidistant from poetic convention and political feeling alike. Technically and aesthetically I became convinced that if I could only detach the lyric mode from traditional romantic elitism and the new feminist angers, then I would be able at last to express that moment.

The precedents for this were in painting rather than poetry. Poetry offered spiritual consolation but not technical example. In the genre paintings of the French eighteenth century—in Jean Baptiste Chardin in particular—I saw what I was looking for. Chardin's paintings were ordinary in the accepted sense of the word. They were unglamourous, workaday, authentic. Yet in his work these objects were not merely described; they were revealed. The hare in its muslin bag, the crusty loaf, the woman fixed between menial tasks and human dreams—these stood out, a commanding text. And I was drawn to that text. Romanticism in the nineteenth century, it seemed to me, had prescribed that beauty be commended as truth. Chardin had done something different. He had taken truth and revealed its beauty.

From painting I learned something else of infinite value to me. Most young poets have bad working habits. They write their poems in fits and starts, by feast or famine. But painters follow the light. They wait for it and do their work by it. They combine artisan practicality with vision. In a house with small children, with no time to waste, I gradually reformed my working habits. I learned that if I could not write a poem, I could make an image, and if I could not make an image, I could take out a word, savor it and store it.

I have gone into all this because to a certain extent, the personal witness of a woman poet is still a necessary part of the evolving criteria by which women and their poetry must be evaluated. Nor do I wish to imply that I solved my dilemma. The dilemma persists; the crosscurrents continue. What I wished most ardently for myself at a certain stage of my work was that I might find my voice where I found my vision. I still think this is what matters most and is threatened most for the woman poet.

I am neither a separatist nor a postfeminist. I believe that the past matters, yet I do not believe we will reach the future without living through the womanly angers which shadow this present. What worries me most is that women poets may lose their touch, may shake off their opportunities because of the pressures and temptations of their present position.

It seems to me, at this particular time, that women have a destiny in the form. Not because they are women; it is not as simple as that. Our suffering, our involvement in the collective silence do not—and never will—of themselves guarantee our achievements as poets. But if we set out in the light of that knowledge and that history, determined to tell the human and poetic truth, and we avoid simplification and self-deception, then I believe we are better equipped than most to discover the deepest possibilities and subversions within poetry itself. Artistic forms are not static. Nor are they radicalized by aesthetes and intellectuals. They are changed, shifted, detonated into deeper patterns only by the sufferings and self-deceptions of those who use them. By this equation, women should break down the barriers in poetry in the same way that poetry will break down the silence of women. In the process it is important not to mistake the easy answer for the long haul.

II

FROM

A Journey with Two Maps

AUTHOR'S PREFACE

This is a book of being and becoming. It is about being a poet. It is also about the long process of becoming one. If these seem in the wrong order there is a reason: the disorder is part of my subject. There is nothing settled about a poet's identity. The becoming doesn't stop because the being has been achieved. They proceed together, attached in ways that are hard to be exact about. For that reason, this is not a scholarly book. I did not approach my subject by finding facts. I approached it by finding myself.

"Ask yourself in the most silent hour of your night: must I write?" said Rilke. Such clarity is hard to come by when you're young. Poetry seemed a magisterial entity back then—not by any means open to a question asked in the silent dark. To start a poem on an ordinary Dublin afternoon was anything but simple. I didn't know how to weigh ideas about poetry. Nothing in the life I lived as a student—and later as wife and mother at the suburban edge of Dublin—suggested I had the wherewithal to do so.

But I did have a unit of measurement. It was the measure of my own life. It was there in the awkward and fanciful assembly of myself as a woman poet in the powerful, resistant literary culture I inherited. Looking back, it seems even now an impossible enterprise: like an early aviator in a remote place, hiding the bulky wings and small wheels in a garage or back garden to protect the odd, presumptuous dream of flight. I was the aviator. I assembled the dream slowly, over years. It was this which gave me some way of understanding my subject; and made this book.

Poetry begins where language starts: in the shadows and accidents of one person's life. And yet many traditional accounts of the making of a poet are over and done with before the reader gets there. Even though I admired those texts when I was young, I regretted they didn't wait for me. The growth of a poet's mind was written about—often with extraordinary power—at its finishing point rather than its source.

I locate those beginnings at an earlier stage here. I push the process back to an origin that some may think too personal. But I wanted to write that record, for the very reason that it has often been unwritten. To do that I knew I needed an alternative critique, one that blended autobiography and analysis. Both seemed necessary. It seemed right that the intimacy and dailyness of experience not be separated from the rigors of criticism, if only because they co-exist in the life of a working poet. They certainly co-existed in mine.

"How shall we tell each other of the poet?" wrote Muriel Rukeyser. In the spirit of that question, the second part of this book is about women poets I've admired and learned from. When I was young some of them were unknown to me, even by name: no part of my education had pointed me towards them. Because of that, a part of my formation happened without the light and example of some of these poems. And so it may be that the real editors of this book are passion and regret.

ONCE I BEGAN TO READ THEM, of course, they became a perspective on everything else. Long before I came to divide my time between California and Dublin I located myself on common ground: in American poetry as well as Irish, and British as well as American. The first women poets I found were from other countries. Their work filled up the silences that troubled me at home. In the sense that my life as a poet has been marked by boundaries this book allows me to unwrite them—moving more freely between countries and poems and histories.

To mark my early discoveries, most of the poems here are not Irish. But I never forgot in reading them—not for one moment—that I was. I make it plain that I understood these texts again and again through my Irishness. They were most often observed through the lens of my life as a woman and poet in a small country most of their authors had never seen; and yet they helped me live it.

Both these parts of the book are held together by a single thread: I have come to believe the journey towards being and becoming a poet cannot happen with one set of directions only. Or, to use the figure I choose here, one map. It seems obvious that ideas of composition or canonicity should never be privileged over even one poem whose voice or style is a challenge. The poem takes precedence. And yet that very precedence can prove disruptive to previous understandings of poetry.

Therefore this book unfolds as clearly as I can the idea of those two maps. I still believe many poets begin in fear and hope: fear that the poetic past will turn out to be a monologue rather than a conversation. And hope that their voice can be heard as that past turns into a future. The first map I followed included a detailed description of the past. The second one provided directions for the future of that voice, and for a new relation with that past.

In these essays, I try to explain exactly what these so-called maps meant to me personally: how at various times I looked at conflicting ideas of a poetic self and an inherited craft and was bewildered at how to balance my obligations to a poetic past with my need to write in the present tense, and out of my own life. And how in the end, for all the inherent contradictions I found, I determined to keep both maps; and to learn from both.

Finally, this book is a tribute to the richness and variety of women's poetry over the last century. I write this knowing the statement itself has built-in tensions. The very category of women poets can and does cause a frank unease. Some people propose it as inevitably reductive: an actual limitation in the way of seeing poetry. I have never shared this view. For me it overlooks something commonsensical. New voices in an old art—and women poets have been that for much more than a century—do not diminish the art through the category. They enrich it. They renew it with common quandaries of craft and innovation. The category simply allows the quandaries to be seen more clearly.

Far from expressing unease, these essays record my excitement at how Sylvia Plath re-stated the nature poem and Gwendolyn Brooks the urban lyric. At the way Elizabeth Bishop re-made the Romantic self and Adrienne Rich re-formed a civic art. Because of them, and others here, something happened for me that I am sure has happened for many readers: an apparently monolithic poetic past was transformed into a conversation I could join and change.

A JOURNEY WITH TWO MAPS

I t might seem odd, even wrongheaded, to begin a book of criticism with a personal narrative. But I have a reason. A story makes a straight path through confusion. It clears the way. And the way needs to be cleared. It would be simpler for every poet if the ethics and aesthetics surrounding them were fixed and signposted. But they're not. Sometimes whatever clarity there is emerges only gradually out of human impulses, human flaws. This piece, very deliberately, is about such flaws; in this case my own. I found them out through a chance encounter, painful, telling and corrective. And since this book is about all the ways poets defy expectations, it seems right to begin with a story about the upending of my own.

My mother was my hero. Without that flat statement, this piece will have no meaning. As an awkward and displaced teenager, I looked up to her. So much so that I made a skewed calendar in my mind: I measured history by her life. 1909, for instance—not the year of the Land Purchase Act but the time her mother died in a fever ward in Dublin. 1915. The year after the Great War started, yes. But more importantly, the year she was called out of class in the Dominican Convent in Dublin to be told her father had drowned in the Bay of Biscay. 1916. The year of the Irish Rising. But also the year she was made a ward of court.

And so it went on. 1928. Not the year before the first Censorship of Publications Act in Ireland. But the time she went to Paris to study art, sitting in the freezing air on the deck of a ferry to Le Havre. Year after year, I counted dates and shifted seasons. And in doing so I allowed the entirely personal to warp the truly eventful.

It wasn't logical. That much I knew. But I was a teenager newly returned to Ireland. The dates and events of its history had little hold on me. My mother's life did. It was her past, to use Elizabeth Bishop's eloquent description of travel, that seemed to me "serious, engraveable." Not the Irish one. And so, without knowing it, I stumbled on one of the essential timekeepers: A magic permission to make time a fiction and the imagined life a fact. A way, in other words, of making a visible history answer to a hidden life.

Two things shaped my relationship with my mother. First the wrenching facts of her life. Born of a mother who died at thirty-one in a fever ward. Of a father who drowned in the Bay of Biscay. Before she left her childhood she had lost most of what determines it for other people. She became a ward of court as a child. She appeared homeless to me, somehow unclaimed. Like Lorna Goodison's grandmother in her poem "Guinea Woman," her future was determined by losses: *It seems her fate was anchored / in the unfathomable sea.*

Second, and just as important, she was an artist. She began drawing and painting early. She left boarding school young. Eventually, she went to the College of Art in the center of Dublin. There she won a scholarship, adjudicated by Yeats's friend,

A. E. Russell. It was called the Henry Higgins Scholarship. It took her to Paris for three years of instruction in the mid-1930s.

Paris was then a city full of studios and teachers. Most Irish art students ended up in the ateliers of teacher-artists like Henri Lhote. My mother did something different. She heard from a friend that a painter had a vacancy for a private student because his American pupil had gone back unexpectedly to the States. She asked him to take her as a replacement. He agreed.

I have some early press cuttings. They detail my mother's first exhibition in Dublin in 1936. By then she was a married woman. They are yellowish and crisp now. And so I have to imagine them in their original context: small, exciting notes in the folded evening newspaper of a provincial city. I have to imagine the convivial gallery party. Feathered hats and maca- bre furs. The half-column in the *Evening Herald* states below her photograph, "First holder of the Henry Higgins Scholarship in Ireland; studied for three years in Paris; swears by——, who taught her."

Those dashes signify a deliberate omission on my part. My mother's teacher was a Cubist, a friend of Modigliani. He had arrived in Paris at the turn of the century. As the mark above shows, he has no name in this piece. He will turn up later here in a strange guise, but perhaps not a discreditable one. Neverthe- less, he should remain nameless. It is part of my subject that the dissolution of his name here belongs to its intrusion elsewhere.

She studied with him, as the press cutting says, for three years. He was considerably older. She was beautiful, in her mid- dle twenties, astray in the world. He was a good teacher. Her palette cleared. Her subjects were fresher. Her style was quicker. But with all the effect of his teaching, he failed to persuade her of one thing. She never became Cubist. She never showed any interest in that fractious, sweet-natured way of reassembling reality. Her heroes were Morisot and Bonnard. Her subjects were objects at the edge of elegy: quick impressions clarified by color but never exempted from it.

My mother hardly ever spoke to me about her painting. We did not talk about aesthetics, or ethics. We had a common bond, not a common language. I did not know how to describe to her the clear view her life gave me—of the past, of art, of Ireland. My rhetoric would have made her uncomfortable. We never talked about influence or authority. In the literary tradition of Ireland I felt restive and often disaffected. I got no such feeling from her. She never talked about those things. Now I wish she had. I wish we had.

But for all that, the question returns: why include this subject here, at the threshold of my accounts of poetry and women? Some of the answer to that question is contained in another story which I include here, but in a shortened form:

My mother loved Berthe Morisot's painting. This in turn made me look more closely at Morisot's life. In the late spring of 1870, Morisot finished a painting for the Salon. Her position among the Impressionists had yet to be solidified. She was still striving for her place in the art world. This was her first submission. She called it *Portrait of the Artist's Mother and Sister*. Her letters show that she worked hard at it. She painted diligently to manage the formal setting. It was not easy. "My work is going badly . . . It is always the same story. I don't know where to start," she wrote to her sister Edma in 1875.

Nevertheless, she finished this painting. It is a studied portrait. It collects surfaces and figures: a lemon-wood table, a small vase of flowers. In the mirror the shapeliness of drawn-wide and bound-back curtains can be seen at the further end of the room. Two women are on the sofa. The younger is Morisot's newly married sister Edma. She is dressed in white, plainly pregnant. Her mother reads a book beside her.

A painting lives in space. The frame closes it in. But when the canvas is stretched and nailed, when the frame closes around it, the life inside continues. I knew that from my mother.

In this case the frame could barely contain the painting. Pushing against those edges was the year, the circumstance, the drama. Paris stood at the edge of the Commune. In twelve weeks, the siege of the city by the Prussians would be established. "Would you believe, I'm getting used to the cannon's noise," wrote Berthe in September.

On the day it was to be submitted to the Salon, Édouard Manet, her friend and mentor, came to the Morisot house. The night before, he had said to Morisot, "Tomorrow after I send off my own painting I'll come see yours, and trust me: I'll tell you what you should do."

If this sounded ominous, it was. "The next day, which was yesterday," wrote Morisot in a letter "he came about one o'clock, said it was fine, except the bottom of the dress; he took the brushes, added a few accents that looked quite good; my mother was in ecstasy. Then began my woes; once he had started, nothing could stop him."

Manet painted out large sections of Morisot's Salon portrait— "from the skirt to the bodice, from the bodice to the head, from the head to the background," as Morisot wrote. "He made a thousand jokes, laughed like a madman, gave me the palette, took it back again, and finally, by five in the evening, we had made the prettiest caricature possible. People were waiting to take it away; willy-nilly he made me put it on the stretcher and I remained dumbfounded."

When I was young, I struggled with authorship, with everything the word meant and failed to mean. Irish poetry was heavy with custom. Sometimes at night, when I tried to write, a ghost hand seemed to hold mine. Where could my life, my language fit in? "For the most part," wrote Nietzsche, "the original ones have also been the name-givers." But was this true? And how could I be original, if I couldn't even provide the name for my life in poetry? At those moments of discouragement, there was a keen temptation to let that ghost hand do the work for me. I could have watched it as it moved fluently across that page, writing out the echoes. Somehow, I resisted that. All the same, I was aware of a shadow under the surface. Of a voice whispering to me: *Who is writing your poem?*

What moved over the canvas of Morisot's painting? What did she see unfolding in front of her as the splashes and pastels of Manet's brushwork corrected her own? A different vision? A higher authority? Those questions would come back: as hauntings, as shadows. When they did, I remembered too late that I had never answered them.

AS TIME WENT ON, I found the shape of my life. I lived in a suburb in Dublin. I raised two small daughters. My husband, Kevin, and I filled the house with books, papers, children's things, our own writing.

It was a source of pleasure to me that the old city—deep in its past—was only four miles away. I imagined it the way I found it when I was fourteen, after a childhood in London and New

York. On winter nights I thought of it as a familiar, unfolding from the lichen and black peat of the Dublin hills all the way to the North Wall. I imagined its freezing rain and stone; the Liffey always flowing to the Irish Sea.

In light traffic, a twenty-minute drive took me into town. If I parked in the center of it, I was in a web of streets which led up to College Green, and back down towards Stephen's Green. Which is where I was when I saw my mother's painting: the subject of this piece.

I was passing a small art gallery. I was on my way back to the car which I had parked at Trinity. The gallery was at a left-hand turn. Its street-facing walls were made of glass. The paintings inside were on show, some stacked against the wall, some hung on it. Shapes and colors making a carnival of a city corner.

Usually, I walked past. But that day a painting stopped me in my tracks: it was middle-sized, clearly visible through the plate-glass window, even in fading light. In the foreground of the canvas was a pair of gloves. Just behind them, in a green wash, was a vase. The light flowed in it, as if its physical surface were a transparency rather than a hindrance. In the vase were small flowers. Lily of the valley. They were my mother's favorite flowers. Their sweet, choking fragrance reminded me of cheap perfumes in London, bought for her on each of her birthdays, but never close to evoking the Paris streets of her youth. I thought of them, if I did, as the flowers of my childish failures.

I knew at once, without a second glance—without study, consideration or hesitation—that it was my mother's painting. The colors were hers. The staging of the objects was hers. And so I went into the gallery and spoke to the man at the end of the long, narrow space. It was a perfunctory, quick exchange.

I indicated nothing at all of my interest. The price was enormous. I asked quickly, again with a disguised casualness, about its provenance.

He announced the painter with an emphasis on the last syllable and with the gallery owner's disdain of the passing enquiry. My mother's teacher. I looked again to be sure. Yes, there was his signature, in the bottom right of the painting, where she usually put her own.

His signature. Her painting. Her vision. His price. And that was that.

I LEFT THE GALLERY and turned up towards Trinity. I had been a student there. I had read poems inside those rooms. I had written them there as well. I had worked in the old airy library above the front gate. I had even taught there as a junior lecturer of twenty-three. Now I walked up to College Green and looked back at the statues of Oliver Goldsmith and Edmund Burke which front the façade.

A poet and an orator. I knew something about them: chiefly, that they were eighteenth-century figures, born in a colony. That they had had no country. That they had a language, a rhetoric. Nothing more. The real nation had eluded them, not just their speech, but their imagination. It had flowed out beyond their shapely paragraphs and wistful cadences. They would speak of it and be spoken of by it. But they would never be its authors.

Suddenly I thought of an earlier time: of coming back to Ireland at fourteen. I had felt awkward. But I still sensed that I belonged somewhere: to the distaff side of Ireland. I was connected to it through my mother. Through her art, her anonymity, her origins in a small town marked on no map. Above all by the signs she made in oils on canvas.

Now that had changed. Standing there, I imagined the scene as it would be a few hours later—a summer darkness folding itself into the trees. Into the bronze ruffle on Goldsmith's jacket. Into the reflections on the windows of the gallery. Once I would have said to the statues, to quote Mary O'Malley's powerful line from her poem "St John's Eve"—*Go back, I want to say, You are in the wrong place.* But not now. I could see that the statues had survived. They stood for a flawed authorship. But they had endured. But on the distaff side? What remained?

For this was the place where I had chosen to locate myself. In a place of shadows I called the past. I had thought about it, written about it. And at its gateway, and pointing to its interior, had always stood my mother. The mystery of her early life folded back and out into the flat lands and ordeals of an earlier Ireland. If I followed that silence, I was sure, I could enter it. Now what?

The truth looked at me coldly. That was her painting. Her authorship. She had assembled those flowers. She had constructed the complicated relationship between their petals and the background. She had worked on it, changed it, assembled it. No doubt she had changed it again. Then he had signed it. She had let him sign it. It was not the signature that shocked me; it was that consent. Down through the years, from a time when I had not even been born, came that faint *yes.*

I drove home. As I opened the door I could see, eye-level, some of my mother's paintings which we owned. But my mind was on only one of them, a few miles away. I thought of its presence there in the summer twilight. How the dark would reach that street and enclose the gallery.

And behind its doors, that painting. I thought of it lying

against the wall: the small gleams of color, the fragmentary evidence of a young woman's life. I thought of those petals and their milky shine. How they would spread their oils and emblems—in that darkness and every one to come—above a false signature.

I asked myself a question. What did it matter that a woman I loved and a man I never knew had exchanged their claims, even their identities, for a brief moment? What did it matter that a young painter had let an older one—in a lost decade in a different country—write his name on her work?

It mattered. I was sure it did. That small canvas had a future as well as a present. That future—I believed this—was nothing less than my mind. Those greens, those imitations of air next to light, belonged to me. Those delicately colored arguments about the traffic between solid and space seemed to me tangled up with my sense of growth and survival. My mother's choice of shade and block were part of my first language. And now it seemed as if a man I never knew had signed my childhood.

But there was more. The shadow world in which I had taken up residence when I was a young poet was more complicated than I allowed. At that time, in that part of my youth, I called it the past. I gave it boundaries and called it by the name of my own country. Ireland. Then I renamed it again and called it my mother's life.

For all those acts of naming and renaming, it was a complicated territory I was setting up house in. The rift between the past and history was real, but it was not simple. In those shadows, in that past, I was well aware that injustices and griefs had happened without any hope of the saving grace of elegy or expression—those things which an official history can count on. Silence was a condition of that past. I accepted it as a circumstance.

But only on certain terms. That the silences were not final. They were not to be forever. That they could be recognized, but also remedied. In my childhood they had been transformed at the end of my mother's day when she picked up an enameled mirror and turned her back to her own painting. Then, staring at a view which was over her right shoulder, she looked at her day's work. Considered it, judged it.

I saw her do this countless times. It would always be near dusk. Light would be leaving the room. When she looked in the mirror, she would have seen a day's worth of mistakes and some satisfactions as well. But as I watched her studying her own work—as I remembered it and reflected on it—it took on a different meaning. The angles, surfaces, compositions she achieved belonged to the craft of a few hours. But the act belonged to her lifetime. And mine.

I had depended on that act. It was the first sign of expressive power I saw as a child. The first article of feminine faith. Later I gave it a broad and glamourous interpretation. As I looked back I designated it as the moment when the hurts of an Irish past, of my mother's motherless life, of my own absence from anything familiar, healed into a little grace of remedy and articulation. A day had gone by. A million lights, refractions, rearrangements had taken place. Here on the canvas, and in the mirror, was a record of it all. But what was that record if, at the last moment, it was not presented as hers?

I remembered Virginia Woolf's bleak comment about the improbability of a woman's authorship: "And undoubtedly, I thought, looking at the shelf where there are no plays by women, her work would have gone unsigned." The problem was my mother's work had been signed. But not by her.

A fuss about nothing? I could ask that question, but I couldn't accept it. For years I brooded about it. The doubts persisted. If anything, they grew. What did I feel had been violated by that long-ago moment? Nothing seemed clear. Whatever deference to hierarchy and authority had made her cede, even for a moment, the rights to her painting, was not what I believed I had inherited from her. The compliant student in Paris was not my obstinate, glowing mother who had opened an elusive past to me.

The mother I saw and understood was a figure of fable, thigh-deep in the mysteries and silences of the country she came from. I had studied that fable. I had learned that mystery. What she did in that studio in Paris was one thing. What I learned from her was another. The problem was I could no longer be sure how one had changed the other.

II

"The trade of authorship is a violent, and indestructible obsession," wrote George Sand. What is it we do when we sign a poem, a painting, a piece of writing? What is it we share when we let someone else do it? What on earth did I think had been changed in that room years ago?

Earth is the operative word. Whether I liked it or not, my life had been shaped by the fact that I came from one part of it. A small country. An island. A place where hundreds of years had passed without a trustworthy signature. The idea of an Ireland whose recent past—in historical terms—had been marred by false ownership had a meaning for me, as for so many others.

And yet, over time, I began to rethink George Sand's obsession. Not just in terms of Irishness. There came a moment when much of what I thought about poetry, language and even origin began to shift. I came to believe that how we see a painting, read a poem or write one can't simply be the outcome of a single fixed viewpoint.

It wasn't sudden or complete, this shift. It happened in increments, in gradual dawnings. The danger of describing it lies in the risk of giving it a coherence the process never had. I changed first. The poems I wrote changed later. Only after that did I add language and ideas. If all three seem to go together here, it's because retrospect flattens chronology. But one thing was clear from the start: change depends on the questions we ask. Always providing we are willing to ask them. And at a certain point, I set out to find those questions.

When I looked at my mother's painting I had yielded to a small outrage. But what was its source? Was it based on a version of authorship? More likely, I thought, on a version of myself. A vast series of impressions goes into the making of any young poet. When I looked back at the nighttime libraries, the wooden tables, the bookshelves I consulted, I could see myself sitting there, with a page turned. I could see, above all, that I was trying to be the author of myself.

But there was no escaping a predetermined narrowness. And no escaping that I learned to be a writer in the shadow of constraining influences. Young as I was, and Irish as I was, I still took most of my ideas from nineteenth-century British Romanticism. These were the texts I read in my convent school, which had found their way into every anthology and were set in stone by college courses. I sat for hours on winter evenings, learning about the fever of this poet and the revelations of that one. I entered my reading the way an echo enters a sound. I never questioned that originality was a primary value.

Yet somewhere beyond those lamps, tables and pages was

a vast and rich world of collaborative forms. A world in which originality was an almost meaningless concept. The ghazals, harvest songs, bardic schools, communal ballads were all there, all waiting. And all invisible to me. I had one template, and one only: the glamour and hubris of the individual poet. "The romantic image of the poet as a vulnerable personage in a hostile universe has not gone out of currency," writes David Lehman. I traded that currency.

At the start, therefore, the notion that poet and audience could blend their purposes, could co-author a poem from deep within a shared communal reality was foreign to me. Above all, the idea that a signature on a painting might be the last sign of an artistic mentorship rather than the first claim on a work of art never crossed my mind. A shadow land of artistic invention where the teacher and the taught, the poet and the listener, the creator and the created object could have fluid boundaries was still closed to me.

This book is about a journey. A journey with two maps. It recognizes my early ignorance of the vast distances of the poetic past—a horizon reaching back far beyond my first sense of it, whose line nevertheless shaped my first map. It is about the dangers and glories of that first set of directions, which seemed to promise a young poet pride of language and exemption from ordinary life. It is also about the growing need for a second map. Another set of guidances in which my own individual voice could be heard. Where the poetic past became something I could participate in, could even change, rather than having it determine my future. It is about making this second map and keeping it ready, while holding on obstinately—and even against advice—to the first. It is, above all, about reading and writing poetry with those two maps—which of course are figures for different or oppositional views—always available.

And yet the truth is, I started with one map. I had no idea there could be any other. That first map opened to me on teenage afternoons, full of enchantment and discovery. On quiet midnights repeating and memorizing poems. Most young poets start out with a reverence for a past defined for them by someone else. Here are the great poems, they are told; these are the exemplars to learn from. A powerful set of suggestions does more than outline a literature. It confirms the young poet in their quest to join it.

For a long time I wanted nothing else. Besides, in those years I thought of myself as merely concerned with writing poems. I applied myself to the craft of a stanza, or to learning a more agile syntax. But the self-limitation failed. I would come to understand there is no poem separable from its source. I began to see that poems are not just an individual florescence. They are also a vast root system growing down into ideas and understandings. Almost unbidden, they tap into the history and evolution of art and language. They seek out their own progenitors. "The form of my poem rises out of a past," wrote Hart Crane. But which one?

I did not ask. At least, not at first. In the beginning, I merely wanted to introduce myself, hopefully and politely, to a single past: the one that awed me. I read continuously. I was sure if I kept reading I would find my name and my life as I looked behind me. And, because of that, I believed in the future. If I could bring together my life and my poems, I was certain I could go there. Despite the fact that by nationality and gender I was likely to be on the margins of the English canon, nevertheless

I refused to feel excluded from its questions—its big, fearless questions. "I ask what is meant by the word Poet? What is a Poet?" wrote Wordsworth.

And so I settled: with one map, with one hope. The corner of a table under a cowled lamp in a library was where I most often found myself. When I went home I wrote poems at a smaller table. And this solitary, self-consciously questing life as a student was just near enough to the lives of poets I was reading—at least in my mind—to make me feel like them. The small proximity made me believe their power and independence could be my own. It was, of course, a false affinity. I was about to find that being a poet is more tangled in circumstance and accident than I would have believed.

"Poets have always known," wrote Muriel Rukeyser, "that one's education has no edges, has no end." At first, the expanding edges of my education looked decidedly everyday. I married. I moved house. I left the literary and confirming center of Dublin and went to live in a new suburb. Suddenly—every parent will understand the word—I had two young daughters. All at once, the library and the table and the friendly helmets of light became a memory. My working day as a poet now happened in the light and shadow of domestic arrangements. The thick notebook I wrote in could be lost and found under newspapers or a child's coat. The glamour and conviction of my first ideas of poetry—the feeling that I could emulate what I admired— began to be tested.

There was something painful about all this. I knew my world had changed. But the change was not clarifying. I loved the sensory world of neighbourly routine and small children. The first delicate smell of an Irish spring which was like crisp linen. Or the fragrance of peat fires in autumn. But inwardly everything was clouded with doubts. I could no longer pretend I was close to the poets I read. I was now at a distance from them, and the distance was growing. I still read my poetry books. I still wrote in my notebook. But I turned the pages now with hands which had come from lifting a child or shutting the back door against a gust of rain. How could I make a text when I had lost a context?

The questions multiplied. Was there, I asked myself, anything of my old free life as a student-poet—anything of all its reading and searching—which remained? Could I even find myself as a poet in my new life? Or had I been an impostor in my old one? In reading the poets of a Romantic past had I learned—laboriously and with a fitful sense of grandiosity—all the wrong things: to invent myself for a world which would not have accepted me, and which could never, in any case, occur again?

It's almost impossible to reconstruct an inner world. I lived a practical day-to-day life as a mother and wife. In my poems, I could echo Sharon Olds's eloquent words about wanting to "make a small embodiment of ordinary life, from a daughter's, wife's, mother's point of view." And if I look back, I could render even now the sloping road of the school run, the sycamore at the top of the hill. I could summon the lost hum of the milk cart. Those are real, actual, describable. But the shadowy questions I lived with are harder to recover.

And so I will try to create a tableau here: a small stage-set of an inner world. A place where ideas of authorship occurred in an atmosphere as vivid as any view outside the window. If I were to describe it accurately, it would be a silent mime. But for the sake of this argument, I will give it words. I can center it around a simple question and a liberating realization. There are hazards in this. It means I have to create an artifice to replicate the way I built my thoughts, as though they happened in sequence, which they didn't. Nevertheless, this seems the only available method, the only way of getting at the subjective mystery: how one poet is made, and how an aesthetic grows in silence and doubt.

"Clearly the mind is always altering its focus," wrote Virginia Woolf in *A Room of One's Own*. Certainly mine was now changed. I had a new life. And yet after a while, for all my doubts and worries, I could see something had indeed survived from the old one. It was there when I went to the back room, late at night, and read a poem or tried to write one. It appeared in front of me, unchanged and confirming.

What was it? It was that shining *I*. That obdurate and central witness of the poet. That first-person pronoun which first signaled my hopes of becoming a poet. It was there, when I went upstairs and took down a book, ready to be found in an image or a cadence. It was there when I opened my own notebook and wrote the first-person pronoun at the start of a line. Written or read, it could still provide me with a lightning-spark. It could still connect the tentative, half-formed entity which was all I yet could lay claim to and the beckoning hope of an achieved poetic self.

But there was a problem. If it was changeless—this pronoun and everything it promised—I was not. I opened a book of poetry now with different expectations. At times I grew restless with that old, glamourous part of speech—that relentless sign of the poet's singular domain. I wanted to see my new life in the old art. I wanted some recognition of the kettle I had just boiled, the sound of rain in the garden—and that they had come with me to the poem. I wanted to see their shadow. When I couldn't I wondered what reality this signal of the poetic self was refusing to encompass. And as I thought about this, I found that another word—an older one—crept out of the pages of poems

I was reading. It shifted, shimmered, dissolved, re-formed and changed again. Not *I* any longer, but *we*.

Of course it had always been there. I had just not looked for it. Now that I did it seemed to be everywhere. Suddenly I was aware of its reach and brightness, of its application to my life. It recalled James Merrill's remark about Rilke: "He never says 'I' but in the *Duino Elegies* he seems to invite his readers into a community of shared suffering, or shared sensitivity. I couldn't wait to accept the invitation. I loved the feeling I got from those first-person plurals, as if one were being consoled and elevated at the same time."

It was a flexible instrument, this new pronoun. It was also inclusive of older histories, older communities. It could be the *we* of the balladeer, recording an event for which I was no longer the audience. Or the *we* of the Middle Ages poet, glued to other words by faith and authority. It might become the *we* of the Renaissance. Then, a few poems on, it might spin around and appear as the *we* of the Irish nation in the poems of Speranza in 1848; or, in another swift turn, manifest itself as a 1930s political poem.

For all its instability, its tendency to vanish in historic change, this new word—this *we*—commended itself. It seemed to include more of my life at that precise moment than the previous *I*. It gathered in the ordinariness of the house, the cheer and heat of the kitchen, the untidiness of the garden. As it did, it gave them a new shape. It spoke to me of down-to-earth communities which had once needed a voice. As mine did now. The time would come when this pronoun too seemed open to criticism, when the world it implied seemed another form of constraint. But for now I was drawn to it.

I have no doubt, even as I write them, that these are small

revelations. And, certainly, they took place in small circumstances. But I promised a stage-set of a mind in process here; a picture of an evolving poet. If these pronouns seem not to provide that, then I have misrepresented them. The truth is, they were critical signs. Within the poem, they marked a vast difference from each other. Outside it, they signaled a growing tension in me. They pointed to alternate histories: towards opposite views of authorship. They were fractional as words; yet as symbols of composition they had enormous meaning. Within their difference I detected shadows of my own choices and dilemmas, and yet saw no hint of how to resolve them.

And so I have to re-imagine myself, back in those days when I was trying to find my own language. I have to remember late-night reading and an open book. And how I hesitated on one page over the silvery *I* of the poetic singular. And then turned back to the hallowed *we* of something older.

In the first instance, I could be upstairs on a winter evening, the curtains drawn, the garden seething with rain. Maybe I was reading "Frost at Midnight" or the tenth book of *The Prelude*, marveling at the way a single poet could stand against storm-forces of history, and be perfectly outlined. Or I could be looking at "The Buried Life" and be moved and persuaded by Arnold's sense of private revelation, of a "true, original course."

And yet the following week I could find myself—the rain turned to sleet, the children fretful and awake—changing my mind. Suddenly I would find myself agreeing with Robert Hass's comment, in his essay on Rilke in *Twentieth Century Pleasures* where he commented on the "sudden, restless revulsion from the whole tradition of nineteenth and early twentieth century poetry, or maybe from lyric poetry as such, because it seemed, finally, to have only one subject, the self, and the self—which is not life."

Then I too would become restless. I would open *Everyman* or *Pearl*, ready for the light and intensity of an earlier, more communal imagination. I would read the lines. I would see for myself how a community co-authored the refrain of a ballad or the shape of a narrative. And so it went on. And so I continued, book by book. Back and forth.

But what exactly was at stake? To answer that, I have to insist again that I am describing a mime here. I was a poet hardly aware of the choices I was making, and yet knowing I had to make them. On a night of learning to read, of trying to write, I was looking for the micro-history of poetry. And yet it was there in front of me, closed into two pronouns.

And certainly, once inside the poem, two apparently tiny parts of speech assumed a larger role. They seemed to reach up from the pages of my books, these pronouns, crying out their different histories like street hawkers. In the first person singular I saw the glamour of the most enticing myths of composition. *Come with me*, it seemed to say. It beckoned me to the silhouette of the hero and the strength of soliloquy. Before I could respond, the *we* interposed itself. In its strength and poise I recognized the old dignity of poetry—its relation to the tribe. Different traditions, different directions. I was hopelessly torn.

And here I could leave it, this story. As a personal narrative, as a chronicle of reading and writing. As an unremarkable account of choices and changes of heart. I could abandon this account, fixed and printed as it is with the image of an indecisive reader and unconvinced poet; a woman shifting here and there between ideas of art and systems of authorship.

I could leave it were it not for one thing: the story changed. There came a cumulative moment which extended and altered it. An inward series of dissents; a growing melody of constraint and skepticism. Finally—still upstairs, still with my books and my children and the sounds of a household—there came into my mind a plainspoken question: *why choose?*

One question. And yet from that simple interrogation came a whole outworks of reason and light. Overdue as it was, it upended my thinking. Looking back, I could see things I had missed. How, for instance, almost from the start, my sense of being a poet had been shadowed by false alternatives. Far as I was from the center, deep as I was in a national rather than an international culture, I had felt a pressure to choose: between the formal stanza and the open one. Between the canon and the tradition. Between modernism and what went before. Between the public poem and the private one. And finally, between two pronouns on a page.

It hardly mattered that the pressure was my own; was an internalized series of figments. The fact was I seemed to have started out as a poet in a world of deliberately crafted division: where modernism chastened indiscipline, and traditionalism scolded modernism. Where poetry fled from the back parlor and the evening recitation; yet no one could quite say where its home was now. Where two parts of speech seemed to hold up different worlds.

WHY CHOOSE? Sometimes I imagine myself walking back into a Dublin twilight. Putting off the years. Shedding office buildings, computers, texting and travelling and the sorrows of aging. In my imagination, I stop on the same corner. By the illogicality and power of memory, the gallery is still there. My mother's painting is there.

And I am the same and not the same. I have had time to practice that refusal to choose. I have grown more comfortable with opposition, even with contradiction. I see more clearly now what I missed then. The elaborations of authorship, for instance. I realize that the *I* and the *we*—and everything they implied— were present even then in a way I failed to notice.

But what I mainly failed to see was my own limited understanding of making, and of being made. The situation unfolded a treasure of complications I never understood at the time: the painting itself was made by one person, signed by another and seen by a third who was herself authored by the first. It existed in a nation which added another element, so that history was woven into the image and my reaction to it. In the end, the laying down of these different authorial layers infinitely complicated the idea of single authorship. So much so that the idea on its own was no longer tenable.

None of these realizations solved the problem of the painting: its provenance remained disturbing and puzzling. In later years I would go back and forth about it. Had it simply been an afternoon's painting, done by the apprentice, but guided by the master and so signed by him? Hadn't my mother once pointedly told me what the strict definition of a masterpiece was? Not a defining work, she said, but the apprentice's final piece before being admitted to the guild? The questions continued; the answers never fit. But they showed me, those questions, that the issues raised were too rich and complex to be confined by a fixed viewpoint. It was not a moment to confuse authorship with ownership. And yet that was exactly what I had done.

The past does not change. But I had changed. If I stood again in the summer twilight on that street, some things would be different. The angle of vision, to start with. The first time I saw the painting I looked at its signature, nothing else. I chose to see only what offended my early belief—that the single artist was the source of art. I allowed the definition of the author to overwhelm the definition of the art.

This time, if I could go back, I would consider both. I would look at the painting: the light wash of green, the quickly brushed petals. This time I would see that the signature and the image were more than just challenges to faith in a single aesthetic. They were separate fields of meaning—rich and problematic and inviting of new perspectives. Above all, their coexistence, even as contradiction, was not only possible but desirable. If art—and indeed poetry—was shaped by the interplay between individual and communal, then here was a chance to look into the fire of those contradictions, as if into a moment of origin. And so the question returns, *why choose?*

And from that question comes the argument of this book. And its advocacy: that we can, and should, draw two maps for the right and difficult art of poetry. That we can and should entertain even conflicted ideas to find a path through contradiction. That we can hold in poise oppositional concepts—I have put them forward here as *I* and *we*, as just one version of a possible opposition, but there are many others—without needing to erase one with the other. That we can take apparently opposed views of the history and practice of this art, and hold them reflectively in our hands as if they were two maps. And yet, in the end, come safely to a single destination.

THE ROOMS OF OTHER WOMEN POETS

I was the fifth child of larger-than-life and wilful parents. I was born in Ireland and even now my parents seem to me perfectly Irish, completely of their time and place. They were eloquent and expressive. They waved their friends off after a late-night party, standing in doorways, framed by noise and laughter, blue cigarette smoke, whiskey kisses. Their life seemed to have happened in their words, before it ever got to their actions. I was their last child.

My father was first a civil servant, then a diplomat. But he thought of himself as the first, as if the second could only be a weak version of the civil servant's reach in a small country: the negotiations for coal, the granting of papers. It was the secret, hidden world of power which attracted him, not the flamboyant one.

My childhood was nomadic. We moved when I was very young, from Dublin to London, from London to New York. My father changed like a landscape. Never exactly handsome, but always high-colored in the face, his voice wounded by an old childhood stammer, but almost always to be feared and listened to.

During those years, my relationship with my parents changed. It was made up of distances, of empty rooms, of knowing they would be back next week or the week after. It was learning to do my lessons by myself, keep my thoughts to myself.

Like all children who are insignificant in a family—the last, the latest, the overlooked—I dreamed of having some surprising importance. But I was not quick at school and there were too many absences around me for me to prove myself to anyone. But even as a child, I felt restless, uneasy, put-upon by this life in strange cities with hard-to-get-at parents.

As I got older I read in random, undirected ways. I liked short poems, pithy stories and, above all, preposterous tales of girlish heroism. I sat up late at night staring at pictures in a Victorian encyclopedia. They were monochrome with a sickly yellow tint at the edge. They were of girls who had saved their town, or defied high water, or endured ordeals or were composed into perfection by virtues I knew even then I did not have and would never have. Patience, for instance. Silence.

I remember that one of them was called Grace Darling. She had saved lives. She had defied weather. The captions to the pictures said that she had gone out in a boat on high seas in some nineteenth-century storm under clouded-over stars. Even her name was a mixture of ornamental beauty and adoring attention. I envied her. I spent long evenings, in rooms I was uneasy in, in a home where I was anything but a heroine, practicing some sort of escape, some sort of immature empathy, looking at the old Victorian book.

What did they mean, those heroines? It was not that they offered any kind of intellectual life. In fact the opposite. Nevertheless, they had gathered around them, and had been the subject of, admirations, attentions, grainy colors and a painter's or photographer's skill. I wanted to be like them. To be that image, that shiny surface of greys and yellows and blacks that fell open in a book opened by some other young girl. I knew it was impossible.

In fact I was at the outermost and final edges of possibility. In those years of the fifties, in London and New York, I lived, without knowing it, in a time when the profoundest changes were happening: when a radical alteration was getting ready to happen in the way a society saw young girls. And, as a consequence, in the way they saw themselves. I know now, as I knew then in some unclear way, that the loneliness of seeking out those strange girls in old books, with their hair blown back by sea gales, or their shiny paper skin cleared by thoughts of sacrifice, was a loneliness that went well beyond me. It was deep in a society which needed to see itself in that skin, that expression. That had needed for hundreds and hundreds of years to offset unease with simplification.

I did not understand those changes. I was not meant to. Coming from a small country, with an intense Catholic idiom, my own language of girlhood was afflicted, was seized-up. Despite my intense awareness of my body, despite my feeling that it was yet another part of me that was displaced, I had no analytical understanding whatsoever. If I had some faraway sense that girlhood was the veiled mirror of a society, a place where it looked to recover its spoiled purity, where it was alternately cruel and grasping in the search for that purity, I could never have articulated it.

And so up in my room, opening the heavy burgundy covers of the encyclopedia, bending over and peering at those girls—

immune as I believed them to be from all my small humiliations and exclusions—I was the last figment of an old world. The hidden and unadmitted sexuality of my own culture would disappear, or so it seemed, almost overnight. In me it lay somewhere between the mind and the body, a lost soul at that point waiting for a definition. That definition would come, swiftly and fiercely. Centuries would extinguish themselves and give out and give up their interpretations of girlhood somewhere between my last boyfriend and my first child. Everywhere, the old-fashioned superstitions would vanish. An entire civilization of crinolines and wasp-waists, of false conversations and choked-back desires, of late-night dreams and short-step dances, of rouge and flattery and simpers and flirtations, was about to disappear. And with it an empire of rude awakenings. But there in my room, at the gates of puberty, I knew nothing about this.

My childhood was ending. I came back to Dublin from New York at fourteen years of age, landed there like some mythical traveller on a magic island without maps or signals. I spent the week at boarding school. On weekends I went in with friends to O'Connell Street and ate in strange-seeming cafés where the food had Italian names but the sausages were plainly Irish. Then back out on the coast road, by train or bus, to boarding school. I was discovering poetry and books. If I was beginning to discover my own sexuality it was still too sunk beneath the reticence and rhetoric of my time and place.

In fact I was a foggy, erratic teenager, a fifth child, the last in the queue for conversation or attention. Yet I knew, I always knew—like a consciousness of an overcast day—that I had a clever and wilful father. It was nothing I could have analyzed. And yet it was impossible not to register that we stood at extreme ends in our family, rigidly positioned there like statuettes: I, the latecomer, the youngest, the fourth girl out of five children. And he, the supremely important and attended-to presence.

There was very little that was sentimental or demonstrative about our relationship. He was a pious father. I was not a confiding daughter. There was no room or time for that. But very early on, in my teenage years, I began to see a measurement and color to his conversation that was different to anyone else's. He knew how to speak. He knew how to address a single listener as if there was something at stake, as if the conversation was more than gossip or anecdote.

He lived in a dramatic world, sometimes a melodramatic one, of late-night phone calls and hurried conferences. His conversation, his speech was reserved for the people in those worlds. But sometimes in New York, on an occasional holiday when I visited from boarding school, he would speak to me across his desk in the room where he worked. It would always seem to me that I was there because the other children were grown. I had his attention by default.

At those times, almost as if I was not present, he would open a book and talk about when he had first read it. Or he would remember a thunderstorm in Ireland when he was a boy. How the lightning had cracked on the roof of their house in Bray, cracked over the Irish Sea and lit up the low line of Howth. How he had been a boy of seven, frightened in the storm, but had still crossed the length of it to comfort his younger brother. How in the morning, on the breakfast table, a small pile of copper pennies had been left there by his father. A reward.

I sat opposite him and listened. At those times, in some strange way, it was as if my skin was made of stone and my eyes were a vacant space. I was not ready to listen to him. I was not even clear why he was speaking to me.

Suddenly I was seventeen, the long years of childhood behind me. It was a warm, clear summer and I was working in a hotel before going to Trinity. I was out of boarding school. The harshly structured days were gone. I was free to look around. I had a summer job. I took the bus to work. I took it home again. After a while I noticed that whatever time of the day it was, they were there too: the iron fathers of the city. Grattan. O'Connell. Parnell. Huge statues, draped in bronze, with ore-colored hands. Standing over their statements, their promises. Looking up every morning I felt like what I was, what I would always be: a daughter.

Then one more year. And at last I was a university student, eighteen years of age. I lived away from home, a short distance from my parents' house. Because I could walk home—Dublin was still eerily safe—I could stay past the last bus, into the small hours. Often my parents were out late and came in, and then the conversation began at midnight. More often than not, I sat in my father's study. Perched on a tiny, awkward trio of steps that went down into the room. It was a small room with high, falsely mullioned windows. The bookshelves behind my father's desk were narrow and steep and full of books on economics and history, on declarations of war and the public testaments of those who fought or prevented them. Outside was a curved, tarmacadam drive and a road that led into the city, into the Dublin he had known and I was just beginning to know. Into the trees of the city, its poplars and willows and sycamores. Into its songs, canal waterways, malice and memories. Into the roads that were bricked, cobbled, surfaced, smoothed over. On cold nights, with the clear frosty air outside, I could almost follow those roads in my mind back into the meeting points and intersections that came together and drew apart and kept moving towards the river. Towards the statues: a crisp skin growing now over the outstretched hands, their icy lips still full of rhetoric.

My mother went to bed. As she left the room, there was always something small and unexpressed, as if I was losing her, as if I was losing myself. She was older now, the line above her eye drawn with less effect, the emblem she was to me much less clear than when I was younger. She did not talk in that high-stakes, clear way my father did. Her talk was more hesitant, more anecdotal. She left. I remained.

My father and I went on talking. One o'clock. Two o'clock. The conversations went in the way they must have done between fathers and daughters for centuries: What he knew. What I did not. What I might learn but could never really use. The depth of seas, the purpose of wars, the events that led to the French Revolution, the sound of gunfire on the Dublin streets in 1920. It was a gorgeous, packed world of facts, figures, histories. I listened. And listened. Did I ever think, once, that not a single fact there was one I knew I could use?

But I was clearer about myself. Or so it seemed to me in those early hours of the morning. A teenager's body, that site of pain and doubt, seemed to be polished away, turned into a mist of syntax and power as I talked. Back in my flat the lipstick, the compact with its pale powder, for flattening the color of skin, still waited for me. And the mirror and my new eyeshadow. But for now, for a few hours of peace, I could disown them. And still the facts, the figures, the shapely histories, the kings, the foreign wars, the famous speeches kept arriving. And I could be part of them, I could be privy to them, I could be sexless, I could be powerful, if . . . If what? What was it I lacked?

Sitting there on the step, listening, trying to nod my comprehension, joining in where I could, was the nearest I had ever come to the flatteries and glamourings of the self I imagined and yearned for in childhood. Those girls in my encyclopedia, dashed by the storm, drawn in sharp inks, were different. They were chosen. Here for a while I was different—plucked by words out of the routines and rituals of young womanhood. Suddenly made complicit in battles and speeches, in the collection of an army in snow-bound Moscow, in a last desperate speech to the Irish Parliament, in the elegy for the Athenian dead.

Book after book was pulled down from the tightly packed shelves. I was shown the titles, told about the authors, invited to listen. More than that, I was being allowed to eavesdrop on great decisions, treated as if I could share their source and their outcome. In a serious, unexpected way I was being encouraged to admire those centers of the earth, of civilization, of culture which had made me. *But was it*, a small voice kept asking at the back of my head, *me they had made? Or my father?* And then the voice would prompt—*But it could be you?*

I remember the hidden seasons outside the small windows. The way the frost made harsh margins on the leaded sections. How the daffodils edged the driveway in spring. How the summer nights were full of stirrings, fidgetings, as if not a single bird or leaf or inch of wind was ready to settle into silence.

The conversations were brilliant and symmetrical on my father's side. They represented not simply a view of the world, but also a view of what was important in it. I sat there on the steps, my knees hunched up, my chin in my hand, listening. And listening. There in that small room, at the edge of that city with its metal and marble orators, a procession of those significances went by. A book would be taken down, a short speech would be read out, or a long one. Grattan to the Irish Parliament. *I found Ireland on her knees. I have watched over her with a paternal solicitude.*

Or Pericles to the Spartan dead. Or Napoleon leaving an ice-bound Moscow. Just occasionally a small detail appeared, like a stowaway on a boat: that his grandmother had come from the Comeragh Mountains. That she had had to walk six miles every day for water. Six miles there. Six miles back.

And then for a moment I would look up, as if someone had called my name from a distance. His grandmother. Walking the hills above Clonmel. That steep, blackish rise of the Comeraghs with its wild broom and hawthorn. Its rough terrain and coarse outline. She had walked there, setting out for water, bringing it back, heavy and necessary. My great-grandmother, knowing nothing about battles and orations. But nothing also about swaying dresses and flirtation and pretence. Just for a moment, in those sentences, I saw something of myself. A narrative I might enter.

But then history would come back: well attired, speaking in sonorous tones. My name would fade. No one, after all, had called me. And the night and the moon would fade too. Sometimes on summer mornings, the light would inch into the sky at 4 A.M. My father would stand up, ready to go, with a fond goodnight. I would get up too and let him go past. And then look around the small room—a few books out on the desk, the ice cubes almost melted in the bucket. I was trying to frame some thought, some clear impression. Where in everything I had heard, in every territory we had covered, was one inch where I could breathe or live?

And yet there was nothing simple about it. It was never clear-cut. For those moments when my father turned and talked to me it was as if some old dream was being prodded into life, even as a new one was put at risk. Those legendary girls, the water dashed on their clothes, their hair streaming in the black-and-white paintings, what after all had made them heroines? This. This very thing. This onset of attention, and powerful talk and arcane knowledge. They had not been—of course I knew it by now—heroines in and of themselves. They had been made heroines. They had been allowed to be heroines.

For so many women there must be one place where the dream of becoming a poet died. There, in one spot, she—whoever she was, whenever she lived—let go of that hope. One house, perhaps. One room. One set of walls, one aspect she can still see when she closes her eyes and thinks bitterly, or sadly, about what she lost.

I did not give it up. But if I had I would have thought back to that place. A small room with steps down, on which I sat night after night in what seemed to be an informal posture. With a dark red carpet and a comfortable armchair and small windows. But which, of course, had more of the domestic updated version of sitting at a great man's feet than I would have ever realized or ever admitted. Where I, the youngest daughter of a clever, wilful and in some ways Victorian man, waited in vain for the big wings of wax.

II

In later years, when I remembered my conversations with my father, I thought of them as providing a theatre: a contest between presence and resistance. I saw that small room as a site where the growth of poetic will was weighed in a delicate balance. Between power and submission. Between authority and independence.

When Adrienne Rich published "Split at the Root," her

beautiful essay on Jewishness and inheritance, I was moved and guided by her honesty. "My father was an amateur musician, read poetry, adored encyclopedic knowledge," she wrote there. "He prowled and pounced over my school papers, insisting I use 'grown-up sources'; he criticized my poems for faulty technique and gave me books on rhyme and metre and form. His investment in my intellect and talent was egotistical, tyrannical, opinionated, and terribly wearing. He taught me, nevertheless, to believe in hard work, to mistrust easy inspiration, to write and rewrite; to feel that I *was* a person of the book, even though a woman; to take ideas seriously. He made me feel at a very young age the power of language and that I could share in it."

The power of language. I had felt it in that room. I had also felt an oppression and loneliness which clung to those words. As time went on, I grew curious. Had the same thing happened to other women poets? If so, I wanted to know. I wanted to see those lives. To find a woman in a room, late at night, a few stars stuck to the window. To witness again late-night talk and unspoken resistance.

I thought back to those evenings, my chin in my hand, words failing me. Where had those failed words ended up? In images? In cadences? All I knew was I had resisted something. But what? Authority? Tradition? I knew that rejecting a body of wisdom could be seen as adolescent. But in memory, it felt like something more substantial: the fending off of the settled products of knowledge in favor of the small beginnings of self-knowledge.

In her book *Scaffolding* Jane Cooper weighs her own struggle to find an inward authority and wonders at her own hesitation. "Is this primarily a political story," she asks herself, "having to do with how hard it is for a woman to feel the freedom that would let her develop as a writer, even when she has it?"

The idea of a woman finding herself as a poet within an unlikely, stay-at-home resistance stayed with me. It had the feel of an intimate allegory. I even began to see my silences in those conversations as revealing. Not so much a chapter in father–daughter relations as the start of a connection between being and becoming a poet. The more I thought of it, the more it became an outline of inverse influence. A wilful detour from the usual narrative of poetic inheritance.

And yet poetic inheritance mattered. I knew it did. Poets manage their growth by opening their minds. They plunder personal circumstance or formal opportunity. "This then is a book and there are more of them!" said Emily Dickinson after one of her first reading adventures. I remembered the silvery, falling-apart pages of my first anthology of poems. The obsessive turning backwards and forwards, looking for old language and new instruction.

So here I was with something of a double vision again. With two maps. On the one hand, the realization that the poetic past is itself a necessary engine of authority. On the other, the knowledge that a poet's resistance to that authority can also be vital. What would I find if I joined those two ideas?

I found Elizabeth Barrett Browning. A troubling, compelling mix of independence and compliance. A poet linked to the tradition and yet in defiance of it. Above all, a writer and a woman that—using one or other map only—I might have overlooked. But now, holding firmly to both, someone I felt I could engage and understand.

She is not easy to understand. Time has not made her clearer. "Fate has not been kind to Mrs. Browning," wrote Virginia Woolf. "Nobody reads her, nobody discusses her, nobody troubles to put her in her place." But I read her. And I wanted to put her in her place. I will start therefore by trying to make a collage, rather than just a collection of facts. Which means beginning with her appearance, as the age did. In her own words, she was "five feet one high . . . eyes of various colors as the sun shines."

But the sun rarely shines in the posed and stiff portraits we have of her. She wears navy dark serge or wool dresses: hard to gather in the hand and yet beautifully stitched. The dress can stand in for all the reticences which are partly chosen in her life and partly habitual. The dress can be a sign of those mornings when visitors were not received. When she refused a friend's calling card. When she chose to lie in a room, the dark serge gathered around her.

But although the dress is a clue, it's not enough in itself. There must be other ways, to paraphrase Woolf, of putting her in her place. And so I add them in. To start with, a harsh backdrop of iron and mill sweat. And then the sound of trains and the sight of sailing ships. It may sound as if these things are irrelevant. But they are not. In this darkened room where the dress gathers around itself, to which the visitor rarely penetrates, there are shadows. The shadows are not just those of poetry. They are also those of empire.

Mill dust and the clang of iron. The making of ships' hulls. The forging of space in which cotton, and paper and steel can be produced. Those sounds fill a whole century. They are noise-makers in an era of change and expansion.

In the room of the so-called poetess these sounds matter. She cannot hear them, cannot identify them. But they were at her cradle. Empire has more to do with her seclusion than she will ever know. Empire, which has touched the merchant and the sailor and the politician, now touches the poet's life. Not just the life of the male poet, although it will do so in the cases of Tennyson and Arnold. But hers as well.

In fact, the poetess—and Elizabeth Barrett Browning almost inaugurated the category—lives in a world defined by empire. The trays which are taken to her room. The noiseless servants protecting her rest. The view from her window of acres which have never been redistributed. These are fractions of it. She herself is another fraction. The role of the poetess is itself a primary fiction of empire. It is a strange mixture of the demands of power and the unease of an age.

This, unfortunately, is where everyone starts to lose patience. I can't agree with Germaine Greer's witty and dismissive comment in *Slip-Shod Sibyls: Recognition, Rejection and the Woman Poet:* "The more women adored poetry the less they were able to write it . . . It is less crucial for women to work out how men did this to women than it is to assess the extent to which women did it to themselves."

But I recognize the challenge she is making, and it deserves an answer. Unfortunately, this phase of Elizabeth Barrett Browning's life does not provide it. She seems merely to have internalized and personalized these power relations. "I am of those weak women who reverence strong men," she wrote in a letter to a friend.

Elizabeth Barrett Browning's first years were spent in the English countryside. She was born in 1806. By her twenties, the intensity and claustrophobia of her life were established. And mostly by her relationship with her father, Edward Moulton Barrett. He was a saturnine man. He had owned estates in Jamaica. He had made and lost money.

He was also darkly possessive. A proprietorial ownership was directed at all his children. But Elizabeth especially. When he refers to her in a letter as "a beloved invalid," the words have an ominous tilt. She was certainly frail. That much is clear. What is not clear is why her frailty evolved from a circumstance into an identity. And then from an identity into a necessary condition. Nor is it clear why, when she fled his house at the age of forty—to marry Robert Browning—he never spoke to her again. "May your father indeed be able to love me a little," she wrote to Browning at that time, "for my father will never love me again."

In the anguish and enclosure of her relation with her father, Elizabeth Barrett Browning proves a point: all women poets have one thing in common. They are all daughters of fathers. Not simply daughters of a natural father, but also daughters within—and therefore sometimes entrapped by— the literature they seek to add to.

What does this mean to the woman who becomes a poet? It could mean, to begin with, an uncomfortable question. A question which must surely have occurred to Browning in the twilight of her room in Wimpole Street: is it possible that the ordinary fate of being a daughter is changed, even subverted, by the extraordinary act of writing a poem? And how is a woman poet to live and think while she steals that fire?

I wanted to imagine more than the personal circumstances around that question. Her solitude, her shrinking were not isolated events. In her time, poetry itself was retracting. A boisterous, robust craft had begun to inch off to the alcove and the ivory tower. An art which had been filled with vitality and ambition in the earlier part of the nineteenth century was starting to be thin-blooded and solitary. The old country of human accident and event was being abandoned. A new country was made called Imagination and poets were sent to live there.

In that sense, the woman who lived in this room—with her nervous avoidance and insistence on vocation—was a tenant of the sacred places in which the poem was now making its home. But she was only a tenant. Elizabeth Barrett Browning did not own in an inch of the land. She had been designated a poetess. Inevitably, she was both elevated and sidelined by the categorization.

And so her headaches and darkened rooms seem especially emblematic of the reduced status of the poet. But for all that, when I read her, I still wanted to imagine that space. I furnished it with images of the rooms I had seen in childhood. I filled it with the conversations I had once had. I imagined an endless dialogue with her saturnine father: complete with anxious-to-please words and ready affirmations of his authority.

I returned to the letters. Her fear and love are plain there, painfully bound together. When she eloped with Robert Browning, Edward Barrett broke with her. He disinherited each of his children who married. She never saw him again.

Her first letter to a friend after her marriage describes the strange atmosphere she had lived in for all her young womanhood. Suddenly, we are staring down into an underworld, the walls jeweled with her needs and nervousness, her sickness and his strength. "Never has he spoken a gentle word to me," she wrote, "or looked a kind look which has not made in me large results of gratitude, and throughout my illness the sound of his step on the stairs has had the power of quickening my pulse."

Elizabeth Barrett Browning, I am afraid, is merely a sidebar in this book. She deserves more space and a closer look. She is a figure of tense and fascinating contradictions. By allowing those contradictions to exist, neither banishing them with certainties nor shutting them down with conclusions, she began to exist for me too. She became too real to be disowned.

And the truth is I could have disowned her. Her submissiveness grated. Her rhetoric could seem forced. But for all that, she corrected and instructed my earliest reading. The Victorian ethos which produced the heroines and storms I once pored over produced her as well. But she was real. They were fantasy.

Where there is heroism to be found, it is in her odd generosities. If she never contested empire, she nevertheless advocated freedom for Italy. If she never disowned the ugly relation with her father, she spoke of him with such warmth and understanding at the end that it seems to heal the old colonial relation between them into a kind of equality.

There is real courage also in the slow unbinding of the pieties which defined her early life. Her gradual taking possession of language and poetry. Her acceptance of a new husband and another country. Not everyone acknowledged her struggle. Virginia Woolf remained acerbic: "We all know how Miss Barrett lay on her sofa; how she escaped from the dark house in Wimpole Street one September morning; how she met health and happiness, freedom, and Robert Browning in the church round the corner." It is plain that Elizabeth Barrett Browning did not meet Woolf's standard of proof.

But to me at least, she proves a different point: the need for two maps. With just one, this poet would disappear into stereotype. With just one, she would become a series of soundbites: less canny than the Victorians, less skeptical than the Romantics.

The second map would not work on its own either. It would make her a ghost in an age of modern women's poetry: a caricature of submission.

Put together however, they direct the reader to a fascinating writer. In the narrow compass of her life, Elizabeth Barrett Browning confronted large things. Whatever her lost conversations with her father contained, we can imagine them as true dramas of Victorian authority: framing an age and being framed by one. In her later work—in poems like "Mother and Poet"— she voiced a contest between the creative and the institutional. It is not hard to guess at the source. She represents alignments of identity and self-discovery that are well worth looking at. And yet the truth is, had I not used these two contradictory sets of directions to go back to her—seeking her out as a traditionalist while also recognizing her as radical and disruptive—I would have lost her.

BECOMING AN IRISH POET

When I was a student I could choose which way to go home. The front gate of Trinity brought me to College Green. The back gate to Nassau Street. On winter nights, I preferred the second way. There was less traffic. It took me down by Clare Street to Merrion Square. The streets would be quiet and empty then. The swan-necked streetlamps were on. The windows looked like stranded moonlit rectangles.

Merrion Square is one of the old treasures of Georgian Dublin. An ambiguous gift of colony. On the nights I walked down to it, it was eerie and silent. But a century earlier it would have been different. The whole neighbourhood was then the center of Dublin professional life. I could easily summon it as I stood there in the dark. Haloed gaslight. Fashionable carriages over the cobbles. The rush and noise of a ruling class.

In the nineteenth century, this was the hub of a garrison city. A place where doctors and lawyers plied a trade guaranteed by their fashionable clientele. The buildings are still lanky and imposing. The fanlights, then as now, spun off down the street, making a vista of semicircles. The topmost windows looked over chestnut trees. The demeanor of it all revealed a purpose. A deceptive grace closing its iron grip of class and dominion over an unreliable nation.

When I came to the edge of the square, I stopped. It was not a place I could or should have wanted to imagine. Far from it. My grandmother had died, a poor sea captain's wife, near there. She was just past thirty. She died in a fever ward, in the lying-in hospital at the end of the street. The generations of women from which she came—products of Boyne Valley townlands and small parishes—were more likely to have entered those houses to clean them than to be entertained.

And yet, as often as not, I stayed looking up. A house stood on the corner. One façade pointed at the trees of the square. Another looked towards Trinity. It was a tall structure, not quite rid—even in the present moment—of the hubris of its origins. But I was not looking up because of a bygone era. I was there for a previous tenant.

Her name was Jane Francesca Elgee. She was the granddaughter of a Church of Ireland archbishop. She would become far better known as the mother of Oscar Wilde. But in the tumultuous decade of the 1840s she was a young woman, still unmarried. She was writing poetry and trying to have it published. She had not yet read her legendary son's comment: "others write the poetry that they dare not realise." For her, there would be no distance between poetry and self-realization.

A few snapshots from contemporary accounts tell the story. A glimpse of her in a drawing room here or there, being introduced or introducing herself, gives a sense of energy and self-importance. Here she is, handsome and insistent in a damp house in Leeson Street in 1846. She is telling the editor of *The Nation*—a fervent patriotic journal—that he must publish her poems.

Now she is in a Dublin courtroom in 1848. It is tense and crowded. This is the critical moment of another about-to-fail Irish rebellion. Jane Elgee is also at a turning point. She has become Speranza. Irish national poet and acting editor of *The Nation*. She sits in court, high-colored and excited.

The Nation is on trial because it has published an anonymous article called "*Jacta Alea Est*" (The Die Is Cast). It is a call to arms, an invitation to Irish insurrection. This is not something to be taken lightly. Charges of treason are in the air. Long prison terms and harsh transportations will soon follow show trials of the organizers of the 1848 rebellion. Under current British law the article in *The Nation* amounts to sedition.

It is hard to recover an age. Its clothes, its transport, its voices. They fade obstinately away. What is left are ghosts of the time: gestures, events. But some features remain the same. Ireland was then, as later, a land of rhetoric and ritual. In Paul Muldoon's lines from "The Old Country": *Every resort was a last resort / with a harbour that harboured an old grudge. / Every sale was a selling short.*

And here, in that climate of rhetoric, was a seditious article. And the young woman who wrote it. Because she was, of course, the author. At that moment, she must have felt she was, in Natasha Trethewey's vivid phrase from her poem "South," in a *state that made a crime / of me*. Speranza's pride and involvement must also have been obvious to everyone in that courtroom. Her face flushed. Her mouth working. But the danger is irrelevant to her. The adventure is uppermost. Finally, she stands up excitedly and claims authorship. She is ignored. Women are not plausibly considered for treason charges at that point in Irish history. But newspapers are: *The Nation* is shut down.

But before that the journal had published her poems. At first, under the male soubriquet of John Fanshawe. They had attracted immediate attention. "Our new contributor promises to rival Mangan in the melody and fullness of his phrases," says the editor. But the male pronoun does not fit Jane Francesca Elgee. She revealed her true identity and took the *nom de guerre* Speranza.

On those cold nights, on my way home, I almost always stopped at the house. The windows glowed out into an Ireland they could no longer beckon. I stood there, looking up. And so I stumbled unwittingly into one of the contradictions of being an Irish poet. To claim her poetic identity in Ireland in 1848 implied an unswerving devotion to nationhood by Speranza. Or at least the fiction of it. And in the making of that identity at that time, rhetoric was encouraged. Hyperbole was welcomed. The results are all too plain to see: Speranza's poems are not good. But no, that does not say it accurately. Speranza's poems are unconvincing.

And yet on those starry, frosty nights it was not her bad poetry I was thinking of. In fact the opposite. I was thinking about two lives—hers and mine. I had moved around as a child. I had lived in other cities. I had learned no dialect of belonging; I knew no idiom of attachment to place or its purpose. Now here was a woman who made no difference between words and purposes. "Once I had caught the national spirit," she wrote, "the literature of Irish songs and sufferings had an enthralling interest for me. Then it was that I discovered that I could write poetry."

How extraordinary that must have been, I said to myself, beating my hands together in the cold. To find a nation through your poems. To acquire your poems through a nation. Never to sense tension or division between them. To be guilty of sedition and yet certain of your own loyalties. To use your words to prove a place and know that proof would become an article of faith to others.

I had yet to understand the meaning of Mark Strand's powerful poem "The Idea" where the definition of origin is reached for and never fully grasped. It appears in his poem as a small, glowing house, stripped back to its Puritan worth and yet somehow inhospitable to visitors, even while being available to their understanding: *But that it was ours by not being ours / And should remain empty. That was the idea.*

On those cold nights, I still believed origin was simple and graspable. I was still convinced, after my own nomadic childhood, that coming to a faith and a cause and place which seemed to embody both was a rich source for a poet's identity. And so when I looked up at Speranza's window in the winter dark, it was not her failures I was imagining. It was her happiness.

It would take years to see my mistake. To understand the difference between the place a poet claims and the place a poem renders. Speranza stated and restated her love for Ireland—in verse, in polemic, in pamphleteering. And yet Ireland—even her high-caste Anglo-Irish version of it—disappeared into her poems. She contributed thirty-nine poems to *The Nation*. They are almost all bellicose and patriotic. Her stance is never less than public and theatrical:

> *What! are there no MEN in your Fatherland,*
> *To confront the tyrant's stormy glare,*
> *With a scorn as deep as the wrongs ye bear,*
> *With defiance as fierce as the oaths they sware*
> *With vengeance as wild as the cries of despair,*
> *That rise from your suffering Fatherland?*

"Lyric cancels out time," wrote Richard Howard in a review of James Wright. It can also cancel out reality. Even so, the extent to which a nation—its complicated history and local suffering—is erased by these lines is sobering. In the nineteenth century the intellectual drift of the poet was usually subsumed in the artifice of a poem. We deduce the aesthetic will of a Tennyson, of a Dickinson, not from what they wrote but from the way they wrote it.

But in Speranza's case the subject consumes everything. Language, tone, syntax all vanish into national sentiment. There is no voice. "We fall back on that term, voice, for all its insufficiencies," writes Louise Glück in *Proofs and Theories*. "It suggests, at least, the sound of an authentic being." But there is no sign of that in Speranza. And none of that reticence implied in the comment by the eminent Irish poet Maire MacEntee about her own work: "In most of my poetry you can see that drawing back, bringing the poem right up to the crisis and pulling back."

Speranza never pulls back. She yields at every turn to the demands of her subject. Finally, it becomes hard not to look at this word-bath of acid, in which details and subtleties are dissolved, without feeling something like horror. This is an Irish political poet—and there were few women in the category—whose poetry is a vanishing act. Nothing is left but the flourish, the quick sweep of the empty cabinet, the self-congratulatory length of the wand.

What happened to Speranza? She was, after all, an accomplished, courageous woman. She was the mother of Oscar Wilde. She lived through a turbulent part of Irish history and recorded it. Yet she emerges as a caricature.

The truth is, a national tradition is a wilful editor. I would later find it oppressive. But as a teenager I was both swept away and lost. I had come back to Ireland at fourteen years of age. I had studied Irish history. I had read speeches from the dock. I had tried to fuse the vivid past of my nation with the lost spaces of my childhood. I had learned the battles, the ballads, the defeats. It never occurred to me that eventually the power and insistence of a national tradition would offer me only a new way of not belonging.

"We are the products of editing rather than authorship," wrote George Wald. In that sense, Speranza was edited. Then again, the compression and reduction of her role, the limitations of her horizon, had been her choice. Through her, I first came to realize that a national agenda could be an editor. I was less aware it could also be a censor. And yet one of the most striking and historic poems in the Irish canon seemed to prove it. If not in the text then clearly in the transmission of the text.

II

The year was 1773.

Eibhlín Dubh Ní Chonaill and Art Ó Laoghaire were a young married couple. He had recently returned from a stint of service in the Hungarian Hussars. The image we have—more a snapshot than an image—is of a truculent Irish noble. We learn that he astonished the local people of Macroom by standing on a rolling barrel down the steep main street, with his sword—illegally according to the harsh British Penal Laws—still buckled on. "I foresaw," wrote one of his relatives, "that his violence and ungovernable temper would infallibly lead him into misfortune."

In that same year Art Ó Laoghaire , already declared an outlaw, was struck down as he galloped across a townland called

Carrigonirtane. He was twenty-eight years of age. A single musket shot killed him. His riderless horse trailed back without him. According to the poem she composed, Eibhlín Dubh Ní Chonaill caught the horse's bridle and rode to the place where her dead husband lay in the briars. Then, in the darkness, she dismounted and went to his lifeless body. She put her hand in his blood. She drank it. And all at once, one of the most celebrated and ambiguous moments of Irish literature is ushered in.

Eibhlín Dubh Ní Chonaill's poem, composed for her murdered husband, is an Irish language lament, a spoken and stylized echo of one of the oldest forms of elegy. And composed in one of the oldest languages. She might have echoed the words of Nuala Ní Dhomhnaill, written in her fine essay "Why I Choose to Write in Irish: The Corpse that Sits Up and Talks Back": "If there is a level to our being that for want of any other word I might call 'soul' (and I believe there is), then for some reason that I can never understand, the language that my soul speaks, and the place it comes from, is Irish."

The soul and the place in this poem are deeply rooted. They are the Ireland of the eighteenth century and the language which was its psyche. But since I did not speak Irish, having been away as a child, my first encounter with the poem was in English. There have been fine translations since, but I came across it in Frank O'Connor's incantatory version: I still remember the musical, furious voice he provided Eibhlín Dubh Ní Chonaill with, and the way he had her describe, in his version, that single extraordinary gesture of lifting her husband's blood to her mouth: *I did not wipe it off / I drank it from my palms.*

A young woman. An expressive grief. But now for the purposes of this argument—I need to swerve away from her. I need to eavesdrop on a lecture given almost two centuries later in

1966. It is Peter Levi's inaugural lecture as Professor of Poetry at Oxford. In the course of it, he describes *The Lament for Art O'Leary* as "the greatest poem written in these islands in the whole eighteenth century." A true accolade. And yet the statement, for all the power of its tribute, serves to erase the poem's identity. *The Lament for Art O'Leary* was not written. It was composed. The difference is crucial.

How did this happen? I suspect the answer is simple: Peter Levi modeled the poem on examples of elegy he knew and understood. The real question his error poses is about which view of authorship—or which combination of views—allows us to return to a text and address the reality of the poem and its maker. Which one will allow us to discover the true identity of Eibhlín Dubh Ní Chonaill: this young woman not yet thirty, her hand dipped in her husband's blood, her lips composing an elegy that reaches far back into oral literature?

I'm able to attempt the question here because of the fine work of an Irish scholar and writer, Angela Bourke. The title of the poem in Irish is *Caoineadh Airt Uí Laoghaire*. The name suggests the origin. The poem is a keen—a subtle re-arrangement of the melodies and repetitions of the Irish *caoineadh*, or keen; an art of the dispossessed.

I never heard the keen. It was reduced to a legend when I was young; another emblem of an Ireland I knew I could never catch up with, and that had almost disappeared. But my father had seen and heard it. As a young man in Galway he watched the emigrant boat get ready to leave for England. A group of old women—these were the keeners—gathered on the pier. As the boat drew out the old women put their shawls over their heads and began the keen. My father remembered the sound as eerie and terrible.

Our first glimpse of Eibhlín Dubh Ní Chonaill is of a new woman using an old art. "We see a chasm opening at her feet," Angela Bourke writes, "a class divide which grew wider through the nineteenth century . . . On the one side of that divide stand orality, the Irish language and poverty; on the other are literacy, English and all the trappings of patriarchal and colonialist modernity. Eibhlín Dubh Ní Chonaill belonged to the class that became modern."

I was fascinated that this almost-modern woman, in her moment of loss, reached for an age-old and communal art form. A poem which is part a fresh spoken grief and part an age-old formula. An elegy poised between worlds. A subtle and powerful negotiation with past laments. If we could only understand it, we might get a deeper insight into poems as far apart as the *Iliad* and *Gawain and the Green Knight*.

But the opposite could also happen. If we misread this poem, then we lose our one and only chance as readers to stand beside Eibhlín Dubh Ní Chonaill. And if we don't take up position there, we lose that precious opportunity to look into the age-old relation between the formulaic part of an art form, and the extempore parts made up by its speaker.

Which is precisely what happened. Throughout the nineteenth century, in the light of new ideas of authorship, Eibhlín Dubh Ní Chonaill begins to disappear. *The Lament for Art O'Leary*, as it came to be known, is pushed, and turned, and remade in the shape of other conventions. Its origins are obscured by contemporary interpretations, most of them British or Anglo-Irish. It is romanticized, glamourized, pulled out of shape. Its author, an Irish woman caught in a moment of historical change, is replaced by a simplified nineteenth-century heroine: a stereotype of Lady Morgan's Wild Irish Girl. Gradually the real woman, the flesh-and-blood aunt of Daniel O'Connell, the young and desperate widow in her late twenties who knew the old arts and availed of them in her grief, vanishes. How did this happen? Again, Angela Bourke provides the explanation: "Nationalist scholars and the literati of the Irish revival were at pains to counter [colonialist] propaganda [. . .] That *The Lament for Art O'Leary* could be read as a text of marital devotion among noble and high-minded Irish people was enough to guarantee it a place in the canon of Irish literature then being formed."

And so, piece by piece, a young woman disappears. A vital clue to our past and our poetry fades out. Like a figure cut out of a photograph, she becomes a missing space, replaced by more comfortable images. Her rich and tense relation with the keen-makers goes. Her historical balancing act goes. Above all, what her art can tell us about the deep connections between a communal archive and a single art—all that goes too.

And so for want of a wider view of authorship, a subtle Irish artist is transfigured into a one-dimensional Victorian heroine. The overwriting of her achievement by ambitious Irish and British canon-makers shows us something we need to keep in mind: that received ideas of authorship can suppress actual ones.

III

One question remained. If a national tradition could edit one woman poet and censor another, how could I myself survive it? I was eighteen when I stood looking up at Speranza's window. My laying out and unweaving of these national threads would come quickly over the next few years. My sense of a national tradition that needed to be challenged followed only years later.

And yet I have deliberately left this account of an earlier moment. Of a nanosecond of influence and alignment. Of an error of empathy, if you will. The fact is, I outgrew the empathy. But I remembered for a long time the yearning folded into it. Far from wanting to forget it entirely, I have written this to try to evoke it.

Becoming a poet in the shadow and light of a powerful nationhood is not simple. I imagine a young poet in some other country, standing even now under another window. I imagine them transposing themselves, as I did, into wayward ideas of passion and conviction. It may be that they also will come to believe that challenging an inherited tradition—extricating a poetic identity from parts of it—is an essential part of growth.

And yet my first feelings, as I've described them here, were far more wistful. Withdrawing from those feelings marked the beginning of a series of questions. And yet I could never have framed the questions if I had not known the feelings. I have described the second. I should now try to be precise about the first:

Two words haunted Irish poetry when I was young. Those two pivotal words for an Irish poet—and for many other poets— were *I* and *we*. I have written elsewhere of the broad tensions between these two words, and their meaning for poets in many contexts. But in the Irish context there were specific tensions. These were the words which had been tested by violence and history. These were the poetic pronouns which had followed a century and a country through its ordeals and violations. These were the words which marked new developments in both Irish poem and Irish poet. In the process they, and their relationship to one another, had been profoundly altered.

The word which showed most signs of distress was not the

I. This was the controversial pronoun, certainly. It was often attacked as denoting autobiography and self-indulgence. It was a target, even in the self-reflexive Ireland of my time. But there remained something solid about it. It had come through the fire. It sheltered in the poem, a vocal and eloquent witness, well aware of its part in a turbulent Irish history: "I only am escaped alone to tell thee," it seemed to say, like the breathless messenger in the Book of Job.

Not so the *we*. A sub-plot in the poetic history of the late nineteenth and twentieth centuries is surely the story of this pronoun's disintegration. Not just in Ireland, either. In an introduction to an anthology of American Civil War poetry, J. D. McClatchy writes eloquently of the way nineteenth-century poetry still had the power "to turn art's moral light on public matters and private deeds." The words look magical, even now. And yet, with time and uncertainty, whole worlds on which that *we* had once depended—from which it spoke in the poem—had vanished. Entire constituencies were gone. Among them Speranza's Ireland, a nation-state rallied by rhetoric: a community bound to it, and bandaged by it.

But the *I* still existed. It had work to do. It remained at the heart of the enterprise. Only the *we* had faltered. Its hinterland was gone. In Ireland it had enclosed a world of undefeated passion. And now the first-person plural had been swept away with the certainties it sheltered. And because the *I* could no longer depend on that *we*—on its urgent and passionate community—the first-person singular became ever more isolated and contested.

When I stood under the window in Merrion Square I knew nothing of this. Poetry was still an ideal to me: a hoped-for symbiosis of old worlds and new possibilities. The sunderings, the wrenchings of a modern era were not visible. And because I did not know them, for a brief moment I was not bound by them. When I looked up at the lighted rectangle I became a self-styled alchemist on a winter night. In my wistfulness for the old purposes of the public poem, I instinctively acted to hold on to my dream: I reinvented that *I* and joined it to the old *we* of a nationalist Ireland which had ceased to exist. I made a brief, forced reunion of something that had long ago been broken apart.

But there was more to it: there was an inescapable irony. I could stand there, hoping to be an Irish poet, precisely because that *we* had faltered. I, who could never have belonged to Speranza's collective national aesthetic, was one of the poets who most benefited in my time by the new and private spaces of the modern Irish lyric. In the disintegration of the Irish public poem the future of poets like myself was made possible. And yet I— created by that very opportunity—stood there on a winter night regretting it.

It was an error. And yet I wouldn't be without that error. For that very reason, it seems right to record it here: that moment when I first realized a cause and its language could be inseparable. When I tried to go back to a place where poetry followed the drum and had the power to elevate even the casual participant into a hero. If it is a seduction, it is also a source of our self-knowledge—even if it sprang from self-deception. Whether we like it or not, it is part of the history of poetry; part of the biography of the poet. Standing where I did, I stood in the old light of epic and praise-song: places where the art attended to the tribe.

It would take time for me to see the damage these intertwinings can cause. The simplification of Eibhlín Dubh Ní Chonaill's legacy is just one example. The way in which a complex achievement was stripped to suit a national purpose is sobering. The way in which a poem was censored in order to make the poet a more reassuring figure is a cautionary tale. In the end, I would find that a national tradition seeks to modify the poet even more than the poem.

And yet ironically it was not the poem I first envied but the poet. It was Speranza. It was that edited version of the public stance which was all the national tradition allowed her; and all she wanted. The role she accepted so readily was made possible by the conjunction between a desperate nationhood and an avid audience.

To my teenage mind, Speranza's identity seemed painlessly constructed. In touch with an audience and in step with history. It was an identity that seemed to reach back to a place where the event and the account of the event were woven from the same cloth. The poet she became knew everything about communality, and nothing at all of the indecision and isolation of a later version of herself. I should know. In many ways, I was that later version. From that perspective, I was right to envy Speranza. And wise to let that envy last for only a short time.

READING AS INTIMIDATION

O ur first child was born in winter. The prospect brought us joy and confusion. Our domestic arrangements were casual. Now we needed to reorder them. We planned a simple nursery in an upstairs room. We moved out a guest bed and put in a crib. We painted the walls a flat ivory color. A friend helped us make a dressing table from chipboard with a fabric curtain.

The room was small and cold. It faced north. At dawn the window was slow to let in light. The shelves of the dressing table stood opposite the window and were plainly useful. The fabric of the curtaining was something more. It seemed to promise something far beyond its stopgap role. It showed a woodland with trees and distances. It gazed into the interior as if the soul of some unexpected pastoral had slipped into plainspoken cotton. A few more shelves near the window held books and an ornament or two. Another opposite the door supported an oddly shaped porcelain cat, its skin crazed with blue flowers.

A room like this lasts a short time. My daughter slept away most of her first hard winter. I rose in the dark and warmed a bottle while the garden was gripped by frost. If I thought those magical standstill hours would continue indefinitely, I was wrong. The season relented. Snowdrops appeared under my neighbour's tree. Then yellow crocuses. Then it was spring. The first days of her life were over.

I was prepared for the beauty and intensity of a small child. I became used to the shelter and scale of the room. But I was unprepared for the way it all fused into a drama of arrival and encounter: a continuous daily adventure of sights and insights. I was instructed by them almost without knowing it. I came to see how well the earth and its objects used one another. The light of the morning. The child's first cry. The last star. The hum of the milkman's cart. They played off each other as sounds and sources all day. They stayed in my mind and marked themselves in my memory. And in the midst of all, the new life which made it visible.

But I learned something else as well: a far less radiant subset of knowledge. I found that even in the midst of this adventure and renewal, which had swept away so many human doubts, I was left with my artistic ones. Radical doubts I did not want to have. There in a room at the center of my life they crept in and out—a sort of underhand questioning. The objects on the shelves glowed by lamplight and clarified at dawn. The shape of a milk bottle defined a curve of space. Moonlight stitched itself into the threads of the curtain. Daylight pushed the walls back. And yet the doubts remained.

They were hard to formulate; they were also constant. For all the instruction of that room—its objects and its new life—I was not sure where or whether they belonged in any poem I might write. I had learned this room. But there were other, older learning processes which seemed in conflict with this new knowledge. All that winter these odd thoughts created a fraction of dissonance. A tiny edge of sorrow came to surround them. What use was an expressive medium if it couldn't shelter an expressive life? What purpose was there in giving voice to an old art if it silenced a new experience?

Under those doubts were other ones. A darker version, in fact. I found that without knowing it I had learned to write poetry, at least in part, by subscribing to a hierarchy of poetic subjects. As though I'd signed on to the repertory choices of a summer theatre company by conceding to a seasonal imperative. For instance, I understood from the first that a poem had permanent, historic residents. The moon, the horizon, shifts of weather and the color of a field—all signaling an inner life as well as an outer circumstance—belonged in a poem. They could enter it as easily as that pastoral slipped into cotton. As subject matter, their welcome had been arranged by centuries of poetry; by custom, by tradition.

Not so this room. However radiant it seemed to me, it was just a room. There were hundreds, thousands of them marching out into the Irish night, lighting up their yellow windows in the dusk of the Dublin suburbs. The growth of population, the building of estates suggested a social shift, not a poetic change. In this new life I had acquired a subject. But no ready-made importance had been ascribed to it. I had to do that for myself. And yet how could I take this private experience and make it as familiar a poetic subject as a planet or landscape? I could see I would have to do more than write this subject; I would have to authorize it. And here, to my surprise, I faltered.

It was a split-second faltering. A moment of hesitation. Nothing more. But later that moment troubled me. Brief as it was, it remained emblematic. I would think back to it. I would remember it as a painful contradiction—that I doubted the importance of this room as a poetic subject at the very moment I was most convinced of its imaginative power. How could I believe that what was compelling outside the poem might not be equally so inside it?

But I had. And I did. Later, I would wonder how it had happened. I would always come to the same question: what part of the process of becoming a poet had led me to that moment of hesitation? What flaw in my development caused that fissure between feeling and expression?

II

The answer, I knew, had to be more than autobiographical. It needed to be formal as well. I would have to begin there. I was a lyric poet. I thought of myself as one. The description was inexact and I knew there was no precise history for the term. Yet when I thought about it, trusting my identity to that imprecise term, I remembered an incident which made it clearer.

One summer morning, I flew to Manchester to record poems for the BBC. It was a short flight out of Dublin. The program itself was not long. And then I was left with one of those cumbersome units of time: too short to do anything substantive with, too long to spend all of it at the airport waiting for a flight back to Dublin. I went to an art museum. I spent an unsatisfactory hour or so, looking from Pre-Raphaelite paintings to my watch, and back again. Then I went to the museum bookshop, bought one or two catalogues and a pamphlet. And went to the airport early, after all.

Airports are not easy places to inhabit. There is only so much steel, so many rotating wheels and passing luggage carts you can ponder. A coffee; a sandwich wrapped in plastic and seemingly composed of it; another coffee. And then you are ready for something more.

So I reached down and took out a pamphlet from my bag. I hardly knew why I'd chosen it. I must have thought it fitted the bill. Its subject was musical boxes at the Victoria and Albert Museum in London, and it was a bright publication. Glossy, distracting, garrulous. Here were the cylinder musical boxes of the wealthy, fashioned out of pearwood and cast steel with glass lids. Here was a description of a thirteenth-century water clock, a marvel of falcons and chimes and hydraulically operated musicians. And here, wonder of wonders, was the eighteenth-century music box of the Sultan of Mysore.

Then I found something else. In black and white, modestly photographed and with a brief note, was the serinette. Even in monochrome, it was an elaborate affair. A beechwood box, veneered with satinwood, standing on ormolu feet and inlaid with a blonde scroll of songbirds and branches. "Small domestic barrel organs known as serinettes," said the note, "were made in France during the eighteenth century for the express purpose of teaching caged birds to sing."

For a moment I pictured myself in an eighteenth-century drawing room. I imagined the whirl of plaster roses and ceiling cherubs. I could see the fireplace, intricately chiselled out of marble. Everything inlaid, decorated, improved upon. The gate legs of the dining table would be the only reminder of the broad-leaved trees and the forest which were once the natural element of this caged bird in the corner, who now had to put up with a dome of stale air and brass bars. That and the lid of the satinwood box. Only this, opened now and again—with artificial woodland notes pouring into the room—provided a heart-breaking reminder of freedom.

I will not be oblique about the connection. The small grotesque image of that box lets me argue that the lyric impulse has something in common with the serinette: that it reaches out to a perceptive area which has fallen silent. For the sake of this argument, let me call perception the bird and time the cage. But not just any kind of time or any kind of perception. It must have a real sense of healed possibility, enclosed and entrapped. Time, after all, is a linear configuration. It proceeds from birth to death, or appears to. It encloses us in the inevitability and claustrophobias of mortality. No wonder then that a particular perceptive area may fall mute within it. The bird does not sing because it cannot fly.

Was it possible that this is what had happened? That I had entered that small room not just as a new mother, but also as a lyric poet? That the lyric form had signaled to a silence, promising all the time to teach it to speak or sing? And yet had failed to do so. I was reluctant to think so. That same form had brought me into my own life. It had been a steadfast companion. But if its failure was not the cause of my hesitation, what was?

III

Where does it start, the wish to be a poet?

For me it began in teenage years. I went to boarding school in Dublin. The building was perched over the Irish Sea. I could see Howth on a sunny day. At night the moon blinded the dormitory windows with water light.

The surroundings were gracious. But the view of a young woman's future—widespread at that time in Ireland—was not. There was a rigid conservatism about it. Not so much in its emphasis on marriage as in its angers about conformity. There was a fixed circle of suggestions. An unspoken insistence on prescribing limits to the body and mind.

I had no words for it. Definitions were not available. It was an atmosphere, nothing more, and hard to articulate. And yet I'm sure my first reading of poetry took place in its shadow. I may not have been able to name those restrictions. But I felt them: I even recognized them as a kind of repression. I also realized, in some unspeaking way, that I could not yet rescue my body. I was years away from that. But I could rescue my mind. I set out to do so.

And so I established a pattern of what I will call here reading as intimidation. I read poems then as I never did again: as a method of self-protection. I read them to persuade myself of something the climate seemed about to deny me. There was nothing wrong with the poems. Some of them, I could see, had reach, beauty, relevance. But I chose them for the wrong reasons. With the result they had the wrong effect: I had no idea that by taking poems out of context, using them as armor against invidious assumptions, I might intimidate myself out of a sense of my own reality.

I see myself again at fourteen years of age. I am staring at the pages of an anthology. The book is worn. The pages are thin and missal-fine. They slip and rustle as I turn them. There is even an old-fashioned silky ribbon to mark the pages. The sleeves of my school cardigan are pushed up. My index finger has inkwell stains on it. Out beyond the window the Irish Sea is turning to a metallic color at dusk. The land mass is disappearing. The visible signs of a country are turning to shadows. It doesn't matter. They hardly existed for me even when visible. It will be years before I allow those shapes beyond the page to enter and inform the poem on it.

And here I am struggling with a single poem. The poet is English. He is long dead, much admired—an icon of the English canon. All prescriptions for a profound disconnect. I am Irish, at the painful end of puberty, unable to read my own body or know my own nation. And here is John Dryden, able to decipher everything, or so it seems. The poem is "A Song for St Cecilia's Day."

> From harmony, from heavenly harmony,
>   This universal frame began:
>   When Nature underneath a heap
>   Of jarring atoms lay,
>   And could not heave her head,
>   The tuneful voice was heard from high,
>   "Arise, ye more than dead!"
>   Then cold, and hot, and moist, and dry,
>   In order to their stations leap,
>   And Music's power obey.

As I read, I don't understand why a man whose life is touched by a civil war would write this slide of rhymes and sounds. Nevertheless, I apply myself to the poem, to its abstract and seemingly cold celebration of music. To its cosmology, which I can't understand, and its religion, which was, at the very moment of its composition, wreaking havoc on my own country.

Ironically, this will all change. Later in life I will come to admire the poem. I will relish Dryden's use of Pythagorean theory to dazzle Platonic thought. Written by this eldest of fourteen children, now fifty-six years of age, who has seen his country broken by war, what I once mistook for coldness I will come to see as a heart-wrenching yearning for order. But I don't see that. I am fourteen years of age, determined to master what small worlds of meaning I can. And so I am reading the poem to gain its power and protection. By doing so, I am missing its point.

And so here it is. An act of reading that becomes a method of intimidation. An act self-selected because I am already intimidated. These are not easy moments to explain. They are fragmentary, lost in a mercurial past and a still more mercurial thought process.

Nevertheless I can find my way back to some of it, even now. The fact is, I am turning in circles in those years. I am trying to break out by disputing a prediction. In my reading, I go instinctively to big subjects that take me away from small concerns. In a culture which warns that the treasures and complications of the mind might be beyond the reach of a young woman, I instinctively look for texts that seem to promise their availability. And I select difficult poems because I feel clever and safe reading them.

This is not the usual account of a poet's reading. It is more usual to provide a narrative of grace: of encountering language and form for the first time. Which did happen; but later. Nevertheless, this earlier, darker version, I am convinced, is less uncommon than it looks. "Reading is a very complex art," wrote Virginia Woolf. Of one thing I am sure: there must have been other young women who read for their own protection. Who were agents of their own intimidation. Who chose poems, as I did, not because they brought them nearer to the life of feeling but because they removed them safely from it. Who felt that the power and distance of language would protect them from the limitations made ready for them.

None of it lasted. Soon enough I set aside such reading and took up the poems of Yeats. But I have remembered my first choices here, and my reasons for them. Later I would trace these strange, small aberrations stubbornly to their source. I would try to align them with ideas and forms. I would go back to the same question. Where did the lyric form come in? Had it helped or hindered? After all, as I remembered it, I had stood in that room alone with my child, at a moment of intense personal history. Surely the history of the lyric should have coincided with it.

IV

And the lyric has a considerable history. It has proved itself to be endlessly adaptable to new environments and changing circumstances. It seems fair to ask, why didn't it adapt to mine, at once and unquestioningly?

The answer is complex; the question itself may be off kilter. We are looking at a form which has fitted itself, on different occasions, to the lyre, to the lute, to the harp. To the small kingdom and the lost tribe. Anyone could find it, if they searched, on the pyramid texts in Egypt. Under the battlements in Picardy. On the back roads of Ireland in a defeated language. It doesn't always occur in the same shape, and rarely in the same words. But it is recognizably the same creature we glimpse. As if we could deduce a mythical animal by its footprint in the snow of high places.

The Irish, like other European nations, have marched and wept and kept their faith and their counsel to the sound and stress of lyrics. William Yeats even floated the idea that the Irish sensibility was better suited to the lyric than the English one. In "A General Introduction for My Work" he wrote about his own early decision to write short poems: he spoke of the Irish preference for "a swift current."

That's not to say the lyric hasn't had its detractors. "Nothing is capable of being well set to music that is not nonsense," wrote the critic Joseph Addison. And today, when the lyric is no longer set to music, his skepticism is still around. Critics have needed little encouragement—especially if, like Addison, they suffer from a surfeit of reason—to take a reductive view of it. To regard it as a pretty and prettified segment of poetic expression. A fossil of times and occasions when the poem was the expressive equivalent of the sweetmeat.

And yet, as a form, its roots go far deeper than fashion or folly. The *Princeton Encyclopedia of Poetry and Poetics* awarded it the most compelling history of all: "At that remote point in time when syllables ceased to be nonsense and became syntactically and connotatively meaningful the first lyric was composed."

There could hardly be a more profound destiny for a form than this: to be a document of the line between language and its negation; to be a venerable witness. It gives the lyric the dignity of having been one of the first theatres of meaning. When a formation is so powerful, so deep in time and history, it is not likely to be erased later. The first lyrics articulated, among other things, the human need for self-expression under the stress of a struggle for existence. We have no exact record of that need. Whatever record there might be is inscribed, not in a book or a chronicle, but in that part of our psyches which corresponds to the listening memory of the caged linnet.

And so, in the end, I stopped suspecting the lyric. It had

not failed me. It was not the form which was responsible for my silence. In fact the opposite. In hunting down reasons for that moment of hesitation, I came to believe something quite different. Gradually, I became sure that a rogue history of ideas—the very same which shaped my early reading—had stood between me and the poem I wanted to write. But what was it?

V

Every poet has an anti-history. A place where some turn was taken that seemed to put their own future in doubt. I had my anti-history. I found it early and kept it late. For me it was that insistence on elevated subject matter described, among others, by Edmund Burke: "Vast objects occasion vast Sensations," he wrote, "and vast Sensations give the Mind a higher Idea of her own powers." It was, in other words, the arc of the sublime—its argument and emphasis—woven in and through all kinds of poems and histories of poems. From the start I resisted it. I had reasons for doing so.

To start with, I was Irish. I was a woman. Once I left school and began to write, I was a poet whose life was lived among the objects of an ordinary existence. It was a safer life than most; and similar to many of the lives lived around me. I wrote my poems upstairs in a room that looked out to a garden. My notebook stayed on a table during the day while I saw to small children. At night with the closing in of the dark, I could go back to writing. It seemed unrestricted and free.

But when I took up a pen, or faced the blank page of my notebook, I understood certain things: I was free to live my life. Compared with many other women, in far more limiting circumstances, I was fortunate. And yet one question kept coming back. I was free to live my life, but was I free to imagine it? Did the poems I had read, or the poetic tradition I had inherited, encourage me to do that? Did the history of these ideas suggest I could live in an eye-level relation to the objects I saw every day around me? Or did something whisper when I took up my pen—*What are you writing? Is it important enough?* I felt a need to critique my doubts. The critique of my doubts inevitably ended in criticism of the sublime. But what did that mean?

It certainly did not mean poring over Longinus or Edmund Burke. If anything, I read them in a glancing way. Some sentences and fragments escaped me; some stayed with me. "For, as if instinctively, our soul is uplifted by the true sublime; it takes a proud flight," wrote Longinus. And yet it was not those words which defined the hollowness of the sublime for me. Nor John Dennis, nor the Earl of Shaftesbury nor Addison.

If it was not those writers and writing I resisted, what was it? The answer was imprecise at one level, but painfully clear to me on another. It was an ethos more than an argument. A slow bending of space. A curving of the scale and size of the poet. It was a painting here, an essay there, a collection of symbols and a growing assent to them. It was a series of brushstrokes, putting the human traveller as small as could be on the ridge of the hill and making the waterfall into an image as big as a dinosaur. It was a series of propositions that seemed to gather force, like an opposing headwind, throughout the nineteenth century. It was not just Kant's "supersensible state" and Hegel's "sublated" means. It was a magic show willingly put on by painters, poets, musicians which made man small and the world large.

The magic show was deceptive; the magicians were hidden. When you looked more closely, a sort of sleight of hand was happening. In reality, the sublime was not an idea that cut the poet down to size. In fact the opposite. It was an idea *made* by the poet. And so, throughout the show, the poet was behind the curtain, defining the very grandeur he appeared to be awed by, and in the process becoming a steward of it. And so a new kind of poet emerged: a master of secrets, a controller of meaning. And, of course, a stake-holder in perpetuating that grandeur.

VI

And so I arrived at my answer. It was not the lyric form that failed me. It was something else: a current of ideas and insistences on which the lyric poem was buoyant, in which it had never capsized. And yet that stream of ideas—I have called it the sublime here—had been powerful enough to intimidate me as a teenager, standing beside me as a ghost of meaning, warning and promising about the significance of inherited knowledge and the fearful diminishment of my own reading and writing if I did not seek its sanction. And it was powerful enough to make me hesitate for that fraction of time when I entered the room in which my first child slept.

The attempt to track back from that small hesitation brought me some questions and a few answers. I have tried to include them here. Writing about these remembered states is elusive. They are so quickly over, so poorly defined that they become like an old photograph. We look at it closely. We're nearly sure that was the tree we saw from the window. We almost believe that was the neighbour who came in to borrow the shears. But the moment is gone.

And yet it all connects up. Recalling my forced connection

with poetry at the age of fourteen made me remember a skepticism about the sublime which came later. Locating myself, even at a young age, in a place where great knowledge made a personal world seem small might look like a common human circumstance. And a world away from the glorious antechamber of the sublime—so argued about, so adhered to from Burke to Poe. But there was a link. I was sure of it.

Coming forward from that time to the most personal moment of a personal world—the existence of a new child—I see again a slim and unproveable connection. Nothing was more important to me than this new life. Yet it had a human scale. It was a small event, however momentous to me. I knew those events registered in the ideology of the sublime as simply ones to be warned against. Unfortunately the girl I was, reading Dryden in a school library, was willing to be warned. The woman I became, entering my child's room, might hesitate for a moment, remembering that warning. But not for long.

When I was young, I thought of aesthetics as an abstract code. I learned later it was a human one. I learned it belongs everywhere, and to no one person. Which means it can be a common possession. Standing in a room in the winter half-light before the wonder of a new child is aesthetics. Hesitating at the meaning of subject matter as fit for poetry is aesthetics. Searching back to the prompts and resistances involved in becoming a poet— the reading, the writing—is also aesthetics. I came to believe there is no meaning to an art form with its grand designs unless it allows the humane to shape the invented, the way gravity is said to bend starlight.

DOMESTIC VIOLENCE

During the 1970s I lived in a suburb south of Dublin. The windows of our house looked to the hills. We were in an incline, in the shelter of a small neighbourhood. Travellers from all over Ireland had once stopped there to take a well-advertised goat's milk cure.

To the east was the coast. If we pointed the car in that direction we could drive onto the crackling surface of Sandymount Strand. There Stephen Dedalus walks and broods at the start of *Ulysses*; there he says, "History is a nightmare from which I am trying to awake." To the south were the roads which wandered to the interior—Meath, Waterford, Kilkenny. To the north were other roads. They travelled ninety miles, all the way to Belfast. The physical journey was short; the imaginative one was infinite.

Our house was part of the new expansion of the city. All by themselves, these suburbs signaled a new Ireland. The previous decades had been hard-pressed and introverted. Now here at last was the outward-looking place which had been promised: American books and French wines. Cars, fragrances. They crept to the edge of the old nation. They beckoned and enticed.

We were southerners, citizens of the Republic. Belfast was a city over which the Union Jack still flew. In the final year of the sixties, a rift between the Northern Irish communities became an abyss. With every month, the north spiraled deeper into violence. The bombings, sniper fire and internments were confined, with few exceptions, to the counties at the top of the island. But the other violence—cultural, political—spilled out and began to stain the whole country.

A place, a moment. It is the late 1970s. I am up at 7 A.M. I have small children. The morning is chilly. I am in the kitchen, looking out my window at a suburban back garden. For the first five minutes, as I turn on the kettle, watch it steam, pour coffee, I can stare at it uninterrupted.

Then I turn on the radio. Guns and armaments fill the kitchen. Hoods, handcuffs, ArmaLites—the paraphernalia of urban struggle slides easily in and out of the newsreader's voice. A blackbird flickers down into the grass. I can see neighbours' rooftops. The voice continues. An odd thought forms in my mind, painful and inexact. I look around the kitchen, lost in contradictions. Then I realize what it is. My coffee is the instant variety, closed in a glass jar made in Huddersfield. My marmalade comes from London. My kettle from Holland. My knife from Germany. My radio from Japan. Only the violence, it seems—only that—is truly Irish.

And yet this piece is not about war or conflict. It is about a poem. I want to attempt a small biography of a genre. I want to revisit, in the later part of my writing life, what bewildered me in an earlier one. I want to uncover a labyrinth of references whose turns and twists lead not to Irish history, but to my own. I want to explore a counter-history. In other words, the so-called domestic poem.

This poem touched the place I lived and was touched by it. I want to argue here for its scope and reach; for its powerful roots in the unseen world it is accused of denying. I want to map the revealing and interesting resistances to it, which are clues to a course poetry set for itself in modern times.

As someone drawn to the domestic poem, I only slowly became aware of the shadow hanging over it. Gradually I realized it had been designated a lesser genre; almost a sub-genre. In fact, in the nineteenth century the domestic poem was a code for something a poetess was likely to write. A short, soft lyric of unearned sentiment. The four-stress, eight-beat line of an obedient music. Those suspicions lingered well into the twentieth century. "The temptation to decorate is great where the theme may be of the slightest," wrote Virginia Woolf.

Worse still, the domestic poem was connected with corrupt feeling as well as with women poets. Neither association was a benefit. "In the nineteenth century," writes Annie Finch, "the term 'poetess' was typically a conventional compliment to, or acknowledgment of, any female poet's femininity. During the twentieth century it became more often a label of contempt and condescension."

And there is more. This is, after all, a personal piece. I was an Irish woman poet in a bardic culture. The political poem and the public one had been twined together in Ireland since the nineteenth century. There was little dialogue with the domestic. My growing belief—that there was a distance between history and the past in Ireland—was strengthened by that disconnect. History was the official version; the past was an archive of silences.

Already I was interested in a sort of poem which did not simply look towards a public world, even as compelling a one as the Irish version. The surface of a drinking glass, the shadow of a tree beside a suburban drive—there seemed to be no vocabulary for these things. In contrast, there was an established lexicon for the public poem. The problem was arranging their co-existence.

But it was more than that. The domestic poem, traditionally barred from the public world, confined to a set script, had been drained of meaning. Yet the meanings were there for the taking. The elements of that poem—intimate, uneasy, charged with a relation which is continuous and unpredictable between bodies and the spaces they inhabit—seemed perfectly set up to register an unwritten past. It was an opportunity for Irish poetry. And yet there was no welcome for it anywhere that I could see.

The violence in the North began in the year of our marriage. 1969. The television showed marches, meetings. Then cracked heads. Then gunfire. Then we went to live in the suburb. It was a ragged pattern in my mind. We moved into our new house, the radio always on, the television telling us that nothing would be the same again.

We were young, in our twenties. We were provincials of a country on the edge of violent change. We couldn't see it; we saw our lives, only that. The country was sundered; we were newly joined. At night, in our new house, we sat and listened. We heard the eerie quiet. The thrashing of the chestnuts and sycamores across the road in the wind from the foothills. We heard whispers of our future: cars pulling up and backing out of drives. A last call for a child to come indoors.

And we quarrelled. It is what young, newly married people do. We loved each other and we quarrelled. And quarrelled. Now, after more than thirty-five years of a close marriage, I try to remember. What was it all about? Our voices—or was it just my voice—high and aggrieved; reproaching, accusing. What was I saying? What was I asking? I forget the details. It was the music of our new life. Or part of it.

BUT I REMEMBERED the fact of it. Increasingly, I was haunted by it. Our children were born. The struggle of wills died. But the memory of that young couple in their new house remained. Their raised voices filling the spaces. The back-echo of new rooms. As time went on, memory changed them. They were no longer an isolated pair in a remote suburb. My mind gilded them with significance. I saw them there, young and infuriated. Above all, I sensed their angry words were connected—by a series of inferences, like an underground tunnel—to the larger quarrel happening on the island they inhabited.

What was it I kept going back to? It was more than their youth and anger. It was a puzzle of art rather than life: a split vision. Each time, I returned to them in memory and with design. I remembered the actual setting: unvarnished floors, a small television. But I also thought of what was outside the windows, the sparse trees and disturbed earth of a new suburb. And beyond that again, a troubled, scarred island.

For a poem to convey any of that, it would have to convey all of it. But there was a problem. The domestic poem had a foreground, not a background. There was no depth of field. It was a poem taken from the nineteenth century, which had granted it only one dimension—and that grudgingly. It was not inclusive.

Yet in my mind, at the edge of my page, I sensed connections. A young couple; an afflicted island. The language spoken and unspoken. The private compact of union; the public one of dissension. It was not an abstraction. These were our lives.

And yet how could I prove this connection where it needed to be proved—that is, in the poem? How could I show the link between private and the public, when the private side of the equation—that front room—belonged to a world of mundane interiors poetry itself had slighted?

In those moments, I knew I wanted to reinterpret the domestic poem. In my house, on a day with tasks and small children, I felt its about-to-be power everywhere. As a painter's daughter I had memories of my mother arranging flowers, fruit, getting them ready for a still life. I wanted the opposite: to feel that those atoms and planes could be thrown into a fever of spatial dissent; that they moved, rearranged themselves, threw off their given shapes. I thought of that as the starting point for my poems. When I came on a line of poetry that recognized the terrain, I was moved, as in Elaine Feinstein's powerful last line to her poem "Email from Wellington (unsent)": *You were always home to me. I long for home.*

But how to explore this? And what would that exploration cost? As an Irish poet, the public world of my country—listened to with horror on morning radio—had a claim on my imagination. But if I wrote this so-called domestic poem, would I be banished to a region of private reference? Would the poem I chose—by nature of its form and history—push me away from writing at the center of what was happening to and in my own nation? Had I—like the nineteenth-century woman poet, with her flowers, her religious piety, her timidity—already been assigned a parameter within which I could write? Was it fixed? And if so, who had fixed it?

In those years, surrounded by questions, I thought wistfully of a poem in which the interior and exterior worlds had a new freedom; a symbiotic negotiation, like shadow and light. Edward

Hirsch's powerful words apply: "In the practical realm of utility and commerce, poetry is inconsequential, but for the interior world, in the hidden realm of our affective lives, it is curiously deep and renewing. Something that might seem fragile—a group of words arranged on a page—turns out to be indestructible."

I wanted the cut flowers on the table to show the wound of their break with the natural. I wanted the voices of those young people to be heard again. I wanted, imaginatively and figuratively—and only, of course, in the realm of the poem—domestic violence. I knew exactly what I intended by that. I had a deep respect for the customary use of the term to denote a tragic relationship, but I needed the words for a different context, to convey an aesthetic association. The old origins of the word *violence*—taking the Latin word *vis* or force, and the past participle of *fero*, which is latus—means to carry out something through force. I wanted the domestic poem to claim that power. To lift its burden, to bear its freight and to advance. To speak aggressively of reality from its private world. To resemble Job's messenger, coming from a mysterious place, saying *I only am escaped alone to tell thee.*

But how? In a BBC interview in 1962 Sylvia Plath noted it. "I feel that in a novel, for example, you can get in toothbrushes and all the paraphernalia that one finds in daily life, and I find this more difficult in poetry. Poetry, I feel, is a tyrannical discipline, you've got to go so far, so fast, in such a small space that you've just got to turn away all the peripherals. And I miss them! I'm a woman, I like my little Lares and Penates."

I missed them too. But where had it happened? When had poetry made that troublesome investment in separating the ordinary world—the small universe of the cup, the open door, the room—from the epic world of violence and civil struggle?

Occasionally in those years I went to the National Gallery in Dublin. Often I stopped in front of this or that painting. Always of an interior: A woman's checked dress. A table with a cup on it. After a while watching the painting, these would become my skirt, my cup left on the kitchen counter that very morning. I would hesitate in front of one painting in particular. It was of a room reaching back into the shadow of a corridor—the door open, inviting. If I followed those shadows what would I find?

It was more than curiosity. It was also yearning. I understood that this chronicling of interiors did two things. It documented a space. But it also spoke for it: for its ferocious importance in the lives of those who lived there. It rolled back the boundaries of spatial meaning and revealed the intimacy of the attachment between the body and its immediate horizon. It said that this attachment doesn't only happen when nature instructs the soul, or art elevates the mind. But when a table is laid, a skirt folded, a door opened into an ordinary evening. It left me—as almost everything did at that time—with questions. What made painting capable of that narrative? And not poetry?

Then I was thirty. Then I was thirty-five. When I read poetry now I noticed something I had never seen in my twenties. An absence. I began to register how few *interiors* there were in the poems of the nineteenth and twentieth centuries. There were cities, bridges, meadows, machines, even skylines. But not interiors. Not, that is, the interiors in which people actually lived.

The more I thought about it, the stranger it seemed. There were a few references, certainly. In "Tears, Idle Tears" Tennyson mentions windows. In "The Eve of St Agnes" Keats constructs a gorgeous, improbable interior. But there is no suggestion that anyone actually lives there. These are theatrical props. In Dickinson there are doors and in one poem, tantalizingly, the cupboard into which she's shut. In Frost, where I looked harder and more expectantly, there are some interiors—but he was a poet who loved to furnish the exterior world.

What made it stranger was that the parallel worlds of fiction and painting were gathering, crowding, pushing those very interiors to the center of the action. Charlotte Brontë doesn't hesitate to describe the "dark coarse drapery" in *Jane Eyre*. Mr. Pecksniff is forthright and unconsciously funny in *Martin Chuzzlewit*: "My daughters' room. A poor first-floor to us, but a bower to them. Very neat. Very airy. Plants you observe; hyacinths; books again; birds," he says. "Such trifles as girls love are here. Nothing more. Those who seek heartless splendor, would seek here in vain."

These are more than references to walls and floors. A whole vista of nuance is here. By now we had had Austen's muslins and dressing tables. George Eliot had shown no difficulty matching "the stony dining room" in *Scenes of Clerical Life* with the weather outside. Elizabeth Gaskell made sure to show the reader the windows "broken and stuffed with rags" in *Mary Barton*. And Trollope's and Thackeray's interiors were about to come into existence. These were fiction writers who had come inside. They were comfortable there. They knew something was happening there which they could not ignore.

When poetry, on the other hand, relents and comes indoors in that era it is to a posed world. Worse still, having lost its access to interiors, it gradually lost a language for them. The poem's ability to speak of domestic spaces and, by inference, of the lives lived in them, was becoming atrophied. A whole teeming world was going on, leaning forward into a future poetry would not share: time was passing and sofas were becoming couches. Swan-necked pitchers and bowls were turning into basins. Streaming water now came from taps. Food was growing simpler, plates were getting smaller. Plants were being excluded from living rooms and more light was allowed in at windows. Lives changed. The rooms they happened in changed. Poetry remained aloof.

The poetic past is a strange terrain—more inner space than outer. It is a fluid mix of echoes, revelations, set-in-stone critiques and written-in-water poems. Like any poet, I was willing to have an experimental present. The problems came in trying to combine that with an exemplary past.

The first place, the natural place to look, was the Irish nineteenth century. But there was no help there. From 1850 to the end of the century—even where the poems were written by women—it was an asymmetric inventory of political poems.

In almost every case, domestic references were overwhelmed by national ones. Speranza—Lady Jane Wilde, Oscar Wilde's mother—was typical. Her oval, composed face stared back at me out of the lithograph on the frontispiece of her 1871 volume, *Poems*. She published her work in Dublin, writing in the house on Merrion Square where she lived with her fashionable doctor husband, Sir William Wilde.

I knew those rooms. I knew their high ceilings, windows blind with light on winter mornings, their lack of heat and strange acoustics. I had stayed in them. I had visited them. I could see her writing there. But no good looking in her poems for a description of them. The details, the exactitude of the interior had been bleached out. All you could find in the poems was rhetoric. Her opening poem, "To Ireland" was enough: *My country wounded to the heart / Could I but flash along thy soul*. The alternate space I was looking for was plainly not there.

And so I did what many poets have done. I began to look for those poems and poets which pointed forward to where I was now. Three in particular struck me, coming at early and later stages of my reading. I offer them here.

One day, reading a volume of poetry published in 1920, I stumbled on something. Not an answer, but a hint. It was a poem about rooms. Not smooth, and not perfect. There was an awkwardness about it. A cartoon stroke here and there. Nevertheless, something held and surprised me. It was called, appropriately, "Rooms":

> *I remember rooms that have had their part*
> *In the steady slowing down of the heart.*
> *The room in Paris, the room at Geneva,*
> *The little damp room with the seaweed smell,*
> *And that ceaseless maddening sound of the tide.*

The cadences were rough yet I felt an energy. What caught my attention was not the description, but the fact that a poet was trying to describe a reach and darkness of feeling; and yet for once placing it inside and not outside. This was not the domestic poem of the nineteenth century. There were no pre-set decorums. The argument was opposite: something had happened in these spaces. Love had died there. Fear was felt there. Death was coming.

The poem was written by Charlotte Mew. She was born in London in 1869 to a family tormented by class and conflict: her father, Fred Mew, was an unqualified architect's assistant, her mother was the daughter of his employer. There were seven children, little money and much grief. Three sons died in childhood. There was an endless scramble to make do: turned collars and darned sleeves.

With adulthood, the real problems began. Her only brother became schizophrenic, soon followed by a much-loved younger sister. Her father died, leaving no money. Her mother, with a tiny inheritance, kept her and her sister alive, in a drifting life-boat of gentility. Mew published articles, made little money, lived as a recluse, and by the first decade of the twentieth century was a strange, eccentric figure.

And here the story is taken up by Alida Monro. In 1915 Mew was invited to the Poetry Bookshop on the Strand, owned by Monro's husband. Through the door came a tiny, odd woman, not more than four foot ten inches. "Her face was a fine oval," writes Munro in her memoir, "and she always wore a little, hard pork-pie hat put on very straight." Mew was nearly fifty when her first book, *The Farmer's Bride*, was published by Harold Monro's press. She lived for only twelve more years. In the spring of 1928, after the death of her sister, she purchased a bottle of Lysol—a creosote mixture—and drank a glass of it. She died a few hours later.

Only a poet of her ilk, so dissident, so lost, so out on a margin of voice, craft and canon—with so little to gain from poetic convention—could prove a category like the nineteenth-century domestic poem so deficient. Her interiors are re-born subjects for the poem. They are real and surreal. There are chairs, bedrooms, windows in her work. Her interiors are places of force, flexing their power against the outdoors; insisting on being named in the same breath. One of the real unshacklings of the domestic poem begins here.

The second poem I read much earlier. It came from a volume called *Another September*, published in 1958 by a then young Irish poet, Thomas Kinsella. I read it when I was scarcely out of my teens, my ears and eyes still dazed by Yeatsian rhetoric. This hardly seemed from the same tradition. In a way it wasn't.

To start with, the setting of the poem is a "country bedroom." A bedroom, moreover, located in the new Ireland, where downright working lives were lived. That Ireland Seán Ó Faoláin once referred to as "the grocer's republic." And since the hinterland of this poem is a nation of plain lives, it goes without saying that the rhetoric of the Irish Revival is nowhere to be seen. When the poem opens, there is only silence and ordinary existence. A husband and wife have fallen asleep. It is a dawn on the edge of autumn. Nothing more. Nothing less.

> *Dreams fled away, this country bedroom, raw*
> *With the touch of the dawn, wrapped in a minor peace,*
> *Hears through an open window the garden draw*
> *Long pitch black breaths, lay bare its apple trees,*
> *Ripe pear trees, brambles, windfall-sweetened soil,*
> *Exhale rough sweetness against the starry slates.*
> *Nearer the river sleeps St John's, all toil*
> *Locked fast inside a dream with iron gates.*

My first reading of the poem, many years ago, was lost to the shock of the familiar. *I know this room*, I said to myself. It was not a literary critique but a visceral reaction. I recognized the simple temper and ordinary dimensions of the space. The Irish bedrooms of that era—so many of them built at the back of a house—were the bedrooms of my early childhood. Sparsely furnished; short on luxuries. Their opulence lay in the fact that, more often than not, they looked to the south-facing gardens of a temperate climate—to sweet grass and bird-pecked fruit trees.

But, reading the poem again, something was different. In the paintings I looked at so wistfully in the National Gallery there was often such an intensity of visual effect that the interior itself ceased to be a mere witness and became a participant. Now here was a room which was an actual character in a poem. The bedroom, raw with dawn, wrapped in peace, listens: *Hears through an open window the garden draw / Long pitch black breaths.*

The final two stanzas of the poem—it is relatively short—achieve a transformation. In this context, the interior, as a poetic figure, encompasses what I mean by domestic violence: an intense moral and imaginative upheaval of the kind associated with external revelation in the poetic tradition, but here happening in a domestic space.

> *Domestic Autumn, like an animal*
> *Long used to handling by those countrymen,*
> *Rubs her kind hide against the bedroom wall*
> *Sensing a fragrant child come back again*
> *—Not this half-tolerated consciousness*
> *That plants its grammar in her yielding weather*
> *But that unspeaking daughter, growing less*
> *Familiar where we fell asleep together.*
>
> *Wakeful moth wings blunder near a chair,*
> *Toss their light shell at the glass, and go*
> *To inhabit the living starlight. Stranded hair*
> *Stirs on still linen. It is as though*
> *The black breathing that billows her sleep, her name,*
> *Drugged under judgment, waned and—bearing daggers*
> *And balances—down the lampless darkness they came,*
> *Moving like women: Justice, Truth, such figures.*

The power of the poem, its action and surprise, lies in the last stanza. "The living starlight" receives the moths. But inside the room, it is "the stranded hair" of a sleeping woman that signals visionary change. From the plain sight of a woman asleep arise the mythic figures of Truth and Justice "moving like women."

In the Irish poem, as I understood it, this was new. The locale of the pastoral had been suddenly and unceremoniously shifted. It was as though someone had pushed the background away between scenes in a local theatre. A real place is inferred. A place of waking and sleeping. A domestic scene where everything is human and from which the demi-gods of the pastoral are banished.

Despite the close, even cluttered rhyme scheme, the metrical march of the lines, there is something quirky and conversational here; a voice rehearsing its new freedoms. Later I would read the poem again and hear that voice in the service of argument, image and large intent. The largeness lay in something the domestic poem could establish supremely well: a tense, combative conversation with poetic convention. A poem talking back to pastoral and elegy.

When I read it more closely years later, looking at it in the light of my own unrest, I realized its originality, its sweet-natured dissent all the more. Had it been a conventional nature poem, revelation would have come from the garden—from earth, nurture, renewal.

Instead the nature poem, which had waited imperiously for centuries for the poet to come out of doors, to make an obeisance to moral instruction and instructive landscape, has to enter a country bedroom. Has to change its colors and its tune. Has to speak the vernacular of an ordinary life. Has to say the words *love* and *vision* in plain speech.

The final poem confirms these points—not as an English language poem, but as an instance of the place the domestic poem meets the public one, so that both can be renewed.

In 1943, a German Jewish poet died in Palestine. Her name was Else Lasker-Schüler. Today she is known as a defining figure of German expressionism, a fascinating dissident. Then, she was a lonely and broken woman.

Lasker-Schüler was born in 1869 in Elberfeld in Westphalia. By her middle twenties she had married, had moved to Berlin and became a noted figure there. She published poems and plays. In 1913 an acclaimed volume *Hebräische Balladen* came out.

The city of Berlin was hospitable to wayward artists. She dressed as Prince Yussuf and a Dada artist remembers her at a poetry reading in 1914: "Suddenly the lights went out, and Else Lasker-Schüler stepped out onto the stage. She wore a robe made of blue silk. Loose-fitting trousers, silver shoes, a kind of baggy jacket, her hair was like silk, pitch black. But her words were hard, crystal clear. They glowed like metal."

Lasker-Schüler's final years were desolate. She fled the Nazis in the early thirties and lived in Jerusalem. Unlike many other poets, who had chosen to live there, she still wrote in her native German. In every sense, she had lost her world. The Israeli writer Yael Lotan was a child then but she remembers her as one of the strange figures in that locale: "There were many such people in Jerusalem in those days, people living a private dream superimposed upon the reality of our city and life . . . She [Else Lasker-Schüler] was a familiar figure on the streets and in the cafés of Jerusalem—tattered and bedizened like a bag-lady, her frail figure bent double. But her eyes still blazed with a black flame and she fed stray cats and dogs when she herself was starving."

There is a painting of Lasker-Schüler, done in 1942, shortly before her death, in which she is looking in the mirror. In it, she has a mask, but also a heavy fur collar in that unlikely climate. Another painting by Ephraim Marcus has a title which describes her plight in those years—*Helpless in an Alien World.*

In 1950 Heinz Politzer, in an article in *Commentary*, left a poignant account of her death and funeral. In her last years, he says, she was "a broken old woman who looked like a solitary exotic nightbird, with enormous eyes in an ageless face." And again: "The Sextons busied themselves with a little bundle smaller than the body of a child."

In 1943, Lasker-Schüler published a final volume of poems. The title poem is called "Mein blaues Klavier" (My Blue Piano). It invokes a world of elegy, of restrained lament. But it is also the exemplary model of a poem in which the boundaries between the domestic and political are made fluid again.

MY BLUE PIANO

At home I have a blue piano.
But I can't play a note.

It's been in the shadow of the cellar door
Ever since the world went rotten.

Four starry hands play harmonies.
The Woman in the Moon sang in her boat.
Now only rats dance to the clanks.

The keyboard is in bits.
I weep for what is blue. Is dead.

Sweet angels I have eaten
Such bitter bread. Push open
The door of heaven. For me, for now—

Although I am still alive—
Although it is not allowed.

In the poem, the piano trembles between the actual and possible, between the lost and recoverable. Put together with the unstable edges of the world it describes, as well as the color blue, it manages to be both surreal and true: a familiar household object and an image of loss. The private world is entrusted to a domestic horizon. This is the piano that was played in a room, in a home. Now it carries extraordinary freight.

As the poem goes on it becomes bolder and stranger. The music is gone. There are rats, there are angels. There is an ominous hinterland of a rotten world. But once again, it is accomplished in an indoors that manages to be both literal and magical, with the memory of an ordinary past blurred into a present made no less desolate by being improbable.

These poems did more than please and console me. I valued them because they resisted an inheritance of perspective I found oppressive: the corrosive effect and tradition of the sublime.

The history of the sublime—enclosing and elusive—has played a central part in poetry. Although the idea may be as old as Longinus, its true moment was the Romantic one. Sixty years before Wordsworth, the eighteenth-century British critic John Baillie wrote of it in this definition: "Vast objects occasion vast Sensations and vast sensations give the Mind a higher Idea of her own Powers."

In Edmund Burke's *Philosophical Enquiry into the Origin of Our*

Ideas of the Sublime and Beautiful, written twenty years later in 1757, Burke redefined the sublime as what appeared greater than us, what we therefore feared and were awestruck by—whether in landscape or literature.

These ideas challenged the inner world of man to equal the outer one. Challenged sensibility and imagination to construct an inner lexicon which reflected the grandeur of outward landscapes. The idea of grandeur, both in language and landscape, began to change the scale of the poem and the ambitions of the poet. Example, illumination, imitation—these were all characteristic modes of the sublime. "Lives of great men all remind us," wrote Longfellow, "we can make our lives sublime." The scale of the poem and the ambitions of the poet shifted. Modesty was no longer a virtue.

And for poetry, there was some gain—at least in part. The critic Thomas Weiskel tells us that "the sublime revives as God withdraws from an immediate participation in the experience of man." As poetry lost its arts of magic, and then its place on the right side of religion, something had to replace it. Hence the sublime.

But for me, when I was a young woman, the sublime was not abstract history: it was a grandiose and off-putting instruction set. A cumbersome warning of how unimportant the ordinary life could be. It was the dark alter ego of my wishes, my ambitions. I woke up in a modest, contemporary suburb in Ireland. The curtains drew back on the ordinary. Light fell on the blue cup. The saucer began its slow continual turn. A child opened its mouth. A tree lost a leaf. Not one of these small events challenged the inner world of man or woman to equal the outer one. Not one of them met the prescriptions of the sublime. Quite the opposite. They invited accuracy, not grandeur. Precision not scale.

Can any one poet say poetry was wrong? Can a single writer challenge a collective past? My answer is simple. Not only can, but should. Poetry should be scrubbed, abraded, cleared, and restated with the old wash stones of argument and resistance. It should happen every generation. Every half-generation. In every working poet's life and practice.

As a young poet I stepped back from aesthetics. It was the era of the New Criticism, of modernism, of ordained poetic authority. The critique of the poem, shadowed and strengthened by sciences of reason and textual analysis, seemed powerful but also alien. Only gradually did I begin to realize that this was beside the point: that every poet has to make their own critique. That authority inheres in that; and only that.

It was easier said than done. The problem is that no young poet goes from theory to practice. Always the other way round. Like so many other young poets, my practice was self-doubting and so my theory was unlikely to be confident. All the same, I was noting things, taking them in, waiting for a day I could be sure.

A poem is a subtle system of references. It codifies, suggests, infers. It gestures outward while staring obdurately inward. Looked at closely, it can tell you about a society. Looked at from a distance, it can reveal a history of evasion. Only later, armed with my own questions, did I feel comfortable enough to challenge some inherited ideas. This essay records those questions. Most of all, I took courage from other poets' questions and answers—often American poets. I heard the clear voice of Adrienne Rich: "Who is to dictate what may be written about and how? Isn't that what everybody fears—the prescriptive, the demand that we write out of certain materials, avoid others"? And Allen Ginsberg: "Poetry is not an expression of the party line. It's that time of night, lying in bed, thinking what you really think, making the private world public, that's what the poet does."

Finally, I made my own questions. Perhaps, as poets, that is all we really have for a critique: an endless, self-renewing series of interrogative thoughts. "The historical sense," wrote Eliot, "involves a perception, not only of the pastness of the past, but of its presence." How had it happened that poetry's historical sense only came alive when it left the house? What did it mean for generation after generation of poets that the world outside was deemed to be a horizon of moral transcendence and pastoral significance? But not a half-empty cup, a child's shoe, a crooked patch of sunlight on carpet?

Finally, I learned to listen for the confirming words of other poets. As for instance these: In a 1999 interview, Philip Levine spoke of Antonio Machado in these terms: "He's able to transform all these essentially simple things into a kind of wholeness and holiness. And it seemed to me that Machado was able to validate these very basic experiences that we all share—and that we begin to think of, in our busy lives, as marginal. But Machado brings them into the center of his experience and his poetry. And I thought, *Oh, what genius that was, to take what we've marginalized and pull it into the center and make it what sheds light on everything else.*"

LETTER TO A
YOUNG WOMAN POET

I wish I knew you. I wish I could stand for a moment in that corridor of craft and doubt where you will spend so much of your time. But I don't and I can't. And given the fact, in poetic terms, that you are the future and I am the past, I never will. Then why write this? It is not, after all, a real letter. It doesn't have an address. I can't put a name at the top of it. So what reason can I have for writing in a form without a basis to a person without a name?

I could answer that the hopes and silences of my first years as a poet are still fresh to me. But that in itself is not an explanation. I could tell you that I am a woman past middle age, writing this on a close summer night in Ireland. But what would that mean to you? If I tell you, however, that my first habitat as a poet is part of your history as a poet: is that twentieth century full of the dangerous indecision about who the poet really is. If I say I saw that century's influence in the small, quarrelsome city where I began as a poet. That I studied its version of the poet and took its oppressions to heart. If I say my present is your past, that my past is already fixed as part of your tradition. And that until we resolve our relation to both past and tradition, we are still hostages to that danger, that indecision. And, finally, that there is something I want to say to you about the present and past of poetry—something that feels as if it needs to be said urgently—then maybe I can justify this letter.

And if some awkwardness remains, rather than trying to disguise it, I want to propose an odd and opposite fiction. If most real letters are conversation by other means, think of this as a different version. Imagine a room at dusk, with daylight almost gone. I can do this because I associate that light, that hour, with ease and conversation. I was born at dusk. Right in the center of Dublin in fact, in a nursing home beside Stephen's Green. Big, cracking heaps of sycamore and birch leaves are burned there in autumn and I like to think of the way blue, bitter smoke must have come the few hundred yards or so towards the room where I was born.

And so I have no difficulty imagining us sitting there and talking in that diminishing light. Maybe the sights of late summer were visible through the window only moments ago. Fuchsia and green leaves, perhaps. But now everything is retreating into skeletal branches and charcoal leaves. My face is in shadow. You cannot see it, although your presence shapes what I am saying. And so in the last light, at the end of the day, what matters is language. Is the unspoken at the edge of the spoken. And so I have made a fiction to sustain what is already a fiction: this talking across time and absence.

But about what? What name will I give it? In the widest sense, I want to talk about the past. The past, that is, of poetry: the place where so much of the truth and power of poetry is stored. "Poetry is the past which breaks out in our hearts," said

Rilke, whose name should be raised whenever one poet writes to another. But the past I want to talk about is more charged and less lyrical than that for women poets. It is, after all, the place where authorship of the poem eluded us. Where poetry itself was defined by and in our absence. There has been a debate since I was a young poet, about whether women poets should engage with that past at all. "For writers, and at this moment for women writers in particular," Adrienne Rich wrote eloquently in "When We Dead Awaken," "there is the challenge and promise of a whole new psychic geography to be explored. But there is also a difficult and dangerous walking on ice, as we try to find language and images for a consciousness we are just coming into and with little in the past to support us."

Then why go there? Why visit the site of our exclusion? We need to go to that past: not to learn from it, but to change it. If we do not change that past, it will change us. And I, for one, do not want to become a grateful daughter in a darkened house. But in order to change the past of poetry, we have to know what happened there. We have to be able to speak about it as poets, and even that can be difficult. Ever since I began as a poet I have heard people say that fixed positions—on gender, on politics of any kind—distort and cloud the question of poetry. In those terms, this letter can seem to be a clouding, a distortion. But poetry is not a pure stream. It will never be sullied by partisan argument. The only danger to poetry is the reticence and silence of poets. This piece is about the past and our right as women poets to avail of it. It is about the art and against the silence. Even so, I still need to find a language with which to approach that past. The only way of doing that, within the terms of this fiction, is to go back to the space you now occupy: in other words, to the beginning.

When I was young I had only a present. I began in a small, literary city. Such a voluble, self-confident place, in fact, that at times it was even possible to believe the city itself would confer a sort of magical, unearned poetic identity. At night the streets were made of wet lights and awkward angles. Occasionally fog came in from the coast, a dense space filled with street-grit and salt and the sound of foghorns. By day things were plainer: a city appeared, trapped by hills and defined by rivers. Its center was a squashed clutter of streets and corners. There were pubs and green buses. Statues of orators. Above all, the cool, solid air of the Irish sea at every turn.

The National Library was a cold, domed and friendly building. The staircase was made of marble and formed an imposing ascent to a much less elaborate interior. Old books, shelves and newspapers crowded a huge room. The tables were scarred oak and small lamps were attached to the edge of them and could be lit by individual readers. As twilight pressed on the glass roof where pigeons slipped and fluttered, the pools of light fell on pages and haloed the faces above them.

I read poetry there. I also read in my flat late at night. But the library was in the center of town. Often it was easier just to stay in and go there and take a bus home later. There was something about the earnest, homeless feel of a big library that comforted me.

I read all kinds of poetry there. I also read about poets. I was eighteen. Then nineteen. Then twenty and twenty-one. I read about Eliot in Paris. And Yeats in Coole. I read Pound and Housman and Auden. It was the reading of my time and my place: Too many men. Not enough women. Too much acceptance. Too few questions.

I memorized poems. I learned poetics—although I had no

use for that word. But I had a real, practical hunger nevertheless for instruction and access in the form. And so I learned something about cadence and rhythm there. And something about the weather and circumstance of tradition as well. If I had known what to look for, I would have had plenty of evidence of the tensions of a tradition as I read about the big, moonlit coldness of Ullswater and the intimacy of Wordsworth's hand-to-hand struggle with the eighteenth century. About the vowel changes in the fifteenth century. About the letters between John Clare and Lord Radstock. "Tell Clare if he still has a recollection of what I have done, and am still doing for him, he must give me unquestionable proofs of being that man I would have him be— he must expunge!"

When I came out of the library, I got on the bus and watched for ten or so minutes as the rainy city went by. During the journey I thought about what I had read. I was not just reading poems at this time, I was beginning to write them. I was looking for that solid land-bridge between writing poems and being a poet. I was taking in information, therefore, at two levels. One was simple enough. I was seeing at first hand the outcome of a hundred years of intense excitement and change in an art form: how the line had altered, how the lyric had opened out. I was also absorbing something that was less easy to define: the idea of the poet. The very thing which should have helped me transit from writing to being. But just as the line and the lyric had opened out and become volatile, the idea of the poet had drawn in, and distanced itself from the very energies the poems were proposing.

This made no sense at all. When I read poems in the library I felt as though a human face was turned towards me, alive with feeling, speaking urgently to me about love and time. But when I came across the idea of the poet I felt as if someone had displaced that speaker with a small, cold sculpture: a face from which the tears and intensity were gone, on which only the pride and self-consciousness of the Poet remained. I had no words for this. And yet I began to wonder if the makers of the poem and the makers of the idea of the poet could be one and the same. It was an amateurish, shot-in-the-dark thought. And yet all I could do was ask questions. What other way had I of dealing with a poetic past whose history I didn't know, and a tradition composed of the seeming assurance that only those it confirmed and recognized would ever be part of it? Besides I felt my questions would bring me, if not to the front, at least to the back entrance of this formidable past. But if these were the gates, who were the gatekeepers?

Stay with the fiction. Imagine the light is less. That we can no longer see the water drops and wasps under the fuchsia. That the talk continues, but in a more mysterious space. I know when I was young I could barely imagine challenging the poetic past. It seemed infinitely remote and untouchable: fixed in place by giant hands.

And yet what a strange argument I am about to make to you. That the past needs us. That very past in poetry which simplified us as women and excluded us as poets now needs us to change it. To bring to it our warm and fractious present: our recent decades of intense debate and excited composition. And we need to do it. After all, stored in that past is a template of poetic identity which still affects us as women. When we are young poets it has the power to make us feel subtly less official, less welcome in the tradition than our male contemporaries. If we are not careful, it is that template we will aspire to, alter ourselves for, warp our self-esteem as poets to fit.

Therefore we need to change the past. Not by intellectual-
izing it. But by eroticizing it. The concept that a template of
poetic authority can actually be changed, altered, radicalized
by those very aspects of humanity which are excluded from it
is at the heart of what I am saying. And yet these ideas are so
difficult, so abstract that I sense them dissolving almost at the
point of articulation. If you were not in a make-believe twilight
in an unreal room in a fictive letter, you might ask a question
here. How can you eroticize a past? My hope is that this story—
this strange story—will make it clearer.

When I was seventeen years of age I found myself, as many
teenagers do, with time to spare between graduating from school
and getting ready for college. Three months in fact of a wet, cool
Irish summer. I lived in Dublin. In those times it wasn't hard
to get summer jobs. So I got a job in a hotel just over the river
on the north side of the city. I worked at housekeeping in the
hotel. I carried keys and straightened out the rooms. The job was
not difficult and the hours were not long. The hotel was placed
above the river Liffey and it was right at the end of one of the
showpiece streets of Ireland. O'Connell Street. Its bridge, the
widest in Europe, had once been a claim to fame when Dublin
was a garrison city. On this street a group of Irish patriots in
1916 had taken their stand against British rule in Ireland. They
had established themselves at the post office just above the river.
The British troops had shelled the building. The position had
fallen after a week of struggle and bloodshed. The patriots in
the post office had been arrested and several of the leaders had
been shot.

It was not hard when I was young to get off the bus on a summer morning beside a sluggish river that ran into the Irish Sea,
and walk straight into Irish history. There was the post office.

Inside it was the bronze statue of Cúchulain with a raven on his shoulder. Here was the stone building and the remembered action. And all up the street, placed only fifty yards or so apart, was statue after statue of Irish patriots and orators. Burke. Grattan. O'Connell. Parnell. Made of stone and bronze and marble and granite. With plaques and wreaths and speeches at their feet. I got off the bus between the river and the hotel. And I walked past them—a seventeen-year-old girl—past their hands, their gestures, their quoted eloquence, all the way to work.

There was a manager in the hotel. He was a quietly spoken middle-aged man. He looked after all the inventory in the hotel and he sat in an old-fashioned office with a ledger and a telephone. One day one of the other girls there, a bit older than I was, told me something strange about him. She told me he had a wound which had never properly healed. Every day, she said, he went up to his room and dressed it and bandaged it. And I was fascinated in a horrified sort of way, by the contrast between this almost demure man, with his dark suit and pinstriped trousers, wearing the formal clothes of small daily ceremonies, hiding his damaged secret.

But what I remember now is not exactly what I'm describing here. And that wounded man is only one part of the story. And the whole of the story is maybe not something I will be able to tell, not because I knew that man. Because I didn't. I spoke to him once or twice. Not more. Once I waited with the voyeuristic curiosity of youth, of which I still feel ashamed, at the top of the stairs to see him climb up to his room to dress that wound. But I never knew him. And never really spoke to him.

The story is something different. It has something to do with realizing that I could change the past. With going in every day to work in that hotel. With having my imagination seized, in a fragmented and distracted way, by a man whose body had not healed. And then, when the drizzling summer day was coming to an end, it had something to do with going out into the long, spacious street and walking down it to the river. Which also meant walking past the statues which had not moved or changed in the day. Which still stood on their columns, above their grandiose claims. It meant leaving the hotel with one idea of a manhood which had been made frail in a mysterious way and walking down a long well-lit street where no such concession could ever be made. Where manhood was made of bronze and granite and marble. Where no one's thigh or side had ever been wounded or ever could be. But where—so intense was my sense of contrast—I could almost imagine that the iron moved and the granite flinched. And where by accident and chance I had walked not only into history, but into the erotics of history.

The erotics of history. In a certain sense I discovered my country by eroticizing it: by plotting those correlatives between maleness and strength, between imagination and power which allowed me not only to enter the story, but to change it. And yet at seventeen my own sexuality was so rudimentary, so unformed that neither I nor anyone else would have thought it could have been an accurate guide to the history I inherited. In fact, it served. I walked down that street of statues, a girl who had come back late to her own country. Who lacked its language. Who was ignorant of its battles. Who knew only a little about its heroes. And yet my skin, my flesh, my sex—without learning any of this—stood as a subversive historian, ready to edit the text.

If you and I were really there in that room with the air darkening around us, this would be a good place to stop. To be quiet for a moment. And then to start again. This time with another question. Is it possible to eroticize a poetic tradition in the way

in which I eroticized my own history? Maybe the real answer
to this is the most obvious one. The only way of entering the
poetic tradition, of confronting its formidable past, is through a
living present. And yet it hardly seems possible that the painful,
complex, single present of any one poet could offer a contest to
a tradition. Despite that, what I am about to tell you is how I
discovered it. Just how tentatively I put together my sense of
being a poet with my sense of a past that did not offer me an easy
definition for it. And how, in a house on a summer night, with
sleeping children, when I wondered how to do it, I would think
back to those summer mornings, that long street with its iron
orators. Of looking up, made subversive by alternative senses
of power and weakness. Of how I asked myself: Would I ever be
able to eroticize this tradition, this formidable past, stretching
back and reaching above, so that I could look up confidently?
Could I make the iron breathe and the granite move? When did
I discover the past? Perhaps the answer should be, which past?

My sense of it as a problematic poetic terrain came late. All
through my first years as a poet it was just the place where
poems I loved had been written, where patterns had been made
which invited an automatic reverence I could not give. And so
I continued to turn to that past to read those poems, but never
to be part of the tradition they belonged to.

But when I married and had small children, when at last I
lived at a distance from any poetic center, things changed. I
started to have an intense engagement with every aspect of
writing a poem. So much so, that the boundaries between the
edges of the poem and the limits of the world began at times to
dissolve. I was fascinated by the page in the notebook on the
table, with a child's cry at its perimeter and the bitterness of
peat smoke at its further edge. I loved the illusion, the convic-

tion, the desire—whatever you want to call it—that the words were agents rather than extensions of reality. That they made my life happen, rather than just recorded it happening.

But what life? My life day to day was lived through ordinary actions and powerful emotions. But the more ordinary a day I lived, the more I lifted a child, conscious of nothing but the sweetness of a child's skin, or the light behind an apple tree, or rain on slates, the more language and poetry came to my assistance. The words that had felt stilted, dutiful and decorative when I was a young and anxious poet, now sang and flew. Finally, I had joined together my life as a woman and a poet. On the best days I lived as a poet, the language at the end of my day—when the children were asleep and the curtains drawn—was the language all through my day: it had waited for me.

What this meant was crucial. For the first time as a poet, I could believe in my life as the source of the language I used, and not the other way around. At last I had the means to challenge what I believed had distorted the idea of the poet: the belief that poetry had the power to dignify and select a life, instead of the reverse. That a life, in other words, became important only because it was the subject matter for a poem.

I knew from everything I had read that the poets who changed the tradition first had to feel they owned the tradition. Instead, I had come slowly and painfully to a number of hard-won positions which did not feel like ownership. First and foremost, I wanted to feel that whatever I lived as a woman I could write as a poet. Once I did that, I felt there was a fusion, a not-to-be-denied indebtedness between those identities: the woman providing the experience, the poet the expression. This fusion in turn created a third entity: the poet, who not only engaged in these actions, but began to develop a critique about them.

This critique may have had its origin in the life of a woman, may have begun in the slanted light of a nursery or a kitchen, but its outcome was about something different. It was about the interior of the poem itself: about tone, distance from the subject, management of the voice. It was about the compromised and complex act of language. It was about the historic freedom of the poet, granted right down through the tradition—the precious and dignified franchise—to return to the past with the discoveries of the present. And then to return triumphant to the present with a changed past.

I did not have that sense of entitlement. The interior sense that I could change poetry, rather than my own poems, was never exactly there. But if the tradition would not admit me, could I change its rules of admission? Either I would have to establish an equal relation with it, or I would have to adopt a submissive posture: admiring its achievements and accepting its exclusions. Yet what tools had I to change the resistances I felt around me and within me? Certainly neither intellectual nor theoretical ones. Gradually I began to believe that the only way to change a tradition was to go to the sources which had made it in the first place: But what were they? Intuitively I felt that the way to touch them was by reaching back into my own imagination, attempting to become not just the author of the poem but the author of myself. The author, that is, of myself as a poet. This in turn meant uncovering and challenging that elusive source of authoring within the tradition which had made not only the poem, but also the identity of the poet.

Who makes a poetic tradition? Who makes the idea of the maker? "We are accustomed to think of the poet," wrote Randall Jarrell ironically, "when we think of him at all, as someone Apart." But customs have to be made. They have to be stored deep in the culture and layered into habits of thought in order to change from custom into customary. Wherever the custom had started, I was certain it was a damaging, limiting one.

Of course it's arguable that I felt this because I was not an author in that past: neither named nor present. But I don't think so. The truth was that in my reading—scattered and inexpert as it was—I had picked up a fault line: something strange and contradictory which I began to follow. Obviously the language I use now is not the outcome of the perceptions I had then. Back then I was young, badly read, just beginning. Nevertheless, I know now that the fault line stretched from the end of the Romantic movement to the end of modernism. That it marked and weakened a strange, confused terrain of technical widening and ethical narrowing. Just as the line and the lyric began to grow plastic, open, volatile, the idea of the poet contracted, became defensive, shrugged off links with the community.

Here for instance is T. S. Eliot: "Our civilization comprehends great variety and complexity . . . The poet must become more and more comprehensive, more allusive, more indirect, in order to force, to dislocate if necessary, language into his meaning."

Our civilization. The poet must. This was too pure for the warm, untidy enterprise of imagination as I understood it. What exactly was our civilization? Why should a poet try to reflect it in a dislocated language, instead of finding a plain and luminous one for standing outside that civilization?

Further back again. Here is Matthew Arnold, seeming to claim for an art the devotions of a sect.

We should conceive of poetry worthily, and more highly than it has been the custom to conceive of it. We should conceive of it as capable of higher uses, and called to higher destinies, than those which in general men have assigned to it hitherto. More and more mankind will discover that we have to turn to poetry to interpret life for us, to console us, to sustain us. Without poetry our science will appear incomplete, and most of what now passes for religion and philosophy will be replaced by poetry.

What higher destinies? What civilization? I repeat these questions only because it seems to me they have something to do with the fault line I spoke about. To read through nineteenth-century poetry, even haphazardly, was to become an eyewitness to the gradual dissolution of the beautiful radicalism of the Romantic movement—where individualism was an adventure which freed the poet to experiment with the self—into a cautious and rigid hubris. Perhaps a sociologist or a historian could explain how the concept of the poet became mixed with ideas of power which had too little to do with art and too much to do with a concept of culture shadowed by empire-building and conservative ideology. And how in the process men like Arnold and Eliot accepted the task of making the poet an outcome of a civilization rather than a subversive within it.

Whatever the causes, the effect was clear. Poetry in the nineteenth century developed an inconsistency which was not resolved in the twentieth. Modernism appeared to be openly anti-authoritarian. "It was not a revolt against form," said Eliot, "but against dead form." But this apparent anti-authoritarianism was built on the contradictions of an authoritarian idea: of the poet as part of our civilization and called to higher destinies. The fault line lay here. The poets of the first part of the twentieth century had dismantled a style: they had not dismantled a self. Without the second, the first was incomplete.

Darkness. No trees. Not even outlines. Just the shadow of a profile and the sense of someone speaking. Let me remind you who I am: a woman on a summer night writing a fictive letter from a real place. Suppose I were now to turn a harsh light on my own propositions, and say why should a great tradition—an historic tradition of poetry—be held accountable to the criticisms of a woman in a suburb?

The answer is simple: However wrongheaded my criticisms, I—no less than any poet who lifts a pen and looks at a page—became an inheritor of tradition the moment I did so. The difference was that as a young woman I did so in circumstances which were relatively new. Not in the London of coffee houses. Or in Greenwich Village. Or even in the city that was four miles away. But in a house with small children. With a washing machine in the background. With a child's antibiotic on a shelf and a spoon beside it.

And the fact is the words of poets and canon-makers—but more canon-makers than poets—had determined the status of my machines and my medicine bottles. They had determined the probable relation between the ordinary object and the achieved poem. They had winnowed and sifted and refined. They had made the authority of the poet conditional upon a view of reality, which then became a prescription about subject matter. They had debated and subtracted and reduced that relation of the ordinary to the poem so that it was harder than I thought proper to record the life I lived in the poems I wrote.

Gradually, it became apparent to me that the ordained authority of the poet had everything to do with permission granted or withheld. Not simply for subject matter, but for any claim that could be made for it. I came to believe that in that nineteenth century where Matthew Arnold proposed his higher destinies, the barriers between religion and poetry had shimmered and dissolved. The religion *of* poetry had ensued. Out of that had come a view that the poem made the experience important; that the experience was not important until the poem had laid hands upon it. I needed to challenge that.

Somewhere in that century, it seemed to me, if I could find it, would be a recognizable turning point, where the poet failed to distinguish between hubris and history. And to which I as a poet—as well as other poets from new and challenging constituencies—needed to return: to argue and engage.

No light at all. Stars somewhere. And if this were a summer darkness in Ireland the morning would already be stored in the midnight: visible in an odd brightness to the east, over towards the Liffey and the heart of the city. I have finished talking. I have to finish also with the fiction of your company, and I am surprised at my regret. Nevertheless, this letter is full of irony and hope. The hope is that you will read in my absence what was shaped by the irony of your non-presence. Despite the fact that this room, with its darkening window and summer shadows, has only been made of words, I will miss it.

Occasionally I see myself, or the ghost of myself, in the places where I first became a poet. On the pavement just beside Stephen's Green, with its wet trees and sharp railings. What I see is not an actual figure, but a sort of remembered loneliness. The poets I knew were not women: the women I knew were not poets. The conversations I had, or wanted to have, were never complete.

Sometimes I think of how time might become magical: How I might get out of the car even now and cross the road and stop that young woman and surprise her with the complete conversation she hardly knew she missed. How I might stand there with her in the dusk, the way neighbours stand on their front steps before they go in to their respective houses for the night: half talking and half leaving. She and I would argue about the past. Would surely disagree about the present.

Time is not magical. The conversation will not happen. Even writing this letter to you has been flawed by similar absences and inventions. And yet there is something poignant and helpful to me in having done it. If women go to the poetic past as I believe they should, if they engage responsibly with it and struggle to change it—seeking no exemption in the process—then they will have the right to influence what is handed on in poetry, as well as the way it is handed on. Then the conversation we have had, the letter I am just finished with, will no longer have to be fictions.

What is more, the strengths that exist in the communal life of women will then be able to refresh and renew the practice and concept of the poetic tradition. Thanks to the women poets in the generation before mine—poets such as Adrienne Rich and Denise Levertov—many of those strengths were there when I started out. But I believe words such as *canon* and *tradition* and *inheritance* will change even more. And with all that, women poets, from generation to generation, will be able to befriend one another. And that, in the end, is the best reason for writing this letter.

III

*Uncollected Prose:
A Selection*

THE WEASEL'S TOOTH

Irish Times 7 June 1974

I have written this article with authentic reluctance. The reluctance springs not from the average difficulties inherent in articulating a difficult idea; nor is it even that reluctance which springs from a sense of the inadequacy of any articulation in certain given circumstances. Rather it is, I am afraid, that most simple and intractable of reluctances which springs from the need to take, in a time of crisis, a cold, reasonable and self-accusing look at oneself, at past beliefs, past mistakes.

I must add, indeed insist, that is not simply a personal, but an entirely private assertion of my instinct of where the writer must look in Ireland now. For within that very privacy—that lack, to use a colloquialism, of safety in numbers—lie, I believe, the last chances of writers now in Ireland to liberate themselves from the myths, the hallucinations of cultural unity, the imaginative anti-patriotism which has maimed Irish writing, even as it has, I believe also, mauled Irish politics.

For as the first has fed the second with fantasies, so the second has projected those fantasies onto the screen of rhetoric and finally into the infinitely tragic sphere of action, of flying limbs, lost lives, broken hearts. Now both stand accused;

both, I believe, have a case to answer. For the public business of the nation others must bear the responsibility; for the private insights, however, the unspoken assumptions which stimulate and have misled that public business I not only can, but must, attempt to make some answer. For I write in Ireland and by that simple and infinitely complex act of structuring words on paper I share the guilt as, one day, I may hope to share the historic acquittal for what has happened.

WHY—any reader may reasonably ask—should a woman of twenty-nine, an apprentice in poetry of this country, speak in such grandiose terms as of guilt and acquittal? Because I have shared in and spread the damaging fantasies—and herein lies part of the reluctance in writing this article—of the writer I have admired and loved most in my life: William Yeats. When I look to find the expression of that fantasy in Yeats's work I find it in one phrase, where he sees the hills of Clare-Galway and sees, dramatized through them, his scheme of Irish culture. This Irish culture he summarizes in a fine and empty phrase as "a community bound together by imaginative possessions."

I believed that once. Now I know it to be arid rhetoric. Had he substituted the word "imaginary" for "imaginative" he would have been nearer to the point. For William Yeats, understandably and regrettably, needed a fantasy of cultural coherence—of Anglo-Irish pride and peasant simplicity—to sustain his one terrible and most harrowing achievement, which is also his final greatness: his ability to look alone into the void of death, in poems such as "The Tower" and "The Circus Animals' Desertion." There, stripped of the heroism he craved, forced to true coherence by the incoherence of bodily disintegration, in his moment of his utmost humiliation he reached the only heroism that matters. Yet his fantasy of cultural coherence has not—more's the pity—been thrown out intellectually by writers with the force and decision with which his final, single achievement has been kept and rightly cherished. In fact it has tipped the pen of many an Irish writer since and, of course, I include myself, with the poison of confusion. For the pity of it is that there are indeed imaginative possessions in this country—and one above all—which should be used. But these possessions, most of which consist in individuality and its creative exercise, have been distorted into a delusion of national cultural coherence. So, imaginatively, our possessions have not liberated us but imprisoned much of our writing. Indeed I recognize much of what is anarchic and worthwhile in our writing as that individuality—the only final imaginative possession worth having—involved in the prison riots which were inevitable once an ideal of cultural hegemony was created. Once and for all I feel we should rid ourselves of Yeats's delusion: let us be rid at last of any longing for cultural unity in a country whose most precious contribution may be precisely its insight into the anguish of disunity; let us be rid of any longing for imaginative collective dignity in a land whose final and only dignity is individuality.

For there is, and at last I recognize it, no unity whatsoever in this culture of ours. And, even more important, I recognize that there is no need whatsoever for such a unity. If we search for it we will, at a crucial moment, be mutilating with fantasy once again the very force we should be liberating with reality: our one strength as writers, the individual voice, speaking in tones of outcry, vengeance, bitterness even, against our disunity, but speaking, for all that, with a cool, tough acceptance of it.

Now any reader of this statement may well ask just what this means for a woman writer, at my age, at this moment in this country? It means, I fear, turning my face away from the philosophy of poetry I have loved, used and abused in such poems as I have written. This philosophy is Romanticism, which sees the poet as a person apart, an exceptional individual voice. For of course the concept of an exceptional individual is a contradiction in terms. The individual, and the poet who writes out of his own individuality honestly, is simply the voice of unheroic, dull and tedious humanity whose dullness and tedium requires to be structured in the tedious craft of words to fight back against that deepest fear of individuals, their fear of anonymity, of the annihilation of self. This unity, this disunity of selfhood, of individuality is, I believe, the only true adventure for poetry—or indeed any writing in this country.

And here, to finish the argument I must be private rather than personal. Recently I wrote a short poem about a baby who died in the recent bomb blasts in Dublin. I wrote it inspired—and I select the word with care—by a photograph I saw two days later on the front of a national newspaper whose most arresting feature was the expression on the face of a fireman who lifted that child, an expression of tenderness as if he were lifting his own child from its cradle to its mother's breast. Perhaps that short poem reached one or two more people than other poems of mine have, simply because they, as parents, citizens, human beings were harrowed by that greatest of obscenities, the murder of the innocent, and were glad to find just one among many other statements of outrage.

I fear it would be easy, all too easy, to continue writing such statements, of temporary healing, of immediate response. For me, unfortunately, I feel the adventure lies in quite the opposite direction: as a lyric poet, particularly as a lyric poet who is also a woman, I feel my contribution must be not to grieve for the child but to explore carefully, sympathetically, finally, with love the evil which could cause that death. For me this means coolly, and with whatever craftsmanship I can muster, exploring what I believe came to be the phenomenon of our time—individual evil. Once again, to relate it to my own work, this means I must search out the evil intrinsic in femininity, that special evil which could cause a Nazi woman to make lampshades of the skins of her sisters, or a girl at an airport to gun down a child she could have borne herself—and I must do it not by patronizing them with my limited cerebral understanding of their motives, but by searching, within my discipline, for the area in myself which could do precisely the same thing. I have no doubt I shall find it; if I can articulate it I shall fulfill whatever potential I may have as a poet.

In this work I shall be nothing so heroic as a pioneer. For this exploration by women of the evil intrinsic in womanhood was started in *Wuthering Heights*, decided in the strange codes of Emily Dickinson's work. It may even be said that Sylvia Plath, by her suicide, by her bravery, by too much identification, fell in the front line of this attempt on new territory.

In such an undramatic way do I feel I can best fulfill my potential: not through the glory of crusade, but within the boredoms of craft; and by such a disappointingly private search do I feel I will discharge whatever public responsibility I have in this country as a writer at this time. And here I must salute my contemporaries and elders in the profession who will be—as *Time* magazine would put it—considerably underwhelmed by my conclusions. I saw it through their eyes before I saw it with my own. But especially I must salute Northern poets, my contemporaries, who need no naming, who with discipline, and against pressure to be superficially coherent, have guarded their own identity well.

If then, I believe, this individuality is guarded in our writing on this island, a genuine contribution may be made: then there may be not an ending, but some resolution to this anguish, a resolution luminously stated by Charles Dickens in a novel about another time of excess and national disgrace, a novel aptly titled for all of us now—*A Tale of Two Cities*:

> *I see a brilliant city and a brilliant people rising from this abyss, and, in their long struggles to be truly free, in their triumphs and defeats, through long years to come, I see the evil of this time and of the previous time of which this is the natural birth gradually making expiation for itself and wearing out.*

VIRTUAL SYNTAX, ACTUAL DREAMS

PN Review March–April 2003

I

I am surprised at how little exists to document the revolution in writing habits of the last twenty years. Almost exactly that long ago I went to interview Mary Lavin for Virago Press. They had decided to bring out a book on just that—the writing habits of women poets and novelists: whether they used a typewriter or a pen, which kind of pen, and so on.

During the course of the interview she told me she had never learned to use a typewriter. That she had sat at a dining room table writing and writing as the pages collected on the floor. I like to think of her even now, using that fast, almost unreadable pen script, making her marvelous short story "The Will." She told me she felt the characters came into existence and deepened simply through this process of scratching out words and discarding sheets. As she spoke I could imagine Lally in that story, disregarding her inheritance, taking on her shabby coat, her way of speaking, those tears in her eyes, as she rose slowly through foolscap and ink.

I interviewed many writers in those years. But this one stayed with me. It was a glimpse: a small window opening onto the secrets of a process. The last twenty years have seen far greater changes. Writers have traversed centuries in decades. Many have left the form of writing they began with as poets or novelists—the pen, the pencil. They have gone to typewriters. Then to word processors. Then to computers. Each change must have made its inward mark: fear or delight or resistance or nostalgia. But there is largely silence about it. And because of that silence we may lose a piece of minor history. For that reason, I have made—at least partially——my own account. It follows here.

2

The scene is a café in Dublin at the beginning of the 1990s. I am reading an evening newspaper. It is a March evening. My daughters are opposite me, in their school uniforms. Suddenly, for no real reason, I look more closely at a classified ad.

It is a couple of lines: terse and easy to miss. It is for a second-hand computer. That in itself, in 1991 in Dublin, is rare enough. There are still only a few in private homes. Even the offices— the homes, the banks and the government buildings—are more or less innocent of them. The old city, with its iron and soot-pitted granite, and mountain-colored distances, is taking one last breath before it is swept away into the new era.

Without a moment's hesitation, I answer the ad. I buy the computer from a round-faced Dutchman who is sad to see it go. I bring it home, unload it carefully and finish the tasks for the day. It waits—ugly, bulky, inert— on the table where I left it. Without my knowing it, a piece of rough magic has entered my house.

3

I got the computer in spring. I kept it upstairs in the room in which I had always worked and not far from the window which looked out on the garden. The circular part of my life gathered all around it. House. Family. Garden.

The laburnum was in bloom. A pure electric yellow assailed me whenever I came in. The bracts hung down, catching and refracting light. Beyond them an Irish summer was collecting its rain and greenness to produce the lilac and blossom and leaves which were the common occasions of the season.

There, in the middle of the room, while the season grew and gathered and put on strength, was this seasonless machine. The laburnum and apple blossom showed up even more the dour plastic casing of the monitor. The soft light at the end of the day fell even more oddly on the bleak line of the casing.

And I was fascinated. Fascinated by the fact that every morning I could turn this machine on. That every morning it would leave with swift heels to carry my small messages around its circuits. And return. And leave again. After an initial moment of strangeness, I no longer saw it as merely a series of angles and intrusions in the old pure space of my room. I saw it as something different: as the mute survivor of an extraordinary journey. And there was more: even then I could see that somehow there had crept into this casing every dream of language, of power, of magic that human beings had ever had.

4

What language does poetry happen in? Is it the language we choose? Or one made out of what we haven't chosen?

The scene changes again: a boarding school on the Dublin coast. It was my last year there and I was seventeen. And if I was reading poetry, it was only in a fitful, here-and-there way. All my intensity—whatever intellectual energy I was capable of—was reserved for Latin. I hardly knew how it had happened. Hardly a year before, I had regarded it as a burden. Now it was a pleasure.

And so I sat in the convent library, on spring evenings, my Latin grammar beside me. Gradually the blunt outline of the Wicklow hills would disappear. All of a sudden, a small array of lights—a fishing boat—would pinpoint a place on the water.

I began my Latin exercises. Immediately there was magic. The sinuous verbs were smoothed by the syntax. The ceiling, the grain in the oak, the color of the windowsill seemed to be smoothed as well. They shimmered with the ablatives, stretched out with the ambitious gerundives, were shut down again into turn-on-a-sixpence meaning. The sentences on the page beckoned, enticed, promised, enchanted. And finally, they marched from the page into the air, the atmosphere, my plain and workaday surroundings: the bay outside the window softened and retreated. The Kish lighthouse with its fog-announcing *boom-boom* was silent. The small fishing boat returned to its almost-black location.

I would never forget those evenings. I would never forget that I had been alone and enchanted in a space mastered by language, deluded by verbs, kept at bay by the compressions of gerundives and ablatives. That I had seen firsthand the ability of language, in the right alignment, to control time. That I had participated, in some small way, in that control. That I had felt my local, frail contemporary moment dissolve in the power of a syntax made somewhere else, and thousands of years earlier.

5

Poetry and magic. A fellowship as old as speech and ambition. The first poets were certainly magicians. Keepers of secrets. Makers of incantations. Coaxers of rain and harvest. Holders of spells. But the dream did not die with the keepers of it.

For poetry, the history of magic has always looked suspiciously like its own shadow. *The Cambridge History of English and American Literature* notes the origins of poetry in magic and traces its shadow to a long lost past. "The songs which have been preserved," it states, "seem to be in the nature of incantations for securing the fertility of the fields . . . Some of them occur in descriptions of the magical ceremonies at which they were sung. We may notice especially the verses used for the blessing of the plough when the first furrow is drawn. They are addressed to 'Erce, the mother of the earth,' and are in the form of a prayer that the Almighty will grant her rich fields full of barley and wheat."

The idea of the poet, under an arc of stars, at the edge of a harvested field, at the center of society has a true charm. But the idea of the poet in possession of a particular language to control all these has more than that. Furthermore, the idea that the poet will find the right name for those constellations, will keep the rain away from the harvest or guarantee a firstborn son is compelling. Not because these things give the poet access to magic. But because they give access to power.

332 | CITIZEN POET

Who wouldn't wish to hold on to it? And so the idea that poetry could retain its magical inheritance as a strengthening, rather than a weakening force—right up to modern times—is sanctioned by critics. Even the most sober-sided. Matthew Arnold, for instance, in 1866 said:

> If I were asked where English poetry got these three things, its turn for style, its turn for melancholy, and its turn for natural magic, for catching and rendering the charm of nature in a wonderfully near and vivid way, I should answer, with some doubt, that it got much of its turn for style from a Celtic source; with less doubt, that it got much of its melancholy from a Celtic source; and with no doubt at all, that from a Celtic source it got nearly all its natural magic.

If the alliance and then division between magic and poetry were just historic then none of this would matter. Times change. Poetry has moved and evolved. But no, the real importance of that old tension is its reenactment in the life of the individual poet. When the old dream of shaping the world through language somehow intrudes on the daily work of the poem.

I am not speaking here about runes or spells. I am simply inferring a longing for that feeling of order and force which comes when a poem seems to echo that ghostly past. When it re-orders a moment. When its cadences shift and slip and undercut the hard, temporary logic we all live by.

Imagine a poet at night, making a poem which resists and resists. Imagine that distance outside the window, crawling with starlight, deep in shadow. Imagine for a moment that the words on this page could once have made those shadows move or named those stars.

In fact, for any poet, the tension between a language of power and a lexicon of true limits is a daily, chastising struggle. The old shadow of magic is merely the map of our own human longing to be without the pain we call time.

Time, power and language: themes shared between the poem and the new technology. And so, when history catches up, when the computer arrives primed with power and language, in a certain sense, and with a certain irony, the poet is particularly well prepared to comment.

6

The architecture of a computer is a mystery. Quite simply, the building process is invisible. There are of course physical signs of a structure, but they are deceptive. There is a motherboard and there are slots which take the sensitive component parts. The sharp simms memory modules—so fragile you can only put them into the computer while earthing and grounding yourself. The modems with their green surfaces and bumps of solder, the hand scanners and graphics boards. Years ago silicon had changed the process forever. It had taken the computing process from the huge, dust-free rooms in which it had begun into small offices and summer rooms like mine, where a table in front of sunlight and green leaves supported what had once taken a concrete building to house.

Years ago, also, the computer had leaped out of the hands of its inventors, refusing to be merely an assembly of mechanical adding parts, casting off the punched cards and the paper tape readers of the 1950s. By the 1970s a computer could check eight binary digits of data with every cycle. A group of such digits was called a byte. A byte contained over two hundred patterns of ones and zeros. And each pattern was urging and instructing the computer to do something. To read. To compare. To remember.

So much for the structure. But the builder, the true architect of the computer was different. It was not really silicon nor plastic nor the hot drip of a soldering iron. It was language itself. Language that had odd names and poignant old-fashioned descriptions. High-level language for instance that made an abstract of machine language, that issued declarations and control statements. Programming language that put together the vital instruction set. And compilers that took the source code made by a program and turned it into machine code; something the machine could work with. But how did all of this affect the individual writer?

When I sat down at the computer, turned it on, issued the dark and plain commands of its operating system, I began to feel that I was not simply instructing a machine but constructing a reality. Syntax—that old magic of language I had first found in my Latin grammar—flowed from my hands into a dumb assembly of plastic parts and soldered pieces. And what was enacted then, in my imagination at least, was nearer to myth than technology. And the myth was the myth of meaning. It was the exchange of language between one who understood it and one who could enact it. It was Orpheus playing his music to round-eyed lions and attentive snakes: altering nature with art.

7

Art. The very word etc. Because, of course, I was a poet and not a computer technician. A poet, moreover, from a country which had prepared its poets to think of language in the context of the bardic and the oracular; within the confines of rhetoric or set free by the music of balladry. When I said to myself with equal conviction that the architecture of a poem was also a mystery, I had in mind a different syntax. I had in mind the days of my late teens and early twenties when I had begun writing my first poems. The excitement and challenge then had also consisted in sensing a way in which syntax could release power. Yet I knew these two structures and syntaxes were utterly different.

That summer, my first with a computer, the poems accumulated slowly. I wrote them as I always had, in a clumsy handwritten script, across pages and pages of a notebook. I crossed out and re-wrote. I circled phrases and underlined stanzas.

In literal terms, the relation of those pages to the computer was exactly the same as to the typewriter. Nearing the end of the composition process I would start to print out the whole poem for further revision. I would look carefully at line lengths and consider the new shape in the light of the older and less clear one. After all, I had had a typewriter since college days. And I had long since taken for granted the shifting of the imagined shape into the written one. The slow and cumbersome procedures by which I began to write, and then worked on what I had written, and then printed out what I had worked on had become some kind of awkward second nature.

I had no reason to think it would change. That summer I went through the same movements, the same arrangements. There was no difference in the method. I wrote the poems on the page. I wrote them out by hand. Then I transcribed them. Then I copied them into the computer. Then I printed them.

But there was a difference. The poems were difficult to write. They had never been easy but now there were new resistances. I was older. My children were growing up. Now when I worked it was outwardly with the same action and involvement, but there were new awarenesses. The language of poetry, which had once seemed to me invincible, now carried its own shadows onto the page. They were my shadows, of course, not those of poetry. But it would take time to realize that. As I struggled to write, I was aware as I never had been before that the language on the page had the power to enact a stay of time, but not to include me in it. That I could construct, through this language, exemptions to the process of time and yet could not avail of them. It was an ordinary and obvious realization, but I had never before been in the circumstances when limits of language seemed so personal a loss.

And with that feeling of loss came another sense, harsh and exact, of the powerlessness of the poet. I could stand at my window, a middle-aged woman, without the ability to rid myself of memory, and see time made green and ominous in my own garden. There was nothing I could do about it. And the little I could do—slow work on the page—seemed unfitted for the task.

Slowly, however, the poems happened. Given my sense of hesitation, I was surprised that I wrote continuously. And yet I did. The poems formed. I copied them onto the page of the notebook. Then it was time to take them to the computer. I would cross the room. I would turn on the switch. The computer would start, the screen would clear. I would sit down and write the few words of the DOS script—by now I was more fluent, more confident. Then I would begin the word processing program and start to write the far less fluent, less confident words of the poems. And so, without realizing it, I engaged each day in two opposites of language; an opposition of history and possibility so intense it became a fearsome dialogue before I was even aware of it.

The first—poetry—was the one I had inherited and loved. It had come, a veteran art, from the nineteenth century, from a struggle it had won and been wounded by: against the decline of faith, against the dethroning of the imagination, against the fracture of meaning. And yet it had survived. I was part of its survival. Until that moment I had not examined the nature of that survival; and I had never doubted it.

The second was a new culture of language, one long implied by science and made inevitable by technology. This was its first, glittering moment of emergence. It was brand new and yet ancient in some of its allusions. When I sat at the screen and used a crude and simple formula of compression—pkzip mine c:\ *.*— and found that the space on the drive was suddenly more, that the documents I had written were suddenly enclosed and shrunk, it was hard not to feel that, for all the banality of plastic, I was being invited back into a realm where the magician and poet were reunited. Where a small act of syntax could lead to a defiance of limitation.

The summer wore on. The poems grew. The computer stored and printed them. Stored and printed them again. One form of language accumulated slowly and painfully. Another gave them shelter with mysterious ease and power. Between them, acting as a link, was myself; was the hand that wrote the poems and the mind that remembered them; that executed the operating language and remembered its commands.

When the summer began they had been separate actions; separate but not opposed. As it wore on, as the season changed, as the contrasts grew, the oppositions between those languages grew more intense in my mind. The part of me that was a poet remained assured and committed, but felt more frail. The part that was gaining ease and confidence with the computer began to see an unlimited horizon, where language led straight to power.

But I was uneasy. Stricken and surprised that after so many years of knowing poetry, of seeing its reach and grace, I should regret any part of its limitation. But I could not be dishonest. This new language had a glamour and force, it had history on its side. And so I began the long and difficult process of comparing those languages while using both. And my mind changed so radically in the process and came to such turbulence and re-assessment that I could see I had, for myself, touched some nerve about the nature of language. And this piece is the result.

8

The date 1475 means little enough now. The name *Recuyell of the Historyes of Troy* means less. Yet in their time they were signs of a watershed. They marked exactly that mixture of chance and personality and the force of the moment which has also marked the more recent watershed.

In 1471 William Caxton finished his translation of *Recuyell of the Histories of Troy*. His French was only passable but the book was popular in the Burgundian court. Many people requested a copy. But copying was a tedious and time-consuming prospect. Caxton had visited Cologne in 1471 where he first saw a working printing press. By 1475 he had his own in Bruges with two fonts of type. There, to forestall the tedious work of copying his translation by hand, he printed it instead.

And so a man and a medium—a crude association of ink and

mind and mobile metal—changed the world. It would never revert. The old cumbersome methods of reading and writing and sharing knowledge had been altered forever.

The past twenty years, as has often been stated, is comparable. But there is a difference. The fifteenth-century revolution in printing rescued a civilized fellowship from isolation. It made the book possible; it made the audience actual. This event is different, especially in its reception. There are relatively few accounts of writers in mid-life for whom this technology arrived, not just as a change of machines, but as a series of profound questions which needed to be addressed. There are essays on the consequences of change. But the down-to-earth, this-happened-to-me accounts of poets and novelists have been slow in coming.

I, for one, like the way writers describe writing. Keats changing his shirt to make a new poem. Yeats walking up and down at Coole Park. Plath in the hard frosts of Devon, writing her best work. They make an equivalence to the physical existence of drafts: they are an informal commentary on a process. And writers, by and large, are not slow to write about the associations between their process and other things: cafés, wine vintages, weathers, new towns and old acquaintances. But about the encounter between that process and this technology they have been far more reticent. The reasons are not clear. They may lie in unease, in resentment, in the belief that this new technology threatens the beloved existence of the book. But these are the very oppositions which will make future writers curious. They will want to know how this generation—which was, so to speak, hit by technological lightning—reacted. They will want to hear their story. If they can't find it, it will seem to them, as it does to me, a loss.

LETTER TO EDITOR

Poetry magazine, January 2004

D ear Editor,
   I'm very sympathetic to several of Averill Curdy's points ("Is Anybody Out There?" December 2003). They are made with eloquence, and some of them have that kind of bold, testing honesty which is particularly difficult and especially admirable. The concept that women might exist in the poetry world, even today, on a shadowy border between being silent and being silenced is both poignant and bleak. I think the questions asked here are brave and necessary.

The main sticking point is the idea of criticism itself. I certainly recognize how crucial it is, and how important its role as a rallying point for each new generation. But the question remains: what does it really mean for a poet to develop and possess a critical voice? For myself, I don't associate such a voice with reviewing, or any routine wish to carve out some kind of position. I think of it as something more urgent, more inward.

All poets face one thing, and they face it alone: the mysterious distance, part cultural and all solitary, between writing poems and being a poet. The way it is navigated is different for every poet. I certainly found the writing of prose essential to managing that distance. But the word "prose" is deceptive. I also reviewed poetry for the *Irish Times* for the best part of twenty years. I valued the books; occasionally I valued the chance to say something about them. But reviewing never helped me travel one inch of that distance I'm describing. It is only the making of a critique which does that. What's the difference? Reviewing is almost always—the "almost" here is important—done from the center. It is the outcome of shared ideas, shared assumptions, even the shared fact of the physical object of the book. Critque-making is almost always—another weight here—done from the margins.

It is the product of that inward, isolated struggle to become a poet, and to leave a record of that becoming. Averill Curdy speaks about the relation of authority and articulation. I think the real relation, in terms of a critical voice, is between authority and risk. The poet who risks standing at his or her own margin, and making a critique from it will have the authority of that act. Even though the critique is inwardly directed, wilful or even self-absorbed, the authority comes from renewing the old covenant between being and becoming a poet.

I should add that afterwards, once this is done, then the civil and communal duties of reviewing and commenting have a real value. Then the poet can move from the margin to the center. Poets can argue, explain, chide and protest in a review. But the essential work, the defining work, is in the initial making of an individual critique. Until a poet knows where he or she stands, they can't know where anyone else does.

How much are gender and generation involved? It's a huge question and well stated in Curdy's essay as a question rather than an answer. I tend to think that gender, even now, plays a role in the flawed permissions that women sense as they try to travel between being and becoming poets. By flawed permissions

I mean a compound of different things: diffidence in the face of a canon a woman poet may feel she has inherited but hasn't shaped; anxiety in the interpretation of the relation of the poet's life to a woman's life; the private attempt to clarify what Averill Curdy says may be the fact that "women have a different way of responding to art." Any or all of these can make a poet hesitate on the edge of making her own critique. But flawed permissions can themselves be the engine of new critical understandings. In that sense, the critique offered by women poets can often possess a new and welcome power.

FROM DAUGHTER

An unpublished draft, circa 2007

his book begins on a summer night. I could begin it anywhere. But this will do. Here is the scene as I saw it then:
an inky sky, softening into the shapes of the Dublin hills.
The air full of the smells of cut grass. The silence noticeable
because the calling of children has stopped. I am a young woman
here. I come outside to pick up a child's toy. I look up at the
window, behind which my small daughters are asleep. I go into
my house again, and up the stairs to a room above the garden.
There I write in a journal. I set aside the journal, and I write
poems. And this is where it begins.

This is a book about a way of life—motherhood—and an
art—poetry—which has made hardly any space for it. It is
about the anger and mystification and finally the curiosity which
made me want to go further with that contradiction. It is about
the years in which I puzzled over the fact that an unhistoric
and given human experience and an old and powerful mode
of expression had not found each other. That is, not enough to
change one another. The effect of this was a deep, personal loss: I
went through my years as a mother without being able to quote

many lines of poetry about it to myself; I continued my work as
a poet with little enough encouragement from within the form to
alter it according to that other life. Part of my motive in writing
this is the hope that it could allay that loss for someone else.

This book is assembled in fragments. The fragments are
deliberate. They echo, retrospectively, the anger, irony and
estrangement I felt as a working poet and a mother, and the
incoherence I felt would make it impossible to draw these two
sides of my life together. Above all, they are intended to probe
the mystery: to lead forward to a place where aesthetics and
argument—at least in my time—refused to go. What is that
place? It is the silence I found, and struggled with, and strained
against. It is the silence I want to fill now with one question:
How did it happen that a great human experience and a great
human art missed one another? Begin with that.

1. LYRIC

I have a daughter like a golden flower.
I would not change her for all the gold in Lydia.

SAPPHO

This cathexis between mother and daughter—essential,
distorted, misused—is the great unwritten story.

ADRIENNE RICH. *Of Woman Born*

There was a little bed, and Marina's younger daughter,
two-year-old Irina, was all alone in it, rocking herself.
Rocking herself and humming. No words, just humming,
but it was surprisingly tuneful and coherent. She adds in

a footnote: "Irina Efron, who was weak and sickly from
birth, died of starvation in winter 1920."

VIKTORIA SCHWEITZER. *Tsvetaeva*

WHAT IS A LYRIC?
Impossibility of Definition.
It is impossible to define a lyric. The faculty that creates
a lyric is too complex, and its functioning is too subtle, for
the psychologist to pin it down with a phrase. The lyric
emotion itself is too vague, too universal almost, to imprison
within the ambit of a few philosophical terms. That is not
to say that definitions have not been given by men who have
made a profound study of aesthetic principles.

PETER F. MCBRIEN. *Higher English: Poetry:*
How to Know Good Poetry, and to Say Why It Is Good

I came to the suburb in my mid-twenties: urban, newly married, bookish and childless. My children were born there. My poems were written there. For a while, the weathers of the place were those of my mind as well. In retrospect, what really happened there?

The reason any poet writes a memoir, a prose statement, is because they believe their circumstances will never happen again. Never in that exact way. As far as the history of poetry goes, they can only be right. Surely I am right in believing the Dublin I found as a student, as a young poet, has gone forever. If I close my eyes I can see its clumsy buses and steamed-up café windows. I can see the sea fogs that came in after dark in November. I can hear the hubris of its literary talk. I see myself—a bookish, estranged, eager-to-please girl—listening to talk about poetry in that city.

Then time spins away. Just as I am ready to be ashamed at the way that girl talks and agrees with men and cuts her cloth, the city disappears. The years rush away. A marriage is made. The scene is changed. The old city, with its malice and history, has developed a hinterland it knows nothing about. The girl is a woman, thirty years of age. She knows something about it. She lives in a suburb, with freshly planted trees and half-completed houses, and the hills right at her doorstep. She is pregnant.

> *I looked on my stomach and saw Frieda Rebecca, white as*
> *flour with the cream that covers new babies, little funny*
> *dark squiggles of hair plastered over her head, with big,*
> *dark-blue eyes. At 5:45 exactly.*
>   SYLVIA PLATH. *Letters Home*

FROM "FIRST LETTER TO A YOUNG WOMAN POET"

I want this letter to come as a shock. I want to tell you about the waste, resistance and exclusions of a great art. At the same time, I don't want to be eloquent or reasonable. Imagine this:

A woman as young as you are. Thirty perhaps? A little older? A spring night in another country. A small neighbourhood in one of those parts of Europe that has neither bitter winters nor hot summers. The snowdrops are over. The daffodils are out. But the sky is still full of winter pointers: Orion. The Bear.

A woman is sitting at a window. She is writing the journal you are about to read. Just behind her head, you can see an outline of doors and other rooms. Her two daughters are asleep there. They are not part of the language in her mind: they are beginning to displace it.

Vera Zvyagintseva, who made friends with Tsvetaeva in
summer 1919 and met her frequently, first heard of Irina
when she once stayed the night at Borisoglebsky Lane. "We
chatted all night, and Marina recited poetry . . . it was
beginning to get light. I saw an armchair heaped with rags,
and a little head sticking out of them. It was Irina, the
youngest daughter, of whose existence I was unaware till then.
Marina put her in some orphanage. And she died there."

VIKTORIA SCHWEITZER. *Tsvetaeva*

So long as you write what you wish to write, that is all
that matters; and whether it matters for ages or only
for hours, nobody can say. But to sacrifice a hair of the
head of your vision, a shade of its color, in deference to
some Headmaster with a silver pot in his hand or to some
professor with a measuring rod up his sleeve, is the most
abject treachery.

VIRGINIA WOOLF. *A Room of One's Own*

We moved in during December. That very first morning, we
woke to a cold prospect. Big, ragged spruces interrupted our
view straight out to the Dublin hills. My first sight of the hundred different blues in the curve and rise of those hills was
absolutely discouraging. I was in a strange place. No theatres,
no talk, no companionship with other poets.

Far from it. It was just a road of half-built houses. If I had
only known it then, I had had the infinite luck to be snatched
away, by one customary life, from the temptations of the other.
My life as a woman—as a wife, as a neighbour, as a cog in an
old history—had brought me to this place. But that good luck
wasn't in the least visible to me.

I was a vain, hand-to-mouth young woman, whose only importance, in her own eyes, had come from a few poems, a few prizes, a first book and the fast food of praise every young poet craves.

How was I to know I had been saved? The language of poetry, the esteem attached to it, had exempted me from a close-up view of the powerlessness of womanhood. Both in society, and in poetry itself. I valued the poetry. Of course I did. But I also, in some deep subconscious, valued and had an ugly need for the exemption. Now, suddenly, blessedly, it had been taken away.

> *Did I want to be a man? Not that I can remember,*
> *certainly not sexually. But I must have thought that*
> *"To be a man, the crowd's hero" was what becoming a*
> *published poet would mean; it was where my ambition*
> *was driving me. Then the definition changes to something*
> *female but disturbing: "Half lover-poet-sybil." How could*
> *you be a sybil by halves? I recognized, though I still did*
> *not fully recognize, the doubleness of my urge to become.*
> *What was expected of me, what I wanted for myself in the*
> *most profound ways, was marriage and children. I saw the*
> *"nets" as "kind" even though they were also the "coils"*
> *of my middle-class heritage . . . I didn't really think you*
> *could be double. At the University of Iowa, some years*
> *later, a classmate told me he believed that to be a woman*
> *poet was a "contradiction in terms."*
>
> JANE COOPER. "Nothing Has Been Used
> in the Manufacture of This Poetry
> That Could Have Been Used in the
> Manufacture of Bread"

PAGES FROM A JOURNAL

April 1977

I find it hard to write about Sarah. Is this because she's still so new? A year and four months old. She stands in her cot, dressed in yellow pajamas with a brown donkey on them, a halo of curls and her cheeks shining. My little daughter. I never expected her. But now I think I always craved her.

Kevin is downstairs watching a Beckett trio on television. Right behind me the summer evening is opening like a fan with a span of peacocks and a frill of new green and magpies strutting and foraging. What wouldn't I give to be a part of this risk, this musk of excitement and danger?

April 22nd

The evening time. The hard part of the day for me. Maybe the reason I don't write poetry at the moment is because I get to it this late in the day. During the winter I tried it differently. But so few poems came out of that. I got up early for a while. I sometimes thought I touched something deep. But there was nothing to show for it.

Sarah has fallen asleep after a sobbing fit. Her fists still folded up with the tension of it. Her cheek is red with a tooth.

April 25th

Somewhere are poems I want to write. But it's too structured in my mind. I behave too consciously to the possibility. That old system of sitting down at the table in the kitchen in Morehampton road. Of writing a lyric at will. It won't do anymore. Not now. But what will?

May 1st 1977

Kevin and I went in to Sarah early. We built colored towers
and banged the toy xylophone. She stood up in a wobbly
sort of way, balancing herself against Kevin's dressing gown,
rummaging in his pocket for papers.

Suddenly, when we were putting the room back to order,
I remembered her at a few weeks old. It was all eerily clear:
The way her night-cry brought me into her room. The high
white walls and the exaggerated shadows. The tick of the
bottle warmer. It all came back. And all the time, outside,
the winter bustling and growing and then giving way and
the light creeping towards the solstice.

But will I ever write the poem I want to about it all?

FROM "First Letter to a Young Woman Poet" (continued)

I was that young woman. By that time, I was also a poet. I had
published two books. I had lived in a literary culture. The discovery of poetry had been the first real adventure of my life. The
making of poems, however flawed, had made me real to myself.

Then my daughters were born. Slowly, with a sense of scandal
and astonishment, I found that this great art—this venerable,
exact, magisterial craft—had no place for the central adventure
of my life. No language. No ethic. No aesthetic. The poems I
wrote in those first years of their life laboured under that sense
of surprise. There was no joy in writing a poem like "Night
Feed." I finished it one summer afternoon. No joy. But maybe
something aggressive and solid. As if I was trying to teach lyric
poetry a new word.

NIGHT FEED

This is dawn.
Believe me
This is your season, little daughter. The moment
  daisies open,
The hour mercurial rainwater
Makes a mirror for sparrows.
It's time we drowned our sorrows.
I tiptoe in.
I lift you up
Wriggling
In your rosy, zipped sleeper. Yes, this is the hour
For the early bird and me
When finder is keeper.
I crook the bottle.
How you suckle!
This is the best I can be,
Housewife
To this nursery
Where you hold on,
Dear life.
A silt of milk.
The last suck.
And now your eyes are open, Birth-
  colored and offended. Earth wakes.
You go back to sleep.
The feed is ended.
Worms turn.
Stars go in.

Even the moon is losing face
Poplars stilt for dawn
And we begin
The long fall from grace.
I tuck you in.

The Prime Essential

But what we want to know, without any straining
after absolute logical precision, is how, roughly, to
recognize the true lyric when we meet it, and how to
pick out from any poem that part of it that strikes the
true lyrical note. It is true that the lyric has certain
characteristics, some of which are more important than
others, but still it has them all. Now, thousands of
second-rate poems are true lyrics, that is, have all these
qualities in combination; whereas there are thousands of
perfect poems that are lyrical and yet have not all these
characteristics in combination. Until you have clearly
grasped this important distinction, you will make no
progress in your study of literature.

FROM MCBRIEN, Higher English: Poetry

Two of the charges most frequently leveled against poetry
by women are lack of range—in subject matter, in
emotional tone—and lack of a sense of humor. And one
could, in individual instances among writers of real talent,
add other aesthetic and moral shortcomings: the spinning
out; the embroidering of trivial themes; a concern with
the mere surfaces of life—that special province of the
feminine talent in prose—hiding from the real agonies of

the spirit; refusing to face up to what existence is; lyric or
religious posturing; running between the boudoir and the
altar, stamping a tiny foot against God; or lapsing into
a sententiousness that implies the author has re-invented
integrity; carrying on excessively about Fate, about time;
lamenting the lot of the woman; caterwauling; writing the
same poem about fifty times, and so on.

THEODORE ROETHKE. *On the Poet and His Craft*

PAGES FROM A JOURNAL

February 2nd 1980

I'm in the dining room. I like it here with the garden window. Kevin is in the front room, his legs crossed, his new book beside him. I've noticed recently that all the dear things seem more typical than particular.

It's the disturbing parts of my own mind that trip me up—not just writing them. Living them, too. Being thirty-five. Being certain I won't have another child. Part of me is that thing nature hates: the broken temple, the stone at the mouth of the grave. How cumbrous I feel. And how finished.

Three years ago—was it that much?—I worked in the room upstairs and I sat at the desk, with everything round me—the muddled shelves and the books and the mesh curtains, and Sarah scarcely more than a baby.

But now—such irony. I sit in this room, the lamp reflecting in the glass. One daughter asleep upstairs. One getting ready to go to bed. And I remember the mystery and peace of three years ago, and how brave I felt getting up early and thinking *I will persevere.*

February 11th 1980

The whole morning has been like this: fractious and ill-tempered and drab. Both wretched with the chicken pox. I feel so sorry for them. Sarah a little better.

Now it's afternoon. Back in the dining room. The trees are still bare. The light is pre-spring. The grass is a flat color as if everything was just restraining itself from dazzle.

I think the worst thing is this: I look back on myself, on my persistence, however erratic. I see myself just beginning—struggling to write about this life.

March 7th 1980

A grey morning. But real spring. Eavan Frances is beside me, scrambling up and down from the chair, then back onto a stool.

She's better. Then the chair again. The gap in her hair, where they cut it away, is almost closed.

Chicken pox, rain, the nights broken. Days and days go by. I write nothing.

Now, just as I'm writing this, she has scrambled right on top of the striped chair. Her little bright eyes are at table level.

This is the life I want to show. This instant, visionary world here—the colors, warmth, the children at the end of the day. How all this found me.

March 14th 1980

It's late at night. The dark has drawn in totally. In the little rectangle of light from the kitchen window, I can see the grass is absolutely packed with daisies. And upstairs my

children with their fists, damp and tight. This is the poem
I've been trying to write.

I used to get up at night in America, and go into the bath-
room. Then I'd see myself in the mirror—my outline, my
thighs, my face—and I would think *it's finished.*
I've been used, I'd think. *I've been discarded.*

> *Love set you going like a fat gold watch.*
> *The midwife slapped your footsoles, and your bald cry*
> *Took its place among the elements.*
>
> SYLVIA PLATH. "Morning Song"

> *On the afternoon of August 31, she was found hanging*
> *from a hook inside the entrance to her hut. As Karlinsky*
> *says: "Marina Tsvetaeva, one of Russia's greatest poets*
> *of this or any century, was buried in Yelabuga in an*
> *unmarked common grave."*
>
> ROBERTA REEDER. *Anna Akhmatova: Poet and Prophet*

PAGES FROM A JOURNAL

March 11th 1980

I keep thinking one thing. So many people have lived—so
many women I mean—with more than my aptitude and
character and spirit. My mother—just to begin with.

But I still don't find in poetry the story I want: which I
suppose is the story of this. My life here. What happened
here. What I've felt in these past few years.

Is it just hopeless presumption to try? Maybe I have
some clerkly aptitude for neat figures, that can reach out to

this disorder of silence that has existed forever about sleeping children, and the world behind and around them. The stacked cups out there. The daisies. I have some capacity for persistence. I keep thinking that all it needs is some subterranean mathematics, some music. Then that silence, or whatever it is, would give way.

Power in the Lyric
When you speak of the power of a lyric you mean
that the poem in question expresses and evokes one clear
emotion; no more. If there is an entanglement or confusion
of emotions, the poem is so far unlyrical. It must have
emotional unity as well as the unity of pattern or design
which is the external symbol of the spiritual unity it is
meant to express. The single emotion, moreover, must be
clear and simple. Any ordinarily sane and healthy person
ought to be able to experience it in his or her own life. Any
ordinarily cultured person on reading the expression of this
emotion in the lyric ought to be able to say: That is just
how I felt; or else: that is just how I would feel.
                    FROM MCBRIEN, *Higher English: Poetry*

The divine breath . . . How did it never pass, even in the
lyrical form, over the lips of a woman? How strange!
And can we deny that it was so? I look everywhere for
grandmothers and see none.
                    ELIZABETH BARRETT BROWNING.
                       The Brownings' Correspondence

So what does she do? What did I do? I read the older
women poets with their peculiar keenness and ambivalence:

Sappho, Christina Rossetti, Emily Dickinson, Elinor Wylie, Edna Millay, H. D. I discovered that the woman poet most admired at the time (by men) was Marianne Moore, who was maidenly, elegant, intellectual, discreet. But even in reading these women I was looking in them for the same things I had found in the poetry of men, because I wanted women poets to be the equals of men, and to be equal was still confused with sounding the same.

ADRIENNE RICH. "When We Dead Awaken"

FROM "FIRST LETTER TO A YOUNG WOMAN POET" (CONTINUED)

If I told you that there wasn't a terrible, tight maleness about the poetic world I first published in, that I wasn't on guard, that I didn't learn to look for a slighting vocabulary—both slighting and intimidatory—I wouldn't be telling the truth.

I came to poetry by the lyric route. I was born in the city that knew that route by heart. I grew up in a poetic world whose roots were almost as deep as the eighteenth century. Dublin was a city of iconoclasm and late night talk. It was not only male. It was bardic. What it valued was history and pessimism and the public poet. What it remembered was not Yeats—he was a relative newcomer—but some bitter world in which history had abandoned the bards. Their language, their life.

What it was comforted by was an idea of the poet cut free from all ties—domestic ones above all—and fixed in a romantic posture, viewing the world from a vantage point where only nature could confirm him, only language could elevate him. After a while I became absolutely firm and clear and indifferent about parts of it. The suggestion that women's poetry was restricted, domestic: that was too customary in the end to have an effect.

What I listened for, what I thought more damaging, was the general version of this particular: that women were bringing into poetry currents of experience which would somehow make it small. One word above any other: autobiography.

The idea that autobiography puts poetry at risk, that it leads to a coarsening and blurring of the line between self-expression and art, is not new. But it had a different intensity when I was young. It stands, even now, as a code that leads poetic argument back to the secrets and mysteries of resistance and priestly ownership. When the code is broken open, the argument is revealed to mean something like this:

Women—so it goes—have not lived the lives which fit them to be the central, defining poets that men can be.

But wait. The argument is much more sophisticated than you think, more than it looks at first. Men are acculturated, by art, history and power—this is how it goes—to control the relation between the inner and outer world. Not only to control it. To define it also. Poetry itself has been defined by that definition. "Before Wordsworth," wrote Trilling, "poetry had a subject. After Wordsworth its subject was the poet's own subjectivity."

With that achieved, inherited control over inner and outer worlds in the back pocket, so to speak, of every young male poet from 1800 to the present day, poetry seemed safe.

Now imagine. Someone, like myself—like you maybe—stays indoors in the rain on an October evening. The fire is lit. There are long shadows on the wall. The children are asleep. The outer world—the trees, the whipping darkness, the clouded-

over stars, the sleeping children—creeps out of its definition. In
defiance of the romantic movement, of the modernist initiative,
of Arnold, of Eliot, of every canonical authority, it takes up its
new identity: it becomes an inner life.
How beautiful. How dangerous!

ENDINGS

A child
shifts in a cot.
No matter what happens now
I'll never fill one again.

It's a night
white things ember in:
Jasmine. And the shine—
flowering, opaline—
of the apple trees.
If I lean
I can see
what it is the branches end in:
The leaf.
The reach.
The blossom.
The abandon.

PAGE FROM A JOURNAL

March 20th 1980
A dream on Friday night. Two sets of people crouching
under a tree. There had been—somehow I knew this in the

dream—two sets of suicides on that ground. I wanted there to be blossom. Before I woke, I felt a fluttering over my head.

Is this a leave-over from Eavan's illness? This is her second spring. There is still a gap where the skin of her head shows through her hair: eggshell fragile. Five months ago—and nothing but that and dreams to remind us that the horror was real.

2. THE DREAM CONVENTION

DREAM-ALLEGORY is one variety of the vision
literature popular in the Middle Ages. The allegory
may vary widely in purpose and extent and is often fused
with other, frequently more interesting, elements. The
framework, however, shows little variety.
　　　　　The Princeton Dictionary of Poetry and Poetics

Darkness. I hear voices. I open my eyes. I hear them
saying: "It was a little girl. Better not show it to her."
All my strength returns. I sit up. The doctor shouts:
"Don't sit up!" "Show me the child!" "Don't show it,"
says the nurse, "it will be bad for her." Nurses try to
make me lie down. My heart is beating so loud I can
hardly hear myself repeating: "Show it to me." The doctor
holds it up. It looks dark and small, like a diminutive
man. But it is a little girl. It has long eyelashes on closed
eyes, it is perfectly made, and all glistening with the
waters of the womb.
　　　　　ANAÏS NIN. "Birth"

The mother does not sleep;
she stares
fixedly into the bright museum.

LOUISE GLÜCK. "The Sick Child"

Our daughter did not die. But at one year and three months of age she contracted meningitis. One moment—this was the way it seemed—she was a lively, vocal baby. The next she lay, with no color in her face, in a clear plastic cot, in the Mercy Hospital in Iowa.

We were far from home. Ireland, our family, our friends were thousands of miles away. We were alone, with our other small daughter, beside a sudden abyss.

Her head was shaved. Antibiotics were dripped into it. For days the fever continued. For days she seemed lifeless. The small head, the brain, the centers of sight and retention I had hoped to fill with language, images, memories, were all under siege by one of the great killers of children.

It was October. The beautiful air of the midwestern town had started to turn cold. The sun shone for the first days of her illness. I went from hospital, to home, to hospital. Pumpkins began to appear on doorsteps. Sometimes in the evening, walking back, I could see a flame flickering weakly behind the cut-out eyes. I turned my eyes away from the wavering, the fragility.

Although I knew, in one part of my mind, that medicine had advanced, that the drugs were strong, that there was hope, another part flew helplessly to the darkest chances: she was so small. The force of this attack on her was so pitiless.

At night I sat by her bed, looking for the child I had known, looking for some recognition from her. Neither were there. I felt my powerlessness as if it had been flesh, skin, a limb that would no longer do what I wanted it to.

For the days that she was ill, in danger, unable to respond, to lift her head, to recognize us, we both struggled with a sense of complete despair. At the edge of that again—an even darker hinterland—was the subversive and terrible recognition, barely kept at bay, of the treasured beauty and importance of this child. Of what we stood to lose.

> *Nnu Ego was the apple of her parents' eyes. She was a beautiful child, fair-skinned like the women from the Aboh and Itsekiri areas. At her birth it was noticed that there was a lump on her head, which in due course was covered with thick, curly, black hair. But suddenly one evening she started to suffer from a strange headache that held her head and shoulder together.*
> BUCHI EMECHETA. *The Joys of Motherhood*

> *Remember what I have often told you, that we never can expect to be exempt, as to our many children, from the afflictions of other parents, and that if—if when you come I should even have to say to you, "Our little baby is dead," you are to do your duty to the rest, and to show yourself worthy of the great trust you hold in them.*
> CHARLES DICKENS. Letter to his wife
> on the death of their daughter, Dora, 1851

> *By spring the child will die.*
> *Then it is wrong, wrong*
> *to hold her—*
> *Let her be alone,*

without memory, as the others wake
terrified, scraping the dark
paint from their faces.

LOUISE GLÜCK. "The Sick Child"

FROM "SECOND LETTER TO A YOUNG WOMAN POET"

Someday you will go up to a room. You will go over to a table, and sit down and begin to write. The window in front of the table will face into the dark of the garden, into a sweet atmosphere full of shadows and winter stars. There is the page. Here is your pen. What can be wrong? Poetry has assembled its critique the way custom assembles laws: slowly, with a self-conscious authority, over-dependent on precedent and slow to break with it. For two hundred years these critiques, naming and re-naming themselves—modernism, post-modernism, romanticism—have taken new initiatives based on old exclusions. But the exclusions are subtly coded. In the nineteenth century they were visible in phrases such as *important* and *immortal* and *imperishable*. Now they are hidden in assumptions about poetic language and the identity of the poet.

You take up your pen. What can stop it marking the page? You are ready to write. You are sure of what you want to write. But something—you are not sure what—prevents you.

> *The Themes of Poetry*
> *It has been said that poetry has but three themes: love,*
> *religion, and war. On first glance many poems would*
> *seem to stand outside this trinal classification; and, since*
> *the time of Wordsworth, much of English nature poetry,*
> *though not all, refuses to fall into any one of the three*

*categories. But on the whole the classification is a good
one and the Wordsworthian preoccupation with Nature
for itself alone can hardly be said to touch any of the
fundamental, primitive emotions of mankind as do the
other three. Very often the three themes are combined in
the one poem as different aspects of the same emotional
fact, as it comes under different qualities of interpretative
illumination. For death is the concomitant of battle, and
death, which is the true focus-point of all religion, means
the bereavement of a loved one.*

FROM McBRIEN, *Higher English: Poetry*

That room would stay in my mind for years. Two windows, one straight ahead and one to my left. The twilights were fast. The light, after dark fell, was burnished, the bulbs shielded in the lamps, and the color of one blue chair in the corner deepened and glowed in the shadow. Beside her were the machines, tubes, drips she depended on. Her cot had a clear, plastic roof. On it lay the inert bear we had bought in Chicago, a dark brown splayed out shape. There was an open space behind me, beyond which was the nurses' station. And then those windows, through which came the mournful sound of the Rock Island Line, and the sweet air of a midwestern autumn, growing quickly colder.

She had been our beautiful second daughter, red-haired, quick to walk, independent and curious. The idea that the small, straight spine, which had grown perfect in me, was under attack, was almost too terrible for understanding, were it not for the succession of drugs, nurses, doctors.

I thought she would die. For three days she lay without movement. No smiles, no recognition. On the first morning she convulsed with terrible, marionette movements. I had no life except at the hospital, often till late. But we both thought, for her sense of security, I should spend the nights at home with her sister. I phoned the hospital at midnight. Then, awake after a few hours' sleep, I phoned the hospital again, usually at 3 A.M. Finally, the night nurse had good news. Our daughter had smiled. Was it strange, I thought in that irrational moment of joy and relief, that she had smiled at that moment? In those low hours? But then, I thought—perhaps equally unreasonably—she was an Irish child. Far away it was not the bleak, low pre-dawn hour, but a full autumn morning in Ireland. The light curving and easing over the coast, the harbour, inland a mile or so to our house, and on to the hills which were the backdrop to her first year. It comforted me more than it should have, to think that in some part of her wounded body, her memory, her infant sense of time, it was an Irish morning that she first began to recover in.

FROM "SECOND LETTER TO A YOUNG WOMAN POET" (CONTINUED)

Say that the day has been cold, that the winter jasmine has begun to flower. Say that at dusk you closed the curtains, put the kettle on, saw that one child was ready for bed and one child was sitting beside the black cat on the bench. The kettle boiled. The windows fogged with the steam. The damp warmth put a skin of wet on your hands, on your arms. Suddenly this room, with its sensory world of damp and children, with your sense of the shut-out stars, the misted over jasmine, becomes the limit and extent of your understanding of beauty and truth. Perhaps not for long. But a moment is enough.

Enough for what? Here, again, is the room, the table, the pen.

Now how will you put that moment in the poem? What is that shadow which suddenly lies across your page?

What if I were to tell you that no book of aesthetics, no essay on metre, no treatise on the art of poetry is as revealing as that shadow? Follow that shadow back to where it came from—track it, chase it, close with it—and you will come to the mysterious inner chamber of the art. The old Druidic center of poetry. The place where its first authority was composed, its first permissions given and refused, its first subject matter decided on. Where the poem was charged with stories, definitions. But not of this one. Not of this room with its kettle and its children and your transforming sense. They are not included. They do not belong there.

> *The Uncultured*
> *Conversely, when you see a person moved by, say, a story that is cheap and shallow, you may at once put him down as being below the average level of culture.*
>
> FROM McBRIEN, *Higher English: Poetry*

Afterwards, without wanting to, I thought of the underworld. As a student in school and college I had studied Latin. In the Sixth book of the *Aeneid* the underworld opens out, beside its polished river and its dangerous alcoves. The Latin is earnest and memorable. Thieves, lovers, warriors speak out of the text. I had read it with pleasure and confidence. It was a construct. A fiction.

In the week in which she began to get better, after she first smiled, I could think of nothing else but her getting better. I sat by her bed and saw her quickly, miraculously, begin to get her strength back. The brown bear came down from the roof of the cot and lay beside her. The tubes and drips hardly interfered with her eating. And as she recovered, something strange began to happen.

The shadows which had occupied my mind, which had stayed with me bodily even when I was half asleep, began to lift. They were not vague entities which are called worries or fears. I felt them as thick, physical shadows: a coldness, a darkness in which I stood, in which I slept, in which I remembered her as a little vivid child. Into which I could see her beginning to disappear.

Now she was recovering, spared, and they were gone. I sat in the small hospital room in a midwestern town looking at her hand, at her closed eyes. Her skin was pink again and a solid sweetness filled out her shape, her outline.

For years afterwards, I would remember those shadows: the thickening dark and cold of that time. Even then, I understood that they united me to a human mystery, that they brought me to an entrance from which, at the last minute, we were turned back. Even then I understood that they were harbingers from a world out of which children never return, out of which our memories and spirits would never have emerged if our daughter had disappeared there.

The underworld, after all, was not a literary fiction. It was this place. These shadows.

But I also knew those shadows connected me to a human past. That they had the power—although this came later—to radicalize my poetic present.

But there was something else: during that time I had felt an aloneness which was not simply to do with being far from home, or having a sick child, or fearing the future. I had no words for this then, and maybe not much consciousness of it either. Later it would become extremely important in my memory of those days.

I was a poet. I had constructed my life, my consciousness, my commitments since I was very young, on love for the art, on a deep faith in its nearness to truth. But where was poetry in that room? In some corner of my mind, when I looked around the room, I knew it was untouched by the language of poetry, had always been starved of that touch.

My thoughts were disconnected. Watching the liquid drip into my child's head I would think *no one has ever written a poem to an antibiotic.*

The power, privilege and consolation of art—why did it leave me and my child so unattended in that room? The more I thought about it, the more the question seemed urgent, huge and ominous.

The days moved towards Halloween, the air grew colder. Slowly, far away from the part of my mind that was simply grateful, I felt the beginnings of a true intellectual anger.

Immediately cries were heard. These were the loud wailing of infant souls weeping at the very entrance-way. Never had they had their share of life's sweetness for the dark day had stolen them from their mothers' breasts and plunged them to a death before their time.

VIRGIL. *The Aeneid*, Book VI

the male child was born dead, strangled by the cord at birth . . . Tennyson could not forget the alabaster perfection of the little corpse as if it was dressed for burial, and he wrote compulsively friend after friend to tell them of the death of his son. He was assured that if Emily had another child there was no reason to believe it would not be born normally, but the infant's death haunted him all his life, so that when he was ill forty years later he wept as he "talked about his firstborn, & broke down describing the fists clenched as if in a struggle for life."

ROBERT BERNARD MARTIN.
Tennyson: The Unquiet Heart

Mrs Arnold got through the long, endless day better than I could have hoped.

MATTHEW ARNOLD to a friend
on the funeral of his son Thomas

She was lying with her eyes fixed—and I knew what was going to happen.

DOROTHY WORDSWORTH on the
death of William's daughter Catherine

Little Clara's convulsions ceased and she grew quiet and died silently about one hour after they had arrived in Venice. Shelley returned to see her die in Mary's arms. Shelley wrote to Claire that Mary was by this "unexpected stroke reduced to a kind of despair. She is better today."

RICHARD HOLMES. *Shelley: The Pursuit*

We came back to Ireland in December and everything seemed different. The moon slicing the early darkness, the snowdrops that escaped frost—for a while everything was an omen, a promise, an emblem.

What was it I had envied in male poets? What was it I had coveted? Only the previous year, with one small child and another just born, I had read a life of John Milton. Closed into the faction and danger of the seventeenth century—pale, slight, driven and finally blind—he had still had a blessed apprenticeship in poetry. When his days as a student were finished, he went to a place called Horton. There for seven years he prepared himself for his destiny as a poet.

Horton? The name had a fragrance, a stillness, a treasurable distance all that year. I imagined it as the garden of England, a place where the days were gracious, endless. I imagined him, with his few exemplary texts, with a candle guttering as dawn reached back into the Malvern hills. One part of me was enough drawn to the arcane history of poetry, to the power and privilege of language itself, to long fiercely for my own Horton.

The truth was I lacked the nation, the gender, the erudition, the time or the leisure to be at Horton. I was a young mother, upstairs in a room facing out towards the unkempt, sodden Dublin hills. My reading was snatched. My writing was snatched. But still that word Horton kept its sweetness.

In that first winter back from Iowa, the name no longer seemed so sweet. I had the authority of some understanding I hardly had words for yet. I came to explain it this way: there are places where a craft can be learned. Horton was one of them. Or a university. Or a poetry workshop. Or a coterie of quick-minded fellow poets.

But now I knew there are also places where an art can be learned. Places of ordeal and grace. Beside my infant daughter, in that small room, with the train whistle of another destination and the darkness of a different hemisphere outside, I had no chance to learn the craft. But I learned something about the art.

I had come to that room unwillingly. I stayed there through fears and darkness of spirit. I saw my child recover, slowly at first. Then hour by hour. Then minute by minute. I felt that I had come to this place of ordeal, powerfully attended by the spirits of other human beings.

But one thing did not attend me. Language. Poetry. Metre. The deepening mystery of loss and pain and reprieve which happened in that room—with all its echoes of myth—had no pre-existing shape in poetic language.

FROM SECOND LETTER TO A YOUNG WOMAN POET (CONTINUED)

How do we see form? How do we look into it? I am convinced this question divides women poets more than any other.

In my time the division could have been called one between separatists and subversives. These are my terms, and they represent only a crude shorthand.

The separatists saw form itself as offering the oppressor's language to women poets—tempting them towards a place where the erasures I have spoken of were so ingrained that the whole project of form could only be corrupt.

There was something poignant and whistle clean about this. A new world opening—new forms, new inclusions.

I could not do it. I believe, as poets, as women, we are constructed by the construct. If form is the poisoned chalice, then we have drunk out of it already.

I became a poet to the accompaniment of poetic forms re-structuring my world even as I read. However bitterly I would accuse those forms later of unwriting my world, the truth is they had also once written it.

The only way forward, for me at least, was to subvert those forms. To force them into the inclusions they had shunned.

In small increments, I came to a drastic and complete understanding: if I could not make my poetry tell this story, then any other story it told was suspect. This was a central moment: a place where the plates under my life had shifted. One part of my relationship with poetry had ruptured in that room in Iowa. Sitting there alone, with the sound of the freight train, and my child's life in the balance, I expected to feel abandoned by circumstance, luck and even life. But not by art.

One result of this was that I would never again feel diffident about the canon or its customs of subject matter and theme. In that room, I was still a poet because I was always a poet. But I was primarily, with every particle of my mind and personality, a mother. I had time for doubt, as well as grief, reflection as well as fear. And it was still remarkable to me, hours and days and years later, that not a line of poetry, not a single poem, came to my mind or memory in that terrible solitude.

For good reason. Hardly any powerful or persuasive poems on the sickness or fragility of children existed. Tennyson wrote a great and subversive poem on his dead friend, Arthur Hallam. But nothing on his dead son. Shelley wrote a memorable lament for a dead poet, but only a text-reader could see the palimpsest of his dead son's shadow in "Adonais." Wordsworth's poems on the death of "Lucy" pre-empted any reference to the death of his daughter Catherine. Matthew Arnold lamented the death of faith in "Dover Beach" but the death of his three sons, within four years of each other, is not recorded.

What prevented them? What decorum was worth this silence? They were feeling men and passionate artists. They had toppled other household gods. Yet they complied, in their own work, with this erasure.

What angered me most of all—an anger that was slow to develop, that went below the surface of dailyness, that lives in me to this day—was that the great conventions of poetry had not prevented this silence. They had been party to it:

THE SILENCE OF ELEGY

William Wordsworth
1770–1850

Catherine Wordsworth
1809–1812
Died of sickness, aged three

Percy Bysshe Shelley
1792–1822

William Shelley 1816–1819
Died of enteric fever, aged 3

Clara Shelley 1817–1818
*Died of enteric fever in Italy,
aged one*

Alfred, Lord Tennyson
1809–1892

Tennyson
A first son, stillborn 1851

Matthew Arnold
1822–1888

Thomas Arnold 1852–1868
*died after a fall from a horse at
16 years of age*

Trevenen Arnold 1853–1872
died of pneumonia at 19 years of age

Basil Arnold 1866–1868
died of fever at two years of age

The underworld: that elite place, constructed by poets and legend-makers and poets again. A place where poetic history and language blatantly tested its power and exclusion. In the dream-convention poem, the poet goes to the underworld. Aeneas goes for Virgil. Dante goes with Virgil. Chaucer falls asleep at his book, confident that he is shifting the boundaries between dream and reality, between poetic language and the emerging poetic self.

In a way, it is the grandest and most hubristic of the poetic conventions. Made by poets to show that poetry prevails even in the world of shadows. The poet does not so much walk into the underworld as strut there, among the spoiled clerics and disgraced lovers.

My underworld was different: meeting Kevin one snowy afternoon in Iowa, everything seemed in doubt. Our human world, composed of love and purpose, hung in the balance. Our child was deathly sick. The metal-colored water behind us, the snow melting in it, suddenly opened a landscape where anything could have happened: the clay sides of the river could have collapsed, the shadows could have rushed in. This was the real underworld.

How could I forgive this dream-convention, this other construct, for the fact that when Aeneas reaches the edge of the river, in Virgil's poem, he goes past the dead infants with a few throwaway lines? That his intentions are not humane, but heroic?

I did not need to forgive it. But I needed to continue that dialogue with it which connected me to my youth, to my first hopes as a poet. I needed to take the form and make it tell my story.

LOVE

Dark falls on this mid-western town
where we once lived when myths collided. Dusk
has hidden the bridge in the river
which slides and deepens
to become the water
the hero passed on his way to hell.
Not far from here is our old apartment.
We had a kitchen and an Amish table.
We had a view. And we discovered there love
  had the feather and muscle of wings and had
    come to live with us,
a brother of fire and air.
We had two infant children one of whom was
    touched by death in this town
and spared: and when the hero
was hailed by his comrades in hell
their mouths opened and their voices failed
  and there is no knowing what they would have
    asked about a
  life they had shared and lost.
I am your wife.
It was years ago.
Our child is healed. We love each other still. Across
our day-to-day and ordinary distances we speak
plainly. We hear each other clearly.
And yet I want to return to you
on the bridge of the Iowa river as you were, with
snow on the shoulders of your coat
and a car passing with its headlights on:

I see you as a hero in a text—
the image blazing and the edges gilded—
and I long to cry out the epic question
my dear companion:

Will we ever live so intensely again?
Will love come to us again and be
so formidable at rest it offered us ascension
even to look at him?
But the words are shadows and you cannot hear me.
You walk away and I cannot follow.

THE JOURNEY

FOR ELIZABETH RYLE

> *Immediately cries were heard. These were the loud*
> *wailing of infant souls weeping at the very entrance-*
> *way; never had they had their share of life's sweetness for*
> *the dark day had stolen them from their mothers' breasts*
> *and plunged them to a death before their time.*
>
> VIRGIL. *The Aeneid,* BOOK VI

And then the dark fell and "there has never"
I said "been a poem to an antibiotic:
never a word to compare with the odes on
the flower of the raw sloe for fever

or the devious Africa-seeking tern
or the protein treasures of the sea-bed.

Depend on it, somewhere a poet is wasting
his sweet uncluttered metres on the obvious

emblem instead of the real thing.
Instead of sulpha we shall have hyssop dipped
in the wild blood of the unblemished lamb,
so every day the language gets less
for the task and we are less with the language."
I finished speaking and the anger faded
and dark fell and the book beside me
lay open at the page Aphrodite

comforts Sappho in her love's duress.
The poplars shifted their music in the garden,
a child startled in a dream,
my room was a mess—

the usual hardcovers, half-finished cups,
clothes piled up on an old chair—
and I was listening out but in my head was
a loosening and sweetening heaviness,

not sleep, but nearly sleep, not dreaming really
but as ready to believe and still
unfevered, calm and unsurprised
when she came and stood beside me

and I would have known her anywhere
and I would have gone with her anywhere
and she came wordlessly
and without a word I went with her

down down down without so much as
ever touching down but always, always
with a sense of mulch beneath us,
the way of stairs winding down to a river

and as we went on the light went on
failing and I looked sideways to be certain
it was she, misshapen, musical—
Sappho—the scholiast's nightingale

and down we went, again down
until we came to a sudden rest
beside a river in what seemed to be
an oppressive suburb of the dawn.

My eyes got slowly used to the bad light.
At first I saw shadows, only shadows.
Then I could make out women and children
and, in the way they were, the grace of love.

"Cholera, typhus, croup, diphtheria"
she said, "in those days they racketed
in every backstreet and alley of old Europe.
Behold the children of the plague."

Then to my horror I could see to each
nipple some had clipped a limpet shape—
suckling darknesses—while others had their arms
weighed down, making terrible pietàs

She took my sleeve and said to me, "be careful.
Do not define these women by their work:
not as washerwomen trussed in dust and sweating,
muscling water into linen by the river's edge

nor as court ladies brailled in silk
on wool and woven with an ivory unicorn
and hung, nor as laundresses tossing cotton,
brisking daylight with lavender and gossip.

But these are women who went out like you
when dusk became a dark sweet with leaves,
recovering the day, stooping, picking up
teddy bears and rag dolls and tricycles and buckets—

love's archaeology—and they too like you
stood boot deep in flowers once in summer
or saw winter come in with a single magpie
in a caul of haws, a solo harlequin."

I stood fixed. I could not reach or speak to them.
Between us was the melancholy river,
the dream water, the narcotic crossing
and they had passed over it, its cold persuasions.

I whispered, "let me be
let me at least be their witness," but she said
"what you have seen is beyond speech,
beyond song, only not beyond love;

remember it, you will remember it"
and I heard her say but she was fading fast
as we emerged under the stars of heaven,
"there are not many of us; you are dear

and stand beside me as my own daughter.
I have brought you here so you will know forever
the silences in which are our beginnings,
in which we have an origin like water,"

and the wind shifted and the window clasp
opened, banged and I woke up to find
the poetry books stacked higgledy piggledy,
my skirt spread out where I had laid it—

nothing was changed; nothing was more clear
but it was wet and the year was late.
The rain was grief in arrears; my children
slept the last dark out safely and I wept.

ISLANDS APART

PN Review November–December 2008

I live in Dublin and California. In both places, on both sets of shelves, I keep the same book. It was published in Ireland in the twenties. Like anyone with a similar passion, I've given up asking people if they have read it—or asking those who have read it if they remember it.

The book is called *The Hidden Ireland*. It's about a townland in Ireland called Sliabh Luachra, a mountainy, rushy district on the Cork–Kerry border. In the eighteenth century it was the home of native-speaking Irish poets such as Aogán Ó Rathaille and Eoghan Rua Ó Súilleabháin. The book tracks their struggle in a dark time.

The author was Daniel Corkery. He was a fierce, contrarian writer from Cork, born in 1878. He regarded Yeats and Lady Gregory with an equal and angry suspicion. He rejected the Irish Revival. "Though we may think of this literature as a homogeneous thing," he wrote plaintively, "we cannot think of it as an indigenous thing."

The Hidden Ireland is an unrepentant elegy for that "indigenous thing." He mourns and celebrates those hard-pressed, Irish-speaking poets of the eighteenth century. He looks back to their dying language, to the lost Gaelic order and writes with a scalding bitterness about that loss.

When I was a teenager, trying to hear other voices, I heard his. Now, when I go back to Ireland and see the new prosperity there, I still hear that voice. Maybe no passage when I was young—not Synge, not Joyce, not even Yeats—moved me more than his furious insistence that a group of ruined Irish poets could remain an inspiration, in a passage which concludes that their poetry is a rich thing, a marvellous inheritance, bright with music, flushed with color, deep with human feeling. To see it against the dark world that threw it up is to be astonished, if not dazzled.

WHO EXACTLY IS A POET? How do we recognize one, even when circumstances seem to deny the possibility of such an existence? Once I thought Corkery had the answer. Now it looks far less simple. When I try to think these days about what Corkery meant, I keep colliding into other definitions. Nothing about the poet's identity or survival looks as clear as it did when I first read *The Hidden Ireland*. And of course nothing looks as singular. It seems to me now there are many definitions of the poet—some of them contradictory to each other.

Maybe it's that I live in two places, or went to school in different countries, or come from an island where two languages produced two very different versions of the poet— whatever it is, these ideas of the poet's identity and existence keep coming to me, keep asking for a clearer definition. And if I can't exactly provide it, I still keep thinking I should try.

The truth is, different ideas of the poet have always existed. Different circumstances make the ideas change, clash, and evolve. I love the story, for instance, of the Irish-born Oliver Goldsmith. To the naked eye, he was an eighteenth-century English poet. He signed up for everything from the civil couplets to the Augustan grace. The British claim him for their own. But he was also the son of a farmer in Kilkenny. He was a student at Trinity College. He left Ireland and went to London and Scotland. He apprenticed himself there to a different way of being a poet. It all shows up in his headlong and haunting poem *The Deserted Village*.

What I relish most is Goldsmith's own story of his return to Ireland and just how astonished and put off he was by the Irish bards of the time. Those were Corkery's poets, historically adrift, Irish-speaking, and disinclined to take the slightest interest in London. Their public stance and communal acceptance were still there, as well as the fragments and ruins of their language. Goldsmith, who comes upon them as they service a birth or death, is bewildered and fascinated: they are, he writes, "still held in great veneration . . . those traditionary heralds are invited to every funeral in order to fill up the intervals of the howl with their songs and harps."

In other words, these two types of poets—just islands apart—could neither recognize each other, nor share the definition of their calling. Their oppositional lives as poets, however, continuing to puzzle all these centuries later, remain a rich and contradictory thing.

THIS YEAR FOR INSTANCE, back in Dublin for Christmas, I went into Grafton Street. It's the old, central meeting place of the city, the backdrop of many lives. "Met her today point blank in Grafton Street. The crowd brought us together. We both stopped," writes Joyce at the end of *A Portrait of the Artist as a Young Man.*

Now it's a pedestrian area—a bustle of mime artists and shoppers. It was perfect winter weather. In Ireland, the pre-Christmas weeks can be a small season of light before the January onslaught.

The old city is a ghost haunting the new, more prosperous one. The same buildings are there, the same cobbled alleys. But the ethos has changed. This is a place that talks success, money, and travel. Its youth is more cosmopolitan, more contemporary.

Not far from the city center, and just three miles from our house, is Merrion Square. There in Oscar Wilde's old neighbourhood are the Georgian houses of the old Ascendancy. When I was young many had become shabby and were subdivided into flats. In one basement, opposite the gates and gardens of the square, was the Lantern Theatre, a venue for plays and arts events. There I began covering poetry readings for the *Irish Times.*

I covered them for years. I did it faithfully and without too much introspection. I was in my early twenties—the right age for it. The reading might be slated for 7:00 P.M. I would turn up on time at the theatre, the pub, the arts center, the secondary school, the gallery. The poets might be there. They might equally not be there. The reading would begin. On time. An hour late. Two hours late. I would listen for the poems. I would shape my piece as I listened—quoting, referring, scribbling.

Then some time around midnight I would climb the stairs of the old *Irish Times* building in Westmoreland Street. And if nothing on the night editor's face suggested that he had been waiting for this arrival, nevertheless I was given a chair and a typewriter. I would type out my article, hand it in and drive home in a city laundered by quiet and moonlight.

Occasionally at those readings I would be enchanted and stirred by what I'd seen. Occasionally I would think I had the answer—or part of it—to that perennial question about the poet's identity. One night in the Peacock Theatre I saw Hugh MacDiarmid, the Scottish poet. He was elderly, dressed in a cord jacket, utterly in the moment. When he read about "the white rose of Scotland," when he said out the lines "So I have gathered unto myself / All the loose ends of Scotland," something seemed to shimmer and open behind his frail figure: a place itself being burned into metaphor.

What stirred me most was not the poetry. I certainly relished his work. All the same, I heard an earnestness in the Marxism and nationalism that now and again shouted down the lyric tact. What moved me was something else.

That something else was hard to define but similar to what I felt recently when I managed to find a first edition of Kenneth Rexroth's *In What Hour* published in 1940, and ordered it online. I opened the book parcel eagerly in the copy room at Stanford. Straight away, in "Autumn in California," Rexroth's words made the landscape around me more legible. "The sooty green eucalyptus" and the way the aspens "glitter like goldfish."

The freshness and insistence of those poems were immediately obvious; also the failures. But the truth is, I saw the first and cared little about the second. In Rexroth's book, a California springtime of the late 1930s—fragrant, menacing, lost—mingled with his activist imagining of the Spanish Civil War. In MacDiarmid's work, outrage and music were bedfellows.

The truth is, in the case of both MacDiarmid and Rexroth, what struck me was Corkery's essential point: the witness of the poet. I could feel it in the encounter with their work, listened to and read. Not that it left no questions behind. As for instance—is there such a thing? If there is, how much of it is shaped by externals—by place and displacement rather than by inward freedoms and the act of writing?

Whether or not those question are answerable, one thing is certain: Both Rexroth and MacDiarmid provided that essential thing, hard to define, but familiar when seen: a wider, more generous meaning to the definition of poet. I took away with me and keep still Rexroth's words: "This is perhaps the primary function of the poet, to give life convincing meaning."

AND I NEEDED THOSE WORDS the summer before last when I finished editing a small book—an introduction to the work of Charlotte Mew—for Carcanet Press in England. Mew is a British poet. She was born in 1869 in London. She died there in 1928.

I stole time for the preface and editing from another project—a wonderful and heartening collaboration with Edward Hirsch on a collection of poems called *The Making of a Sonnet: A Norton Anthology*. During the daylight hours a river of emails—and sonnets—went back and forth. Day after day, it was a surefire thrill to see the sheer rightness of fourteen lines after fourteen lines emerge unscathed from electronic mailboxes and burned-up mail servers.

But when the day ended, when the time zones folded back into themselves, I went to the Mew book. I sorted it—for the time it took to do—in that Irish summer interlude which happens between 11 P.M. and dawn in late June, when the sky never actually gets dark.

It was a strange transit. There was a charm and promise about the sonnets which seemed to vanish as soon as I opened

Mew's poems. Going from one to the other felt like a descent. A figurative darkening, as well as a real one. A climbing down from possibility into tragedy.

Mew's life was terrible. Her daily existence was one of bitter gentility, freelancing articles and occasionally publishing poems. In Victorian and Edwardian London it was impossible to express a different sexual choice—and Mew was lesbian. Her friends were few. One sister and a brother were institutionalized for mental illness.

In the early weeks of 1928, she entered a London nursing home. She stayed there a short time. Finally she went out one spring morning and bought a bottle of creosote. She drank it and died foaming at the mouth a few hours later. At that point in the preface, in the presence of that event, I wrote in frustration, "there is no bleaker death in the history of poetry." Perhaps there is. But at that point I couldn't imagine it.

And yet Mew's poems are much more than a fever chart of a harsh existence. They are also a powerful and dissenting conversation with English poetry. She was a rhetorical maverick, with little loyalty to narrative or lyric. Her tone owes almost nothing to the Victorians. It unfolds through big, wilful lines that are always on the verge of a prescient, pre-modernist fragmentation.

Most of all, Mew suggests a different way of being a poet. After the nineteenth-century subplot of poetesses, with their restrictive assignments of religious and domestic themes, here was a total subversion of the category: a poet with so little investment in the society that created the poetess that she could break the mould.

Recently I took a long plane journey and brought a book on tape to go with it. It was an obscure Trollope novel called

An Old Man's Love. I don't associate Anthony Trollope with concerns about poets or poetry; nevertheless, the plot of this book dropped me suddenly and unceremoniously back into that shadow world of competing definitions.

Mr. William Whittlestaff—the central character—is an aging Victorian anti-hero. We learn that he's had two great reverses in his life. He's been jilted by his first love, and his attempts at writing poetry have failed. Both feel like disgrace to him. Trollope, perhaps wisely, doesn't quote the unsuccessful work. But he makes his failed poet a sympathetic character—growing older, remote from reality, embarking on a last attempt at love.

The novel may be little known, but I suspect Mr. Whittlestaff—or his ilk—was a familiar enough figure at the end of the nineteenth century. I imagine there were plenty of them. Gentleman amateurs. Sheltered men who idealized the role of the poet but couldn't enact it. It might be that no one wanted to read their work. But they had recognized virtues. They hadn't been atheists or vegetarians or stirrers-up of European revolutions, or prone to elope with poetesses.

I sometimes wonder these days whether there is a new Mr. Whittlestaff in existence. But a reverse of Trollope's template. Society now—to use the term loosely and inaccurately—is insistent that poetry is of little use. By a strange irony this seems to have led to the demand that actual poets, as against their work, be more visibly useful than ever before.

WHETHER WE LIKE IT OR NOT, the contemporary poet is increasingly skill-based. Or expected to be. He or she can—or should—lecture, lead a workshop, run an introductory class, teach composition, write a review, give a conference paper. In pursuit of all this, he or she is also expected to travel neatly, punctually, and soberly.

I should add that I don't mean to confine this at all to American terms. I mean it in Irish and British terms also. I think it is a development that is peculiar to the art rather than to any national version of it.

I want to be clear here. These are not negligible skills for the poet in the world. I certainly wanted to acquire them when I was young. All of them seemed to me a way of talking about or living with poetry. They still do. And I still believe many if not most poets engage them for exactly that reason.

Nevertheless, I'm nagged at by the thought that many of the poets I admired when I was young were not skill-based. The opposite in fact. To think of Patrick Kavanagh or Charlotte Mew leading workshops or flying to a strange city to give a reading is to stumble straight into anomaly.

And yet skills are an integral part of the poet's world—and prospects—today. The Stegner Fellows in poetry at Stanford, for instance, are working writers, and many have gone on to become very fine poets. Many of them also go on to teach, to edit, to coordinate, or to administer.

Over the years, I've seen their zest for doing this, their pleasure in finding the right job, the right role. I've seen the contributions they've made. And the fact that they are motivated to make those contributions. I've no doubt the motives derive from the reasons I've mentioned: because it widens the conversation about poetry, and allows them—as many young poets want to be—to be part of it.

But there is always a fraction—even if it's just a small minority—of poets out in the world who don't want to do any of these things. If there's a conversation, they're having it with themselves, with their own poems. They don't want to extend it, share it, structure it. They are private, inward, and dissociated from the skills on offer or in demand.

Once I thought there was a broad tolerance for this. Now I'm not so sure. In Ireland, or the US or the UK, the tilt is towards the poet who can navigate the worlds of the university, the institution, the community, the reading series, the community workshop, the literary festival. There has been a gradual, perhaps calcifying professionalism which requires of a poet a standard of behavior and communality which poets were once exempted from. I was never uncritical of that exemption. But now, somehow, I wish I saw more of it.

"When one burns one's bridges, what a very nice fire it makes," wrote Dylan Thomas. It's a winning statement, suggesting the kind of disregard for convention and orthodoxy poets were once associated with. But his statement has to be weighed against Patrick Kavanagh's words, published at the start of the 1964 edition of his *Collected Poems*. In his author's note, Kavanagh comments that the only true tragedy for the poet is poverty. "On many occasions I literally starved in Dublin," he writes. "I often borrowed a 'shilling for the gas' when in fact I wanted the coin to buy a chop."

That chill reminder of economic vulnerability puts skills in a different light. It doesn't seem right to forget that often they are a lifeline for a poet—a way of buying time and living with dignity.

And yet it seems right to ask—if the skill-based poet is a contemporary figure, then who or what is the antithesis? Who, in other words, is losing out? Is it possible to suggest a category, a grouping, even an individual poet who might be marginalized by such an emphasis? It's a rhetorical question. But here, at least, I can think of some answers.

I think the genuinely avant-garde poet, even in this time of widespread institutional support for "experimentalism," might well find a world of skills onerous. Their work, perhaps more often in process than not, might not be easily available to an audience. Or even to a workshop.

The down-to-earth question of availability might affect women poets. For instance, a younger writer with children might well look with dread at the opportunities offered by scheduled readings, believing that she herself might just not be able to manage the fixed times or even the travel.

The shy poet, the private poet, the anti-social poet, the curmudgeon, the introvert, and the fastidious craft worker—I could see all of these, in various degrees, at various times, looking with skepticism on a world of skills.

And to press the point a bit further: is there a series of shelters, reprieves, spaces of quiet that also offer an unpressured lack of expectation which could suit these poets? The answer has to be partly and quickly in the affirmative. In the US and—increasingly—outside it, there are generous prizes and fellowships. They buy time. They create a buffer zone. They are often judged by poets. They allow the less skill-based poet to resist performance and competence with safety.

That's as it should be. It's always seemed to me right that one side of the poetic world should try to protect the other. Public poets draw sustenance from private ones. Formalists are nourished by experimentalists. But it has become easier and harder to do, to offer that protection. And yet I like to think that in today's climate of debate and questioning, there might be a zone of comfort for a Patrick Kavanagh. And even—who knows?—Charlotte Mew.

STILL THOUGH IT'S USEFUL and even essential to think about alternatives, the truth is that there have always been quirks and absurdities about the poet's fit in the world. There probably always will be. And maybe some of them we wouldn't want to do without.

I. A. Richards, for instance, in an essay on T. S. Eliot, cannot resist retelling his conversation with a bank supervisor he met on holiday in Switzerland who worked at that time in Henrietta Street. A fellow employee was the young Eliot who was then a diligent, if misplaced, bank official.

Mr W., the bank supervisor—as he is described in the anecdote—is neither imaginative nor aware of his co-worker's prospects. In fact, at one point he asks Richards if he thinks his young colleague is a good poet. Richards says, well, yes he is. Then Mr W. responds:

> Whatever his hobby may be, it's all the better if he is really keen on it and does it well. I think it helps him with his work. If you see our young friend, you might tell him that we think he's doing quite well at the Bank. In fact, if he goes on as he has been doing, I don't see why—in time, of course, in time—he mightn't even become a Branch Manager.

A WOMAN WITHOUT
A COUNTRY: A DETAIL

PN Review November–December 2014

I t was winter. I was a student in the National Library, waiting for my call number. The library was a Dublin institution, managing its circular lending room with Victorian grace and delay. You found your book by searching through heavy catalogues. You scribbled its number in pencil on lined paper and handed it in. And waited.

I was starting out as a poet. I was beginning to publish poems here and there. Almost all my reading had been in the poetry of the Irish Revival. Especially Yeats. Sometimes only Yeats. Now I was beginning to see the gaps in my knowledge, especially of contemporary poetry.

My catalogue searches were not yet targeted to individual poets. The books whose numbers I penciled in were chosen for survey rather than specificity. Most likely the poem I stumbled on was in an anthology and not a single volume. It was called "Pike" by the British poet Ted Hughes.

It wasn't long. Eleven stanzas of four lines. In the first four, the pike—a fish I'd never seen—was described: its eerie grin, its gold-green stripes, its killer jaws. Later I would find it was a fish that could be found in Irish rivers, the Lee, the Barrow, the Erne. For now it only existed on the page.

In the second stanza the pike changes again. It becomes a creature of "submarine delicacy and horror." In the third it holds quite still, "hung in an amber cavern of weeds." In the fourth stanza the ferocity of nature, together with the poet's purpose, emerge together: "A life subdued to its instrument; / The gills kneading quietly, and the pectorals."

The fish, the pond, the twilight are elaborately staged. By the time the poem finishes, the speaker is afraid to cast in the darkness, "with the hair frozen on my head." But just at that moment I became distracted, brought to a halt where the poem shifts from pike to place.

It happens in the eighth stanza. The speaker describes "a pond I fished." He remembers its gloom; how the tench and lilies had outlasted the stones and structures of those who built the surroundings. How deep it was, how cold:

> Stilled legendary depth:
> It was as deep as England.

I remember my hand on the page, not ready to turn it. I remember the energy and surprise of the words: *as deep as England.* When I looked up the words kept their power, marching out from this single statement into distances of riddle and wonder. Outside in the winter dark, past the wooden doors and steep, grand steps of the library the city of Dublin unfolded through surfaces of history, colony, survival. It unfolded west and east into the Irish Sea, to the very edges of the island. My island.

But here came the meaning together with the riddle. Even

supposing that I found a cold, deep water late at night, could I write similar words? Could I have made a phrase in which so large a claim lay under such a slight felicity? Could I have said that anything was *as deep as Ireland*?

No, I decided, I could not. Some ghostly resistance seemed to stand between me and the very idea. In order to write those words, you had to be confident of that unit of measurement. You had to have some ownership of the phrase. I had neither. I closed the book, handed it in over the counter, packed my book bag and went home.

II

A simple question. Why have so few women, in the history of poetry, been citizen-poets? Why have so few set up their poems with country, nation, nationhood, placing themselves at the center of those themes? "Words are women, deeds are men," writes George Herbert. And so it would appear.

Nor is the answer easy. In seventeenth-century America, Anne Bradstreet wrote with a sharp awareness of the social texture of the Massachusetts Bay Colony. She was the daughter of one of its Governors, the wife of another. She managed an artful balance of devotion and assertion. But never with a reference to the nation-making going on all around her.

In nineteenth-century Britain Elizabeth Barrett Browning wrote the superb, scathing "Mother and Poet." She also declared in a letter "I am of those weak women who reverence strong men." It is hard to put the two modes together. But for her, as for many women poets of that time, a sense of nation seemed out of reach. Perhaps even out of mind.

There was no encouragement off the page either. Sir Samuel Evans in the House of Commons in Britain in 1906 remarked that "all the public duties of citizenship ought to be imposed upon man and man alone." In the same debate, the Speaker of the House of Commons—the issue was women's suffrage—said he was "too fond" of women "to drag them into the political arena and to ask them to undertake responsibilities, duties, and obligations which they did not understand and which they did not care for."

Did not understand. Did not care for. The terms prompt a counter-question. Why should women want to be citizen-poets? Setting aside the parliamentary language, there is an obvious reason. From Wordsworth's yearning address to Milton— "England hath need of thee"—to Allen Ginsberg's fond invitation to Walt Whitman to stroll "the lost America of love" to Yeats's trenchant "Out of Ireland have we come," there is a rich, confirming tradition of national reference in male poetry. More importantly, within that tradition it's clear that male poets in England, Ireland and America are not just drawing on words and names when they refer to their countries. They are also pulling up a deeply sunk reference-hoard of power, nation and poetry.

Here is Whitman, from "The Preface to Leaves of Grass": "The American poets are to enclose old and new for America is the race of races." And now Philip Larkin: "And that will be England gone, / The shadows, the meadows, the lanes, / The guildhalls, the carved choirs." Or Shelley in a high temper in his poem "England 1819," writing of "An old, mad, blind, despised, and dying King; / Princes, the dregs of their dull race." Even when the national reference is one of dissent, with Langston Hughes writing "America never was America to me," there is a circuit of recognition provided just by giving the local habitation a name.

There is also an obvious ease and confidence in these comments. As there was in Ted Hughes's lines on the monastery lake. They show how national reference in poetry can amount to a language of shared values, almost to a *lingua franca*. Not to be able to speak it amounts to losing access to a dominant poetic dialect.

Nor is the dialect itself at fault. There is something musical and consoling even now in reading these gestures towards rootedness. Something heart-lifting in the evocations of country and context. "And did those feet in ancient time / Walk upon England's mountains green?" Blake's question domesticates the wondrous to the local. The far-fetched to the near at hand. The improbable lends a shine to the available.

And yet it's hard to find the equivalent in women poets of the eighteenth and nineteenth centuries. Towards the end of the twentieth century activist writers such as Audre Lorde and Adrienne Rich and Denise Levertov were changing the picture. But further back in time, while there are occasional mentions, there is hardly any focus. There are national balladeers, such as Speranza in Ireland, or regional writers such as Rebecca Hammond Lard or self-styled laureates such as Julia Ward Howe. But they reflect the male paradigm: they don't amend it.

As a drama of contrast, we can take the years between 1850 and 1870 when Walt Whitman and Emily Dickinson confronted different realities in a similar time frame. "I hear America singing, the varied carols I hear," writes Whitman. Not so Dickinson. A single gesture towards nationhood in her work is compelling but also irrelevant. "I've seen him from an ample nation choose one," she wrote in one of her strongest poems. But the nation referred to is not earthly. It is a region of chill and powerful speculation. It is not America.

The contrasts accumulate. While Tennyson wrote "The

Charge of the Light Brigade" and Robert Browning "The Lost Leader," Christina Rossetti was either released or reduced—depending on your point of view—to writing poems about departures, flowers, prayers. Inevitably, these absences and silences prompt an aesthetic speculation: was it possible that the national references in male canonical poems had built a virtual, shadowy realm: a kingdom of entitlement and ownership in which there was no place for a woman poet's imagining?

The more I wrote poetry, the more I read those women poets from past centuries with a deep pleasure and instruction: Dickinson's cryptic lightning. Rossetti's management of a stanza, Bradstreet's bold, deceptive tone. But I was also troubled. When I looked at a particular poem, my mind would turn to the poet who wrote it. There with her book in my hand—with all the advantage of hindsight—I would be distracted trying to summon the wars, treaties, large events and small decisions that once governed her life. Weren't those the years of the gold rush, I would ask myself? Wasn't that beautiful lyric about determinism written in the same year as the Women's Property Act? After a while, however much I liked the poem, what was beyond it—what was unavailable to it—fell like a shadow across the lines. Sometimes when I put the book down, its author seemed to me a woman without a country.

III

Nadia Anjuman was born in 1980 in Herat, the largest city in western Afghanistan. A city so ancient that Ptolemy recorded it on a map. So prosperous that Herodotus claimed it could feed Central Asia. In the Baba mountains, part of the Hindu Kush system, the river Hari rises and flows south of the city. Herat lies on the great trade routes of the Middle East. Its roads are a gateway to Iran; in a different direction they lead towards Turkmenistan. This is an intersection, a meeting point, a crossroads of history and cultures.

Over the centuries, Herat became a center of literary culture. When Robert Byron, a somewhat irascible traveller, came on Herat in 1933 he wrote lyrically about first catching sight of the city: "This was the pure essence of green, insoluble, the colour of life itself. The sun was warm, the larks were singing up above. Behind us rose the misty Alpine blue of the wooded Elburze. In front, the glowing verdure stretched out to the rim of the earth."

Among its most confident possessions, Herat holds the shrine of Jami, the fifteenth-century Sufi master. Like other Sufi poets, Jami wrote of the search for knowledge, gained through mystical union. "Without a veil your countenance cannot be seen," he wrote, "Without a veil your eyes cannot be seen."

His words were almost certainly intended as a figure for how the mind apprehends truth. Nevertheless, five centuries later, they throw a shadow of irony. Of all cities, Herat should have been the most sustaining for a contemporary Afghan poet. And in fact Nadia Anjuman began to write there, as a young woman, at the beginning of the twenty-first century.

She first comes into view as a member of the celebrated sewing circles of Herat. In these a professor at the university, Muhammad Ali Rahyab, taught women literature in secret. She appears in a *New York Times* article called "Afghan Poets Revive a Literary Tradition" written by Amy Waldman in December 2001: "Swathed in black, she curled up like a cat in her professor's study, black eyes peering from an elfin face. She is twenty years old and has written sixty or seventy poems. As the first person in her family to love words, she has had to fight, like a number of Professor Rahyab's students, for her family's cooperation. She has fought, too, to stave off marriage, fearing it will limit her freedom to write. 'I think I've been quite successful,' she said . . . She writes mostly about women's lives, 'because we have suffered a lot.'"

Anjuman published her first book of poems—*Gul-e-dodi* ("Dark Red Flower")—in Herat in early 2005. She died on 4 November of that year at the age of twenty-five, the victim of an apparent honor killing. Her husband of fifteen months, Farid Ahmad Majid Mia, a lecturer in philology at the university, was arrested and charged with her killing, as was his mother. Anjuman was in her third year at Herat University studying Literature and Humane Science when she died. She left a six-month-old son behind. There is no record of a trial or a conviction.

I first heard her story from a remarkable Afghan student of mine, herself a fine poet, for whom Anjuman had been a continuous inspiration. I won't name this student since she is away from her country. But learning of Anjuman through her younger countrywoman was important. It situated Anjuman for me. I was able, through my student's account, to imagine—at least partly—the courage, the fear, the secret meetings in Herat, the hidden pages. Above all, the determination to succeed as a poet.

But even this knowledge was out of date by the time I got it: I had missed a central biographical detail, published in the *New York Times* in 2005:

Nadia Anjuman, who had been gaining a name for herself as a poet in Afghan literary circles, died over the weekend in the western city of Herat after being beaten by her husband, police officials said Monday.

Inevitably, Anjuman's story, and my student's account of it, made me think back to my own beginnings as a poet. At twenty-five, I had finished a first book, as she had. I was married the previous year, as she was. I was starting to see flaws and silences in my environment in Ireland. I was learning to question the hierarchies and exclusions that were in place there, that I sensed would affect any woman poet trying to define herself. But never once did I feel physically unsafe. I assumed a future in which I could continue to write and publish. Anjuman had neither the assumption nor the future.

Information about Anjuman was scarce at first. It is still not plentiful or detailed. I have no knowledge of Farsi, or of Anjuman's dialect of it which is Dari. In a case like this—a different language, a distant culture—I was painfully aware of chance mistakes or errors. For that reason I'm indebted here to other writers and scholars and poets, whose names I've provided wherever I could. And above all to the translators who have made available the charged, painful lyrics from her first book.

To start with, Fritt Ord, the Norwegian activist foundation, was a platform for details and translations. Later, Marilyn Turkovich, an educational activist, provided information and access to Anjuman's poems on her Charter for Compassion website.

There has been some actual publication. In 2010 an organization called HAWCA (Humanitarian Assistance for the Women and Children of Afghanistan) brought out a volume called *Caged Bird: Stories from Safe House and Nadia Anjuman's Poems*. Their annual report states: "We were able to publish a book *Caged Bird: Stories from Safe House and Nadia Anjuman's Poems* to let the world know about the plight still going on of Afghan women and as a tribute to Nadia Anjuman who was fighting for equality of women in society through her amazing poems."

Julie R. Enszer, a feminist, scholar and poet, provided an early and thoughtful essay about Anjuman. She opened with a summary of the facts:

> The circumstances of her death are contested by her husband and family. Despite that, it seems that she was murdered by her husband. He contends that he only hit her and that she was alive when he left after which she committed suicide; however, confirmation of the cause of Anjuman's death will never be obtained as her family declined an autopsy. More than one western news report noted that some members of Anjuman's family believe that her book with poems about love and beauty "brought shame to the family." In spite of the views of some family members, Anjuman's book, *Gul-e-dodi*, translated as "Dark Red Flower" and published while a student at Herat University, was well received and popular in her homeland.

The journalist Christina Lamb, author of the valuable book *The Sewing Circles of Herat*, added to this: "Friends say her family was furious, believing that the publication of poetry *by a woman* about love and beauty had brought shame on it."

IV

Having come this far, I should make clear what this piece is not. My subject is not the Middle East. Nor the politics of Central Asia. Nor is it cultural identity or nationalism. My subject is reading. How we read a poem. How we fail to read it. Beyond that, my subject is the moral responsibility of the poetry reader—an idea without wide currency at this moment.

Surprisingly little time or study has been spent on this reader. Yet this is the same reader who has followed the poem, has shared its history, has endured its disruptions. Who in many ways is a compass point for all that has happened in the past hundred years. Knowing more would surely tell us more about poetry itself. But what methods, what tools do we have to define that reader?

Writers have tried. "If I read a book and it makes my whole body so cold no fire can ever warm me, I know that is poetry," writes Emily Dickinson. "The right reader of a good poem can tell the moment it strikes him that he has taken an immortal wound," adds Robert Frost. In both cases the words are eloquent and almost deliberately imprecise. T. S. Eliot assigned a more sober task: "Pound is not one of those poets who make no demand of the reader." Adrienne Rich, on the other hand, widening both audience and empathy in her poem "Dedication," suggested: "I know you are reading this poem / in a room where too much has happened for you to bear."

All this falls short of definition. Can we have an exact image of the poetry reader in our mind? Occasionally we are pushed into it when an individual reader comes into sudden focus, as Virginia Woolf does here:

> The poem is cracked in the middle. Look, it comes apart in my hands: here is reality on one side, here is beauty on the other; and instead of acquiring a whole object rounded and entire, I am left with broken parts in my hands which, since my reason has been roused and my imagination has not been

404 | CITIZEN POET

allowed to take entire possession of me, I contemplate coldly, critically, and with distaste.

As it happens I have a version of the poetry reader in my own mind. And have had for some time. Not a comforting image either; but a contentious one. A figment, certainly; and yet one with which I have kept up some kind of fractious one-sided conversation over many years. One I blame occasionally for what has gone wrong with the transmission of the art.

This version of the reader is familiar enough. It is the one implied by anthologies, articles, biographical sketches, encyclopedia entries. In other words, the nineteenth-century reader. The one who held on tight as poetry careened wildly through that century, when it was a sociable, exciting time to be reading poetry. When the poem was equally welcome at the christening font or the Sunday sermon, at the Victorian court or the novel of courtship. We can even see that reader's shadow when Marianne in Jane Austen's *Sense and Sensibility* dismisses Edward because he couldn't read Cowper: "To hear those beautiful lines which have frequently almost driven me wild, pronounced with such impenetrable calmness, such dreadful indifference!"

In historical terms, this reader has a fine profile—is seen as attentive and encouraging, a lover of poetry, an enthusiast for its entry into popular society. And always plainspoken about the importance of poetry, even to the extent of blending it with the sacred. "The strongest part of our religion today," wrote Matthew Arnold in the middle of that century, "is its unconscious poetry."

But there is a critique that can and should be made. To start with, these readers were not outsiders. They were not men and women without a country. Far from it. They thought of themselves as having a country and in some cases an empire. They were creatures of their moment, maybe even abettors of its power. Often they exercised their own: in the early nineteenth century when John Clare began a passage with the line "accurs'd wealth o'erbounding human laws" Lord Radstock, his patron, immediately protested Clare's "radical and ungrateful sentiments." The line was removed from the fourth edition of Clare's work. The story is not unique.

In the tectonic movement that came to poetry after 1800— the grinding shift from subject to subjectivity—these readers took up their position: editing, approving, disapproving. They shared their world with the poem: their loyalties remained beyond it. Their limitations had consequences. Their pieties collided with their poetry. Which meant that all too often their reading deferred to an external value system—one that intruded on the poem's interpretation and transmission. "Whatever was the immediate prompting of *In Memoriam*," wrote George Eliot, "whatever the form under which the author represented his aim to himself, the deepest significance of the poem is the sanctification of human love as a religion."

I believe these readers, when they allowed their values to limit their understanding, failed the poem. Is that too harsh? I don't think so. The fact remains that any reader, as soon as they start to read a poem, becomes complicit in the binding and loosing, giving and taking, bestowing and removing of contexts in which a text can breathe, can live. Which leads to the question: does the poetry reader have a moral responsibility? To the text, to the context? The question might seem outlandish given the resistance in any aesthetic discussion to the idea of a moral stance.

For all the contemporary skepticism about poetry, I believe we still want to configure that man or woman who goes to a bookshelf late at night, according to our best hopes. We still believe when they turn the page, and turn it again, that they hold so much more than that in their hands: they hold an encounter with meaning, an act of assent, a compliance with understanding.

This constitutes a moral responsibility. And at this particular moment when poetry is frequently accused of irrelevance or worse, that responsibility persists: to take the poem—both text and context—on its own terms. To remain open to its truths. To step out of the orthodoxies of a familiar world so as to follow Goethe's paradigm: "Who wants to understand the poem / Must go to the land of poetry."

Nadia Anjuman's work tests the reader's responsibility. The contexts are unfamiliar. The circumstances are terrible and distracting. There is the additional complication that although we can translate the poem—this is especially true in the Farsi tradition—we might not be able to translate the poet. Anjuman's work is often unsettling: oracular and distant in a way we don't easily recognize. But none of that prevents us having a responsibility to it. New poetry requires fresh resources. From poet and reader, both. Those resources will be necessary if we are to read an emergent generation of women poets whose poems are rising out of the deepest contentions of history. And who need us to listen.

V

As an Afghan poet, Nadia Anjuman plainly cared about her heritage. In the poems in *Gul-e-dodi* she chooses the discipline of the ghazal over and over again. Other poems, other forms are there as well. But she returns to the ghazal for some of her most important statements.

The ghazal, with its ancient patterning of couplet and refrain, was used by Sufi masters such as Jami and Hafiz. And it is plain, even in translation, how deftly Anjuman used the form to explore both affinity and dissent. Her poems deploy the traditional ghazal relations between couplets: strictly connected and as strictly separated, achieving small, beautifully managed shock-waves of repetition and statement as the poem goes forward.

These poems circle back to the same question. Was Nadia Anjuman a woman without a country? At first glance, there seems to be a country, even a nation in her poems. But her work and death suggest something else: the country she wrote about was not the country she lived in. Was she then a citizen-poet? Once again the answer seems in doubt. The citizenship she proposed for herself, part activist and part aesthetic, was not available to her.

Nadia Anjuman's claim to be both an Afghan woman and an Afghan poet put her in the path of danger. If she had really had her own country she would almost certainly never have posed the threat she did when she walked out of objectification into authorship. As it was she appeared to be trespassing on an already existing country—one that was constructed in her absence and made to perpetuate it.

But the issue is poetry and not nationhood. It is easier to think of Nadia Anjuman's death as an honor killing than as a prompt for questions about the art she practiced. The truth is that she lost her life in a city whose main square honored the poem, its practice and history. What Nadia Anjuman forces us to consider above all is that no art is theoretical.

And here, even though it is unfinished, I leave her story. Already poets, translators and commentators are making her work more available: bringing this wrenching allegory of a poet and her poetry—and its cost—into the light of translation and analysis. Much more will be written about her, and should be. In the meantime, in the absence of the living poet, what she and her poetry deserve is what has been the subject of this piece: a readership.

VI

And so I come back to where I started. To the National Library in winter and to the poem by Ted Hughes I first read there. And to the years when I too often read a poem quickly or carelessly—although that was never my intention. But since this piece contains a reproach to poetry readers, it seems only right I should finish it by including myself in that critique.

The poem in front of me that evening was not the one I read. The one I read was clouded by my subjectivity and by a frank sense of my own limits. I felt that the phrase Ted Hughes used—*as deep as England*—was one I couldn't use about my own landscape, my own country; that it implied an ownership I couldn't claim. Inasmuch as I felt shut out by this perception, I did what I have criticized the nineteenth-century reader here for doing: instead of allowing myself to be changed by the poem, I changed the poem.

I read it as a claim, a separable statement of entitlement, a disclosure of ownership. But of course it's not. Ted Hughes's poem on the pike starts out by invoking a world of nature in which the human element is enhanced but not privileged. It then becomes a subtle unsettling of the whole idea of location. The pike that begins in its own water with its tiger-stripes and clamping jaws has to yield in the eighth stanza to a different habitat. The speaker is remembering "a pond I fished." The imagined water in turn becomes an analogue of memory: it has—with its tench and its lilies—survived and shaken off the circumstances of its own creation.

And so the speaker locates that water in a context that provides both identity and disruption.

> Stilled legendary depth:
> It was as deep as England.

If I had read the words carefully back then I would have seen that the lines imply not a statement of nationhood, but a subversion of it. In nine words the conventions of a national context are stripped back, are exposed to the deep, cold water that has resisted all the directives of origin: that has, in the words of the previous stanza, "outlasted every visible stone / Of the monastery that planted them." If I had looked more closely I might have seen that the words come closer to a renunciation than a claim.

But I didn't. I did exactly what I accuse others of doing in this article. I read the poem through my own values and erased its meanings when they unsettled my own. At which point, I ceased to be the poem's reader and became its editor. I have few excuses. I was young. I should have known better. Fortunately I was dealing with one of the most forgiving of forms: all you need to do if you mis-read a poem is re-read it. Which I did.

THE CONSCRIPTED POET

Poetry Ireland Review 122, 2017

In his 1974 volume called *Out of My Time*, John Hewitt included a memorable poem called "The Scar." It's just sixteen lines long and has the slight look of a sonnet that outgrew its living quarters. Nevertheless, short as it is, it records a powerful drama.

The poem's narrative notes the death of Hewitt's great-grandmother who went to the window during the 1847 famine intending to help a famine victim. Instead, she caught a fever from him and died. Hewitt summarizes the effect of this history on his own identity in two beautiful lines:

> . . . that chance meeting, that brief confrontation,
> conscribed me of the Irishry for ever.

That word "conscribed"—arcane and complicated though it may be—is compelling, both in and beyond the poem. It has caught my attention again while editing *Poetry Ireland Review*. The idea of the conscripted poet is always a controversial one, but never irrelevant. It remains central to the idea of a poet's role. But not always comfortably so, as a small, painful anecdote shows. It involves W. H. Auden, who went to the front in the Spanish Civil War. He then published a chapbook called *Spain*—really an extended poem just twelve pages long—in the key year of 1937. The last lines of the poem extend the Marxist conversation of that moment:

> History to the defeated
> May say Alas but cannot help or pardon.

Two years later Auden left Britain for the US. He went to say goodbye to his friend Stephen Spender. In Spender's account, Auden, catching sight of the chapbook on Spender's mantelpiece, went over and opened it to the last page. He then took out his pen, struck out the final lines and wrote in the margin: *This is a lie.*

This seems to me now both an act of honesty and a cautionary tale. It shows the fear a conscripted poet might have—conscripted that is by external forces—that their art might eventually be compromised in the cause of morality.

What the poet owes or doesn't owe to the world around him or her is a familiar subject. Conscription adds another layer: conscribing a poet to a cause, or an event, or an occasion, or an ideology, may sound coercive.

But the fact remains that many poets of worth and reach have been taken out of their comfort zone by an occasion or commitment and have documented that transit with powerful work. Yet today, so much has changed—so many new voices, so many different tonal registers—that the idea of the conscripted poet has had to change as well.

Today's conscripted poet still exists of course—and in the old version of the concept: poets of color, environmentalist poets, political activists and others are still everywhere called to large questions and to make powerful, unsettling poems in the light of them. But in a new context, the poet we see today may also be conscribed differently: less by history or an external cause than by the subterranean conversation within poetry itself.

Patrick Kavanagh's comments on the Irish Revival—resisting it at every point—which I quote in a tribute in this issue, can be seen in this light as a form of counter-conscription. Alvy Carragher's bold persona poem—she is the featured poet in this issue—gestures towards a partly hidden poetic conversation, where definitions of the page and the performance vie with each other for clarification. Richard Murphy's rich and thoughtful interview in this issue describes the inward power of migration, geographical and imaginative. And there are many other poems in this issue where the poet is plainly and eloquently struggling to balance lyric poise with large ideas. It makes for exciting reading.

Does this mean that the idea of the conscripted poet is no longer of use? I don't think so. Looking at this issue of PIR is a reminder that the definition of the conscripted poet doesn't need to be abandoned, just broadened. In that sense the demands on the poet, the tensions within the poem, remain similar if not exactly the same. What is the same is the need for poetic rigor and thoughtfulness. No poet, after all, wants to accuse their words of falsehood in the margin of their own poem.

COLLABORATE

Poetry Ireland Review 123, 2017

S ome years ago I was teaching poetry to a large group. At
the front of my class was a profoundly deaf student who
attended with two women who signed the class for her.
This student was always present, always engaged. I made sure
to be in her clear line of sight so her signers could bring the class
to her as quickly as possible.

Quite often students brought in their own favorite poems.
One day she asked if she could bring in a sign language poem.
The following week she did. The poem she chose was printed
on a page which was copied and handed out. Then she presented
that same poem through sign language—a beautiful choreogra-
phy of voice—through her signers—and hand gestures. It was
intensely moving.

The students were galvanized—drawn in as I was by the
courage and composure through which limitation had become
an unlimited aesthetic. But more than that. They were also
struck to be watching a collaboration between two languages:
the auditory reading of the poem and the visual language which
was signed—the two translating each other to further texture

and depth, a collaboration as old as poetry, reaching back into its associations with music and magic.

Collaboration is not a word that is associated with poetry as readily as it is with music, drama or the visual arts. Certainly when I was young it was strongly suggested that the best, if not the only collaborative project, was the encounter between poet and page. Which of course remains central. But it seems to me that something is lost if past and present collectives and collaborations are not brought back to be part of the conversation.

For example, there was the 1930 Surrealist experiment known as *Ralentir Travaux* (Slow Down Men Working, in English)—a series of poems written over five days by André Breton, Paul Éluard, and René Char. The three men met in Avignon, and worked in the Rich Tavern. They drove together around the Vaucluse, talking, arguing, composing. And the title of the project came from a road signal they glimpsed on the way to Caumont-sur-Durance—a reminder of just how improvisational collaboration can be.

In pre-modern Japan there was the *renga*, with its chain linking and multiple authors, from whose first stanza, the *hokku*, today's *haiku* emerged. Or in the contemporary moment, American poets like Matthew Rohrer and Joshua Beckman, whose 2002 volume *Nice Hat* was a mutual writing project. Their comments remain relevant: "We've always been interested in collaboration and the idea that being an artist or a writer in a community becomes a form of collaboration—not just working in dialogue with people, but actually writing with them. We also thought of our audiences as collaborators."

In Ireland, editing *Poetry Ireland Review*, I'm often struck by separate energies that don't quite intersect, but yet are clearly present and seem to promise good things to one another if they only could engage. On the one hand there is the page: the values of the hermetic poem are at the center of all poetry. Page poetry will always rightly shelter the private poet who seeks a reach and distance in their work that keeps it at angles to public statement, or the expectations of an audience.

On the other hand, the vivid forays into the public poem represented both in the US and Ireland—and many other places—by collectives such as Spoken Word have energized and given power to new definitions of the poem and the poet. New relations with the audience have emerged from this, which are in fact contemporary revisions of the old relations, where the poet spoke with and for that audience.

Yet despite these excellent energies, there remains almost everywhere—in the US, Ireland, the UK—some tension, some suspicion, between the poets of the page and those of performance or the public poem. They are not divided by acrimony but by custom and tradition: deeply layered choices and commitments that not only change the poem but also the identity of the poet.

In the US, even on a campus, I can hear these suspicions expressed on both sides. The performance poet, whose connections with an audience are deep and sustaining, can feel that the contemporary moment is theirs in a unique way, that they should be allowed to refresh outdated curricula, revise subject matter, and challenge the academy. The page poet can feel— and sometimes say openly—that the public poet is exempt from the challenges and nuances of private work, of words and forms whose life on the page have a more testing and more timeless relation with the reader.

Both make important points. But it seems to me at times that their mutual suspicion might stand in the way of something valuable: a meeting point where these historic formations in poetry might actually find one another and share their energies. That certainly would be a worthwhile and exciting collaboration.

DIVERSITY IN POETRY

Poetry Ireland Review 125, 2018

In September of last year, Poetry Ireland hosted a focus group of poets, activists, critics, students, and teachers to discuss diversity. The Poetry Ireland team ably coordinated an event with many voices and differing perspectives. Earlier in the year, in May 2017, Poetry Ireland had re-stated its commitment to promote the "best practice models on diversity and gender balance across all areas of our work." The focus group was one outcome of this commitment. I was present with others at the discussion in September, as was the American poet Kevin Young. The conversation that day mirrored some of the concerns of the West Coast in the US where I work. The issues raised are central now to poetry everywhere. They are issues of inclusion and permission. They already affect many of the emerging poets this journal publishes. So it seems worthwhile to register some of the arguments here.

The conversation in September was informative. The details were often surprising and compelling, and the conversation often eloquent and moving. Poets in the room with an awareness of ethnicity, of gender, of disability, of sexual difference, voiced their sense that their poetry spoke from and should record these realities; poets who valued performance and others who relied on the page spoke about this; poets who led urban workshops and some who fostered online communications described their different knowledges. They advocated for these experiences not only because they formed their identities, but because those identities were forming a richer sense of the poems they wrote.

I was a listener there. Many of the details I didn't know and wouldn't presume to comment on. But if I didn't know the occasion, I certainly knew the conversation. I have known it for a long time. There is no more difficult and no more important ongoing discussion in the arts. Yet anyone who knows the poetry world knows how powerful is the resistance to this conversation about diversity. Many of the holders of conservative opinions see themselves as gate-keepers and hold positions of influence and access: publishers, editors, prize committee members. They are able to resist change under the banner of standards and to marginalize dissent with the argument that these energies amount to little but social engineering. For many emerging poets—poets of color, of gender diversity, of sexual difference, of aesthetic dissent—this resistance can be daunting.

Diversity in poetry is interpreted by skeptics as being merely about social change. In reality, it is about formal and artistic renewal. Anyone reading twentieth-century poetry from Allen Ginsberg to Adrienne Rich to Medbh McGuckian has to know that the margin re-defines the center, and not the other way around. But that margin has to be visible, has to be vocal, has to be sustained by new critiques as well as new poems. If not, poetry will be held hostage to outdated critiques in which are coded old resistances. For that reason, diversity has to be recognized and supported. When I was younger, the coded critiques suggesting that the expressive lives of women would distort the

Irish poem seemed to me wrong then. And wrong now. The contemporary codes today inferring that diversity is a social project not a poetic one seem equally wrong.

We need to emphasize the importance of diversity not simply because it's about the future of society, but because it points to the future of poetry. The old conservative mantra that self-expression is not art leaves a question hanging. Who is to arbitrate that difference? Who is to say when one becomes the other? Without a generous vital conversation about diversity, such as Poetry Ireland is undertaking, the question will remain stalled, mired in divisive and limiting arguments.

Despite my own disagreements with purists in the profession over many years, I've often recognized their sincerity, their love for the craft, their deep frustration with what they see as the blurring of lines separating an old art from a contemporary society. But the past is a safe place; the future a far more unsettled one. For all the present distrust that certainly exists, I hope that the future in poetry will be a shared one where division becomes debate, and a living speech—open to change—helps to change poetry.

WHAT DOES THE POET LOOK LIKE

Poetry Ireland Review 126, 2019

What does a poet look like? That question, which seems so out of place now, was once less so. Years ago poets' appearances were noted, their likenesses commented on in letters, novels, poems. Often the poet was the mirror of the moment. Or at least thought to be. "I am of those weak women who reverence strong men," wrote Elizabeth Barrett Browning in a letter to a friend. A strange statement from this deeply independent poet, but not an unusual one in the Victorian era. "The greatest men, whether poets or historians," wrote Ruskin, "live entirely in their own age."

In fact, for 150 years each society, each decade, seemed to dress a poet in its own hopes and concerns. In this context poets, almost exclusively male, were slightly less respectably costumed than the mainstream variant. For all that, their departures from the norm, their apparent freedoms were on a short leash. The ages they lived in were leashed as well. Then and later, appearances mattered. The American poet Louise Bogan, who wrote poetry reviews for the *New Yorker*, commented on Yeats. "William Butler Yeats," she wrote, "first appears, in the memories of his contemporaries, as a rarefied human being: a tall, dark-visaged young man who walked the streets of Dublin and London in a poetic hat, cloak, and flowing tie, intoning verses." Appearances also seemed to denote the inner world as well as the outer one. "Come to lunch," Virginia Woolf wrote to a friend. "Eliot will be there in a four-piece suit."

What does this mean? For the working poet, for the active reader? And was there anything wrong with describing what poets wore fifty years ago, how they looked, how they were observed? I think there was. Lying under those sentimental or sardonic comments, littered throughout novels, newspapers, letters, was a darker outline. A different query lay under the more obvious one. If asking what a poet looked like was one variant then another was a shadow-shape in the water, unspoken but related: Who didn't look like a poet?

In the last two centuries, that shadow question has had a difficult history. Women, minorities, communities on the margins of a society—at first none of them looked like poets. Therefore, the logic went, they couldn't be poets. None of them was included in the inventory of descriptions, word-portraits, commentaries on a poet's life in the world. To be poets they had to be approved. And they weren't.

Because poetry is associated with free expression, many people resist thinking a society could have the power to issue or withhold permissions about a poet's identity. That such permissions, or their denial, could be mediated through comments about appearance. But they could and they were.

One of the pleasures of editing *Poetry Ireland Review*—the same is true of the Stegner workshop at Stanford—is the chance to see close-up these categories disappearing, and just how little tolerance is left for them. There are no easy definitions now, no agreed cut-outs. Part of the reason is that the social consensus that underpinned those divisions has broken down. The woman in traffic, the man at the gym, the teenager seeming to limp along with a sporting injury, the trans writer, the hermetic one, the emerging writer of color—any or all of them could be poets.

Maybe the larger reason for this is that poetry has grown tired of its own exclusions. New energies have come to the threshold of an old art. Clearly they should be welcomed. In Poetry Ireland they certainly have been. The democratic sparkle of spoken word platforms, the intensity of interdisciplinary collaborations where music and language meet, the power of performance and the proper loneliness of the page—all of these are factors in our much wider sense today of who is a poet, who can be a poet, who looks like a poet. This may seem like a small thing. But small things in the arts can sometimes turn out to be saving graces. This may be one of them.

THE POET AND COMMUNITY

Poetry Ireland Review 128, 2019

I n the early 1940s the Russian poet Anna Akhmatova was writing her elegy "Requiem." It recorded the grief and dispossession of the Stalin purges. It was also a dangerous enterprise.
She feared the secret police, the discovery of her manuscript
and what might follow.

Her solution was makeshift and workable. She wrote down
fragments. She gave them to friends. Her friends memorized
them. Then the paper was burned. Her friend Lydia Chu-
kovskaya, a poet and dissident, was one of those who helped.
"It was like a ritual," she later recalled. "Hands, matches, an
ashtray. A ritual beautiful and bitter."

In 2007, at the Hay Festival, the distinguished novelist Martin Amis gave another view. "You may have noticed that poetry
is dead," he said. "The obituary has already been written . . . I
mean, it goes on, and its funny, ghoulish afterlife is in the form of
tours and readings and poetry slams and all the rest of it, but not
many people now curl up in the evening with a book of poetry."

Those passionate, chosen friends of Anna Akhmatova were
certainly not living a so-called ghoulish afterlife. They lived in
a knife-edge present. In that space they may have doubted their

survival under a regime which confused poets with enemies of
the state. But they did not doubt the life of poetry. They lent
to it their own memories, their own belief that the words they
memorized were necessary. They lent to it their courage and
their faith in an essential art.

These events and opinions are separated by decades. What
happened in between? One answer lies in the argument that a
powerful popular culture, with its emphasis on dailyness and
details, turned out to be no ally of a great and complex art.
Martin Amis's views could not have been given a hundred years
earlier, maybe not even fifty years earlier. But in the moment he
offered them, for some people at least, poetry seemed to be in
the shadows: its language and existence still vital to many, but
its place in their culture and society poorly defined.

With the heavy contrast between these actions and statements, an emerging poet might well feel less than comfortable
with the present state of things. The art they practice may seem
called into question too often. They might also ask—is there a
remedy? Is there something a new poet can do, or an established
one, to take on the challenges of their time and engage with the
questions around them?

I think there is. The remedy lies in the very shift that has
occurred over the past decades. Once a poet was thought of
as solitary, as closed in a private world. As a vendor of private
perceptions and visions. That solitude was a source of esteem
in the outside world. But a great deal has changed. Now poets
are able to draw some part of their identity from the communal,
the public, the gathering places—from panels to performance—
which reinforce their identity and make visible their purpose.

Nor are such communities makeshift or temporary. Poetry
Ireland has provided a remarkable community for decades,

together with innovative ideas on how to strengthen it and sustain it. The Poetry Foundation and the Academy of American Poets in the US have the same purpose. If a popular culture was no help to the art, the digital age has proved to be the opposite: providing tools that offer sanctuary and assistance to poets at every stage. All a poet needs to do is engage with the idea of community: from sharing work across boundaries and territories, to entering the debates and arguments which give the poetic conversation its vitality. The remedy, it turns out, adds a dimension to the traditional life of the poet: the building of communities where poets can exchange their work and provide a witness to their lives as poets.

More From
EAVAN BOLAND

Winner of the Costa Poetry Award

"This book is alive as a legacy for all readers—and for the future where Eavan Boland's greatness will endure."
—Carol Muske-Dukes

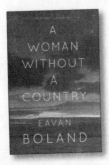

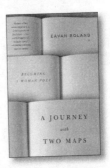

"Masterful . . . I felt, reading *A Woman Without a Country*, that I was having . . . that beautiful kind of conversation where you can't nod enthusiastically enough."
—Amal El-Mohtar, NPR

"[*A Journey with Two Maps*] attempts to rewrite history in a more fair and truthful manner."
—*San Francisco Chronicle*